BRAIN PORN

THE BEST OF DAILY MAVERICK

Tafelberg

Tafelberg
An imprint of NB Publishers, a Division of Media24 Boeke (Pty) Ltd,
40 Heerengracht, Cape Town
www.tafelberg.com
Text © Daily Maverick (2014)
Images (p. 79, 80, 83) © Greg Marinovich

All rights reserved.
No part of this book may be reproduced or transmitted in any form or by any electronic or mechanical means, including photocopying and recording, or by any information storage or retrieval system, without written permission from the publisher.

Cover design: Mike Cruywagen
Book design: Cheymaxim Creative
Editing: Angela Voges
Proofreading: Glynne Newlands

Printed and bound by Paarl Media Paarl, Jan van Riebeeck Drive, Paarl, South Africa

First edition, first impression 2014

ISBN: 978-0-624-07067-2
Epub: 978-0-624-07068-9
Mobi: 978-0-624-07069-6

CONTENTS

Foreword by Max du Preez — ix

Introduction — xii

1 The Gupta house of cards

Exclusive: Gupta nuptials guest memo
RICHARD POPLAK — 1

The Guptas and the man called Gedleyihlekisa
RANJENI MUNUSAMY — 4

Message to cabinet: It is not just a wedding
KALIM RAJAB — 11

The top spooks' Gupta warning
RANJENI MUNUSAMY — 15

ANN7: Car-crash viewing, but no laughing matter
REBECCA DAVIS — 21

2 Reporter's notebook

The lessons no journalism school can teach you
SIPHO HLONGWANE — 28

A thin line between fear and hate
BRANKO BRKIC — 33

The day the Cape Winelands burned
REBECCA DAVIS — 38

Julius Malema and the rally that rocked
RICHARD POPLAK — 47

3 A homestead in the hills

An uncontrolled creep – Zuma, busted by Madonsela
RICHARD POPLAK — 54

Madonsela: It's *Animal Farm*, and the pigs are feeding
SIMON ALLISON — 59

Open letter to President Jacob Gedleyihlekisa Zuma
STEPHEN GROOTES   62

Goodbye, democracy; so long, accountability;
hello, Zumocracy
RANJENI MUNUSAMY   67

Requiem for a dream: On loving and leaving the ANC
SISONKE MSIMANG   72

4 Thirty-four human beings died that night

The cold murder fields of Marikana
GREG MARINOVICH   78

A film every South African should see, and never forget
MARIANNE THAMM   90

Twelve-point-bloody-five
GREG NICOLSON   95

We're not in Eden any more, South Africa
J BROOKS SPECTOR   100

5 People in the news

My friend, the war photographer
GREG MARINOVICH   106

The beautiful mind of Jonathan Jansen
MANDY DE WAAL   109

Bad cops, assassins, Czech fugitives: The meaning of
Paul O'Sullivan
MARIANNE THAMM   116

Talking 'bout a revolution
RANJENI MUNUSAMY   124

Walking with Kathrada: A journey to Robben Island
RANJENI MUNUSAMY   130

6 Princess Thuli and Co.

Best of Daily Maverick's illustrations   139

7 Think again

Karoo fracking scandal exposed
IVO VEGTER … 150

Mamphela Ramphele, the future for South Africa? Nope
VUKANI MDE … 162

To my generation: Listen. Listen very carefully
JAY NAIDOO … 173

Palin, Malema and the rise of the unread
KEVIN BLOOM … 178

Malema's manufactured money
GREG NICOLSON … 184

Lessons from a Zambian vice president
SIMON ALLISON … 188

My coming-out story
STYLI CHARALAMBOUS … 192

8 Lessons from a murder

After the media circus has moved on …
MANDY WIENER … 197

A conversation about violence
SISONKE MSIMANG … 201

What got lost in the Oscar Pistorius frenzy
REBECCA DAVIS … 204

9 Our scourge

Anene Booysen: The agony of South Africa's daughter
RANJENI MUNUSAMY … 209

Watch. Pray. South Africa.
GREG NICOLSON … 215

Thought I'd say 'Hi' to a couple of rapists
ANONYMOUS … 218

In defence of a lion killer
IVO VEGTER … 223

10 The R-word

Black anger and white obliviousness
OSIAME MOLEFE — 231

Racism killed the rainbow nation
PAUL BERKOWITZ — 237

Should South Africa's black people get over apartheid? Hell, no!
SIPHO HLONGWANE — 242

The myth of the competent apartheid government
IVO VEGTER — 245

11 Madiba

Madiba, I let you go
MARELISE VAN DER MERWE — 252

Open letter to South Africa from foreign media
RICHARD POPLAK — 256

A stadium full of truths
STEPHEN GROOTES — 259

Fog donkey: The only honest man in a stadium of fools
RICHARD POPLAK — 263

My old South African flag
IVO VEGTER — 268

List of contributors — 287

FOREWORD

I was sitting around a table with some fellow hacks the other day (the kind, mostly, who like to start sentences with 'In my day …' – veterans, as we prefer to be called), lamenting the state of the media in South Africa. Then someone said, 'At least there's Daily Maverick.' We all nodded, and ordered another round.

Not long ago, I was chastised by a group of politicians (who, having reached the age of my fellow hacks, call themselves stalwarts) about the way in which the press has been reporting on South African politics. Then I said, 'At least there's Daily Maverick.' They all nodded, and asked me to buy another round.

Yes, at least there's Daily Maverick. Brain porn, indeed – a dependable weekday offering that lifts my foul mood when the morning papers don't arrive at my door. In five years, Daily Maverick has shown outfits here and elsewhere – outfits with much better backing and bigger budgets – how online news and opinion should be done. And it's done this in great style: energetically and with constant innovation.

I get my breaking news and updates from the radio and social media. With my first early-morning double espresso, I don't need a rehash of what happened yesterday – I want to know how I should understand and make sense of it. I want someone to give me the broader picture, and I want intelligent, well-reasoned opinions about the state of my world. When I'm done, I want to feel prepared to see beyond the inevitable smoke and mirrors of my day.

We've reached a point, in South Africa, at which you need to remind yourself who owns the media product you're consuming so that you can decode what you're reading or listening to. This is not true of Daily Maverick. The small Daily Maverick team contains some of the very brightest bulbs in the chandelier of South African journalism. I don't need to agree with everything I read, but I do insist on intellectual integrity and good writing. I demand that reporters have a memory that extends further than the previous decade, even if they were still at school at that time or not yet born.

Every now and then a voice from outside journalism pops up in Daily Maverick's offering: a bright young voice like Kalim Rajab, or a wise older voice like Jay Naidoo or Raymond Suttner. And, unlike most other online news sources, the comments section is a place where real debate can take place. As its reminder to those who comment says: 'Here, we don't pity the fool. We remove them.'

South Africa has become a confusing place in which to live. There's a lot of shouting, too many charlatans, too much posturing, too much obfuscation and not enough reasoning and truth-telling; there's not nearly enough digging below the surface (read Greg Marinovich's brilliant piece from September 2012, 'The cold murder fields of Marikana', for an example of how this digging should be done). As Phaedrus said to

FOREWORD

Socrates in Plato's *Phaedrus*, 'Things are not always what they seem; the first appearance deceives many; the intelligence of a few perceives what has been carefully hidden.'

In five short years, Daily Maverick has become a must-read for all who want an informed and stimulated opinion about their political and social environment. After reading this collection of the best of Daily Maverick, I nodded and said to myself, 'At least there's Daily Maverick.'

Long live!

Max du Preez

INTRODUCTION

On 30 October 2009, a simple message entered the Twitterverse – *@dailymaverick: www.dailymaverick.co.za now live.* What followed was an incredible journey that brought us exhilarating heights and equally depressing lows. It was for real, this trek from obscurity to being a recognised brand in the news space. It was never anything less than the truth to the best of our ability. We tried our best to provide our readers with snapshots of future history, every day, all the time. And we gave the same readers magazine-quality stuff, daily.

Reading through Daily Maverick's massive opus (more than 10 000 stories), it became obvious to us that our snapshots of history had matured well, and that most of them still felt fresh and original all of these years later.

Choosing the best 46 essays to include in this book was no easy task. How does one choose from a herculean effort of continuous originality that some would also call a blurry haze of journalistic folly? Cherry-picking the essays in this selection was a laborious and emotional task, akin to asking a parent to choose a favourite child.

It turned out to be an impossible job. To make it easier, we approached the process from different angles, starting off by looking at the most-read articles – a process somewhat flawed in determining our best efforts, but one that provided, nonetheless, a point from which to begin the journey.

INTRODUCTION

I say 'flawed' mostly because as a daily publication whose audience has almost doubled every year since its launch, Daily Maverick's early masterpieces would have recorded far fewer reads than later articles. And because the most-read pieces aren't always the ones we'd consider our best work. (We have serious reservations about any newsroom that uses 'hits' as the barometer of performance or quality. Or desirability.)

Another angle we took was to consider the major themes that Daily Maverick had covered over the course of its existence. From the various Gupta scandals to the uncontrolled creep that brought us Nkandla, the Oscar Pistorius media circus, the passing of the nation's father and, of course, the massacre of Marikana, we wanted to select the essays that best encapsulated our own stormy journey through these milestone events.

This collection is not only a tangible recollection of our works, but also a snapshot of the space–time continuum that shaped this country between 2009 and 2014. Each of the events described in this book is like a sonar beacon, plotting our course in the sea of madness that is South Africa's daily reality. (To the talented observer, this country's current affairs and politics truly constitute the gift that keeps on giving.)

And yet, compiling this book has been, in its own way, therapeutic. It has forced us to sit back and reflect on what this incredibly special – and massively talented – family of journalists has managed to achieve with fewer resources than most university newspapers have at their disposal. The daily grind of each day's analysis and opinion doesn't allow us the luxury of retrospection.

Perhaps this is a good thing, because Daily Maverick is like a shark that needs to keep moving to survive. Maybe if we had stopped along the way and tried to understand the enormity of the challenge we had so readily, and foolishly, accepted, the part of our brains that processes reason would have imploded.

But it certainly hasn't been all tough times and hard work. What this book won't show you is the behind-the-scenes escapades, the mad late-night group-chat exchanges and the cholesterol- and coffee-laden editorial meetings that have fuelled this journey. Those stories are for another day, another book. But it would be negligent of me, as editor-in-chief of this motley crew of hacks, not to acknowledge the special bond that runs through our editorial team, this cabal that has produced pieces of such high quality and vast quantity. I use the words 'cabal' and 'family' above 'team' because without that feeling of belonging to a common cause, to an ideal greater than just a pay cheque at the end of the month, none of this would have been possible.

There are so many good essays, written by better authors, that we could not include in the compilation – which is why, after compiling a shortish list, we left the final decision to our publishers. You know, for plausible deniability.

But enough posturing. Let's get to the good stuff, the reason you picked this book up in the first place. Strap yourself in and get ready to channel your inner Joker.

Showtime.

Branko Brkic
Editor-in-chief, Daily Maverick

1

THE GUPTA HOUSE OF CARDS

EXCLUSIVE: GUPTA NUPTIALS GUEST MEMO

You may not have heard, but according to an ANC statement, 'some wedding at Sun City' is being hosted by 'a family'. Many of the guests for the Gupta nuptials are coming from afar, and seeing that South Africa is a baffling place, it makes sense that they'd require a primer. After much deliberation, Daily Maverick has decided to publish a top-secret Gupta wedding memo to be handed out to all overseas attendees.

RICHARD POPLAK, MAY 2013

Welcome, dearest guests, to the sunny shores of Guptastan, more commonly known in the global vernacular as South Africa. You have been flown here to celebrate the wedding of Vega Gupta to a very lucky young man whose name escapes us. And while you are probably aware that the land in which you now stand functions as the Gupta's private estate, there are some rules that must be adhered to in order not to upset the locals, who can be quite touchy. Please read the following memorandum carefully:

When the privately chartered Gupta Airways Wedding

Express touches down, you'll note that you are not alighting in a modern civilian airport, but on a military base. Don't worry – this is not a mistake, as we have full use of all local army and air force facilities should we need them. Please do refrain from tipping the personnel you encounter on the ground – they have recently returned from a combat mission in a nearby country, and may interpret your sudden movement as an act of aggression. PTSD can be so troublesome.

When you arrive at the nearby Sun City entertainment complex, you'll notice the prevalence of casinos on the site. This is not meant as a cheeky reference to how we view the South African economy. We promise.

Should you somehow injure a local on your drive over, or back into one with your golf cart, or in any way harm an indigenous person, do not panic. Please log in to your Twitter account, write #Mayday plus your GPS co-ordinates, and make sure to include @guptaweddingcoverup.

In the classic Indian tradition, the nuptials will drag out over four long days. Sun City has all the amenities for those who may not have the stamina for such events, such as spas, personalised valet services and sturdy balcony rails from which to hang oneself.

As you may have read, the Guptas have in their employ numerous government ministers and bigwigs, not least of whom is the president of South Africa. They are not difficult to identify – you will know officials and members of the ruling party by the bottles of Johnny Walker Blue Label they carry at all times.

When presenting a gift to the wedding party, please make

sure to include your name on the *outside* of the envelope. When presenting a gift to a government official, it is best not to include your name at all.

Yes, all of the women at the president's table are his wives. Please do not make light of this – whatever makes him happy makes us happy. Besides, we've learned a lot about wedding logistics from his various ceremonies.

In accordance with the custom of some of the guests present, a display of Indian treats will be laid out on several scantily clad Bollywood models, from which you should feel free to eat until sated. However, please refrain from making eye contact with the models – we must make some concessions to Hindu piety.

As noted, we are not Muslim, but Hindu. Still – no Boston Bombing jokes. Too soon.

Every morning, with your breakfast, you must read a publication called *The New Age*, which you will find has been slipped under your hotel room door. This is non-negotiable. While reading, lean back in your chair, rubbing your chin in thoughtful repose. When this task has been completed, close the paper ostentatiously and say, 'Exactly!'

If you do happen to encounter any white South Africans at the event, by all means share sly jokes at the expense of the powers that be, and enjoy a mutual, knowing sneer at the obvious corruption around you. But *by no means* joke about the country's dwindling rhino population. This will result in social exclusion, and possibly a lawsuit.

In all online commentary, please refer to the event as 'the wedding of the century'. Here, we are referring specifically to the eighteenth century.

Have a good time, take a load off, and enjoy! This is, after all, a business conference, by which we mean 'wedding'. Jump at the opportunity to ingratiate yourself with our employees in government and the ruling party. You will, we believe, find them most amenable in almost every respect.

And, finally, do not feed the locals. It just gives them ideas.

THE GUPTAS AND THE MAN CALLED GEDLEYIHLEKISA

It took a statement from a rather cross Gwede Mantashe to bring the whole Gupta house of cards tumbling down. Before that, the Gupta overlords had been untouchable (in the non-Indian-caste sense) and nobody in the ANC or the government had dared to cross them. But the political and diplomatic fallout from the illegal use of Waterkloof Air Force Base by the Gupta family has been spectacular.

RANJENI MUNUSAMY, MAY 2013

Because this is such a special occasion, let's go back to that great reference point in President Jacob Zuma's life: the Schabir Shaik trial. The reason why Shaik and Zuma were both charged with corruption was because of the way in which they each abused their relationship for material gain. Shaik would flaunt his self-styled position as Zuma's financial advisor to get ahead in the business world; Zuma would allow him to do so – and nod on cue in the presence of businesspeople – in exchange for the privilege of having a sponsor on call. It was a mutually beneficial relationship and they both coasted along happily until the National Prosecuting Authority disrupted the party.

Their relationship, particularly according to the amended Corruption Act, was deemed to be corrupt, and Shaik was sentenced to 15 years in prison as a result. Into the breach stepped the Gupta brothers, until then a relatively unknown family who left India to set up base in Johannesburg some 20 years ago. And the Guptas made Shaik look like an amateur. They are highly ambitious, crusading businessmen who do everything on a grand scale. They commandeered Zuma's family, his Cabinet, government departments and parastatals – and had no qualms about doing so.

Since the start of the Zuma presidency, rumours have circulated about ANC leaders learning of their Cabinet appointments via the Gupta brothers and directors general being summoned to the Guptas' Saxonwold compound to receive instructions on how to direct major government contracts the Guptas' way.

Despite media revelations about millions of rands from parastatals being channelled into the Gupta-owned *The New Age* newspaper through the Guptas' business breakfasts, the arrangement has continued, with Cabinet ministers on constant parade to keep the funds rolling in.

The Guptas seemed unfazed by bad publicity and allegations of illicit dealings. They conduct their business with an air of invincibility and are forthright in the way they use their political connections.

They do not name-drop: they instruct those whose names others drop what to do. They do so with the confidence of people who own the most powerful in the land.

While several high-ranking people in the state and the

ANC have spoken off the record about the inordinate power wielded by the Gupta brothers, nobody has dared openly to break the sacred covenant of the goings-on behind the high walls in Saxonwold. Those who have been exposed to their bullying and arrogance fear being victimised or losing their jobs due to the family's proximity to the president and its ability to use that relationship continually for its benefit.

And then the wedding came, and with it a moment in the space–time continuum when over the top became just too much.

It was designed to be an ostentatious spectacle, something that would get tongues wagging in South Africa and India. Weddings in India are normally grand and protracted affairs but the wedding of Vega Gupta and Aakash Jahajgarhia was meant to flaunt the family's substantial riches and status as pseudo-royalty in a four-day extravaganza at Sun City, designed by the Gavin Rajah Concept. Apart from the lavish arrangements, dance and pageantry to rival a Bollywood production, it was to be a gathering of the Guptas' elite political and business connections in South Africa and India.

About 200 guests, apparently including Indian ministers of state, were flown to South Africa from New Delhi. Nothing wrong with booking flights for your wedding guests; nothing wrong with chartering a jet to fly them over either. Nothing wrong with any of it – if you can afford it, of course. But with the Guptas, it couldn't stop there – not with all of their political connections in the South African state open to them.

They pulled strings, leaned on a few people, snapped their fingers and – *voilà!* – managed to wangle clearance to land a Jet Airways Airbus A330-203 passenger jet at Waterkloof Air Force Base in Pretoria. When they were first denied permission to land at the national key point by the Department of Defence, they asked Indian High Commissioner Virendra Gupta to get authorisation from the Department of International Relations and Cooperation (Dirco). Speaking on SABC television on the following Thursday night, the High Commissioner said the arrangements had been made to use Waterkloof for the arrival of the wedding guests for 'security' and 'convenience'.

When news broke of the jet having landed at a national key point on Tuesday 30 April, there was no official response from the government to explain the protocol and security anomaly. Although the media were asking questions, which opposition parties were bound to chase up, the issue could probably have been kept shrouded under the legislation governing national key points, as has been the case with the president's Nkandla residence.

But then, at about 9 p.m. on Tuesday 30 April, ANC Secretary General Gwede Mantashe issued a media statement that opened the sluice gates. Most ANC statements are issued in the name of ANC National Spokesman Jackson Mthembu. Only under special circumstances are they issued by the secretary general. The language in the terse three-paragraph statement was also vintage Mantashe – brash, minus any attempt at niceties. It was either written directly by him or dictated to someone by him.

'The African National Congress has learnt that guests of a family hosting some wedding at Sun City landed at the

Waterkloof Air Force Base today,' the statement began, going on to explain the significance of a national key point.

'The African National Congress waited patiently for the South African National Defence Force (SANDF), the body delegated with authority over the Waterkloof Air Force Base, to explain to the nation how these private individuals managed to land aircraft at Waterkloof. Up until now, no explanation has been forthcoming. The African National Congress, driven by the concern for the safety and sovereignty of South Africa, shall never allow a situation where our ports of entry and national key points are penetrated with impunity.

'We demand that those who are responsible for granting access to land aircraft in our country also explain the basis upon which such permission was granted, particularly to land at Waterkloof Air Force Base. Those who cannot account must be brought to book,' Mantashe said.

He went on to say that the ANC 'will never rest where there is any indication that all and sundry may be permitted to undermine the Republic, its citizens and its borders'.

The ANC statement on the Gupta jet late on that Tuesday was unprecedented. The ANC had never before been as forthright in demanding answers from the Zuma administration. It could be that Mantashe had simply had enough of the Guptas running the state and ruining his organisation, and decided to stamp his authority on the situation.

There have also been rumours of a widening schism between the Zuma camp and Mantashe. This could have resulted in the ANC secretary general being less cautious about upsetting the president's friends. It is also possible that

Mantashe could have called Zuma to interrogate how this happened, as he is prone to do with ANC leaders when trouble is on the horizon. Zuma, obviously, would have denied knowledge or responsibility, prompting Mantashe to rattle cages in the state.

But Zuma is also an enigma in his relations with those close to him. He could have called the hit. He could have become angered that the Guptas used their proximity to him to muscle their way onto a military air base and decided to teach them a lesson.

Whatever the motivation, Mantashe cranked open the vault that houses the secret workings of the Gupta dynasty. Cosatu, the SACP and the ANC Youth League interim task team issued statements condemning the use of the air force base and demanding answers about how the violation of a national key point was allowed to happen.

In the state, too, all sorts of investigations began, admissions were forthcoming and dramatic action taken in record time – never before witnessed in the Zuma administration.

By the morning of Thursday 2 May, it had become clear that five government departments were involved and needed to provide answers – Dirco, Home Affairs, Defence, the South African Revenue Service and the SAPS. While the first four would be involved in the landing and entry of the Indian nationals into the country, the SAPS was on the spot to explain why they were involved in escorting the guests to Sun City in blue-light convoys.

Dirco promptly suspended the Chief of State Protocol, Ambassador Bruce Koloane, who is alleged to have facilitated landing rights for the jet at Waterkloof. Defence Minister Nosiviwe Mapisa-Nqakula ordered the jet to be removed from the air force base and on the afternoon of Thursday 2 May it was pictured taking off.

The government was unusually talkative about the matter. Departmental spokespeople made themselves available for interviews and even Cabinet ministers, who are difficult to pin down in times of crisis, were speaking to the media.

During the post-Cabinet media briefing, Minister in the Presidency Collins Chabane said the incident was 'very serious' and that high-level investigations were underway to get answers. Later, Minister of Police Nathi Mthethwa announced that he had instructed the National Police Commissioner, Riah Phiyega, to investigate the matter and admitted possible transgressions by police officials in the deployment of resources to the Gupta wedding.

'[There was also] possible abuse of SA Police Service (SAPS) blue lights ... [There were] unconfirmed reports indicating that some of the vehicles used in transporting guests were not SAPS vehicles but private vehicles which were fitted with police blue lights,' Mthethwa said in a statement.

The Guptas, it would seem, just pushed too far this time. While they have been making a mockery of the South African state for a while by trading on their relationship with Zuma, they were caught out this time compromising a national security installation. It also seems that too many people in the alliance and in government were fed up with the special treatment of, and being pushed around by, the swaggering family.

Now that Mantashe has gone where no ANC man has gone before, there is a stampede behind him to lay bare the den of unsavoury dealings. After such a crass abuse of political connections to show off for a wedding, the Guptas will have a hard time scrambling back to the position of privilege. Once the guests have left, they will have to do some hard lobbying to crawl back into favour.

But all this will be dependent on the one man who hadn't yet spoken on the issue by 3 May 2013, the man who gave the Guptas their free rein and quite possibly decided to trip them. Even the Guptas will never know if it was Zuma who rained on their parade.

He is not called Gedleyihlekisa (one who smiles while grinding his enemies) for nothing.

MESSAGE TO CABINET:
IT IS NOT JUST A WEDDING

In May 2010, during a state visit to India, a banquet was given for the great and the good of the subcontinental diplomatic and trade world. From the South African side, the president was accompanied by the usual mix of industrialists, BEE beneficiaries, trade delegates and motley acolytes. In a public forum, the president made clear his love of samoosas, the strong bond the two countries shared ... and, not so subtly, that for the multitude of heavyweight Indian titans in the room who were thinking of investing in South Africa, the suitable way of channelling investments would be through the Gupta family.

KALIM RAJAB, MAY 2013

I'm not sure if there are any historical precedents for such a blatant (and downright dodgy) show of support by an administration towards politically connected businessmen, but at first it didn't seem to have the required effect. Several top Indian industrialists left in disgust. At the time, it was perhaps not surprising. After all, few of them would have heard of the Gupta family or thought of them as major players. Before arriving in South Africa, the Guptas had been a middleweight family in the power stakes on the subcontinent. Those in the know used to scoff at them for having embellished their credentials through a clever sleight of hand – by naming their companies outside India 'Sahara' and trading off the powerful (and unconnected) brand name of the famous billionaire Subrata Roy's Sahara Group. Rumours (never proven, but then few such things ever are in Indian courts) swirled around of the Gupta family providing money-laundering facilities in Dubai. Good stuff, as far as dodginess goes, but relatively small potatoes in India's high-octane world of corruption. Yet now, it seemed, they were about to be seriously made. Having the imprimatur of a president of a G-20 country was an impressive – and lucrative – thing indeed.

For some reason, the South African media didn't pick up on the statements made during the state visit; perhaps they were preoccupied with the other, major, scandal of the tour. Remember it? Perhaps not, after all of these years. Our president had to leave India early to deal with the embarrassing speculation that he had been cheated on by one of his wives with his bodyguard. The bodyguard had subsequently committed suicide and the second lady was pregnant.

It's funny how such scandals fade into collective oblivion after a few months – but only because they're always replaced by new ones. Ah, for those heady few days in May, before Nkandlagate, or Petrogate, or Limpopo-textbook-gate, when all we had to worry about were the amorous goings-on of the presidential bed. We could console ourselves that the looming plague of the Guptas was a worry for another day.

In the week preceding 6 May 2013, I was reminded of these two incidents because, whether we liked it or not, the plague of the Guptas had struck and, as everyone within the ANC and the alliance now belatedly admits, this plague had been with us for quite a while. Those Indian businessmen who snorted at the Guptas in 2010 now probably pay obeisance. Our state organs, judging by the actions of that week, certainly pay obeisance. Without fully realising it, our whole country has sleepwalked into being enslaved into obeisance. For despite the questions being asked only now about why civilians were able to get flying-squad and blue-light escorts, I've been present at several functions dating back to 2009 in which the Guptas received these same escorts. Notwithstanding the questions about the Guptas and landing rights, I've previously seen the Sahara helicopter land with impunity at Zoo Lake near the Gupta compound, flouting all manner of municipal and security laws.

There are, of course, so many worrying things about this new power elite, which has already attracted many inches of column width over the past few days. But, for me, the worrying thing was not only the plane landing at Waterkloof, or how it was allowed there. It was also how so many of our Cabinet ministers seemingly saw no conflict in being so publicly associated with the Guptas – at a time when evidence of them holding incredible sway over the Cabinet and the administration had become increasingly obvious.

What was a member of the SACP like Minister Rob Davies (supposedly bent on achieving a 'national democratic revolution') doing cavorting with the family behind Imperial Crown Trading (whose venal brand of capitalism appears bent on achieving exactly the opposite), other than hoping to soak up some of the patronage that would come his way? What was Malusi Gigaba doing there, so soon after the *Sunday Times*'s exposé that one of his temporary appointments at SAA was the victim of an attempted bribe by Tony Gupta? We can suspend our disbelief when it comes to the attendance of former Mbeki henchman Essop Pahad ('I'm just here to enjoy myself') because he is now effectively in the employ of the Guptas, who bankroll his magazine.

But my heart really sank when I heard that Naledi Pandor, one of the more cerebral minds in an otherwise lacklustre Cabinet, had also attended. 'It's only a wedding,' she was purported to have said. Actually, Minister Pandor, it is not. For the sake of your country and your administration's stated aim of fighting corruption, it is much more than that.

Some say history repeats itself; others say not. The South African optimist in me hopes that, in our case, it just might. In 1971, while his country groaned and burned under the weight of poverty and oppression, the decadent last shah of Iran celebrated the 2 500th anniversary of the Persian Empire. Next to the ancient ruins of Persepolis, he ordered $100 million to be spent to create a tent city of 160 acres. Dancers were flown in from the great capitals of the world. Now, Persepolis lies very close to mud-hut villages of squalor and misery, but the specially flown-in guests would hardly have noticed – or cared – as they sipped champagne in Baccarat crystal and dipped into beluga caviar. Along with the shah, many were beneficiaries of the country's massive oil wealth, and they basked in his patronage. As his guests bowed and grovelled and toasted the next 2 500 years, it would have been easy for the shah to believe them, and to drown out the growing voices of discontent. But before the decade was out, in 1979, he was overthrown. As much as the optimist in me hopes for the same for the family whose members have now proven themselves to be the real power centre in South Africa, the cynic in me says, 'But do we have to wait for close on a decade before it happens?'

THE TOP SPOOKS' GUPTA WARNING

A persistent question following the Gupta jet being allowed to land at Waterkloof Air Force Base is: How could this have happened? In 2011, intelligence heads tried to warn the government that the Gupta brothers posed a possible threat to national security. But their investigation was stymied, leading to them losing their jobs. Therefore, the phalanx of Cabinet ministers and senior government officials now claiming to be mystified about the security breach needs to look no further than Minister of State Security Siyabonga Cwele and President Jacob Zuma.

RANJENI MUNUSAMY, MAY 2013

The only direct comments by President Jacob Zuma on the raging controversy surrounding the Gupta family were that the situation should be handled with care so as not to jeopardise diplomatic relations with India. In an interview with the SABC after a visit to the Democratic Republic of Congo, Zuma said the Indian High Commission could not be blamed.

In an effort to limit the diplomatic fallout following the irregular and private use of a national key point by Gupta wedding guests, Zuma said the High Commission had made an application requesting to land at Waterkloof Air Force Base, but that the application had been incorrectly handled.

'But of course it's important to know that you are dealing with citizens of another country, India, there are diplomatic relations so the manner in which we handle it must be handled in that understanding,' Zuma said.

Fair enough. It would not be in South Africa's interests to raise enough of a stink over the role and conduct of India's diplomat in the matter to cause a strain in relations between the two countries – both partners in BRICS. While South Africa is considering issuing a démarche, the highest diplomatic rebuke, due to Indian High Commissioner Virendra Gupta's circumventing normal procedures to secure landing rights for the private jet, it would not want to dent relations, particularly trade relations, with the Indian government.

During the interview, the opportunity presented itself for President Zuma to say, 'However, I take exception to businesspeople, whoever they might be, using my name and my relationship with them to secure special privileges and abusing state facilities.'

That is all it would have taken to extricate the office of the president from the muck and to set the record straight. But even though Zuma is said to be angered by the behaviour of the Gupta family in this instance, and is clearly supporting the multi-departmental probe into what, exactly, transpired, he will still not cut the brothers loose.

The relationship between Zuma and the Gupta brothers has befuddled even Zuma's closest comrades in the ANC and the alliance structures. While Zuma has always had less than savoury relationships with businesspeople, including those found to have contributed to the initial renovations at his Nkandla home, there is something extraordinary about the connection to the Guptas.

Whatever hold the Guptas have on Zuma has even resulted in the destruction of relationships forged during the liberation struggle.

Gibson Njenje, the former head of the State Security Agency's domestic branch (previously called the National Intelligence Agency), was hand-picked by Zuma to serve as his intelligence head when he became president. Njenje is highly respected in ANC intelligence circles, having served as deputy head of counterintelligence in the ANC's department of intelligence and security in the underground.

While Zuma consulted with other leaders in the ANC, the SACP and Cosatu over other high-profile portfolios in his administration, Njenje was his first and only choice for the job. Njenje left the business sector to return to the civil service at Zuma's invitation.

Several months later, Zuma appointed Mo Shaik as his

foreign intelligence head. Shaik and his brother Yunis ran a covert intelligence unit under Zuma when he was head of ANC intelligence. They became close comrades and friends, which led to Zuma being introduced to older brother Schabir. Even after Zuma and Schabir's relationship was found to be corrupt by Judge Hilary Squires during Schabir's corruption trial, Mo maintained his relationship with Zuma, acting as the president's confidant on political and private matters.

Jeff Maqetuka, who also served in the ANC Department of Intelligence and Security from 1979 when he went into exile, was a director general of the State Security Agency. Maqetuka completed Zuma's intelligence dream team, a triumvirate of directors general he trusted unequivocally.

A few months apart, starting in 2011, all three resigned after a fallout with Minister of State Security Siyabonga Cwele. The source of the conflict, it turns out, was the Gupta family.

Alarm bells started ringing in the intelligence agencies about the conduct and dealings of the Gupta brothers and Njenje ordered an investigation into the family's inappropriate influence on South Africa's top political leaders and government officials.

When Cwele learned of this, he ordered the investigation to be stopped immediately. Njenje, backed by the other two directors general, tried to warn that the Guptas' behaviour constituted a 'threat to national security' and, if allowed to continue, would compromise the credibility of the state. Cwele refused to listen or to see whether there was legitimate cause for the investigation.

This soured relations between Cwele and the directors

general, which, over the next few months, deteriorated to the extent that the minister asked them to leave.

It was not as if Cwele pulled the plug on the investigation because Zuma told him to do so. He would not entertain any discussion about the Guptas being investigated because he was cognisant of the special relationship between the family and the president, and concluded that they needed to be protected from scrutiny.

During the standoff, Zuma became aware of the trouble between his three trusted spooks and his minister, and the source of the trouble. He did not intervene to stop their departure, leaving Njenje, Shaik and Maqetuka to hang out to dry. The Guptas continued with their wayward behaviour, unhindered, while Zuma's three comrades washed their hands of the matter – and of him.

Two years later, in 2013, the warnings Njenje gave about the Guptas compromising the integrity and credibility of the state by bullying and influencing senior officials came back to haunt the Zuma administration. The family pulled off the most brazen act, arranging landing rights for their private jet at Waterkloof Air Force Base without fear of reprisals. The Guptas became aware of the attempted intelligence investigation against them and the punishment meted out to the three directors general. Therefore, if they were not swaggering enough already, that incident showed them, and everyone else in government, that they were beyond reproach.

Their previous stunts allegedly include trying to strong-arm a former senior Government Communications and Information System official to buy government advertisements in their newspaper, *The New Age*, and instructing other directors general on how they should award government contracts.

For the Guptas there have been no repercussions, while those at the receiving end of their bullying have been fearful about complaining to their seniors. Njenje, Shaik and Maqetuka are not the only senior officials to have lost their jobs as a result of the Guptas – several others who balked at the Guptas' instructions were shown the door.

The security breach at the national key point, however, provoked alarm and an extraordinary reaction by the government. Five senior officials were suspended or put on special leave and the security cluster of ministers promised a swift investigation to determine how the plane was able to land and the 200 passengers were able to enter the country.

However, all the ministers and officials who were trotted out to show how seriously the government is taking the matter know full well why the Guptas had got away with interfering with the state until that time. They could have been stopped in their tracks in 2011 if the government had taken heed of the warnings of the intelligence heads. Ironically, the acting head of the Department of State Security, Dennis Dlomo, was among the high-powered team of top government officials tasked with investigating the Waterkloof landing. Perhaps Dlomo's task would be to come up with different information from the information that came up in the aborted investigation in 2011.

But if the government really wants answers, it needs to look in its intelligence archives. And if President Zuma really wants to preserve the integrity of the state, and to put our country's interests above everybody else's, he needs to look into his own friends first. The Gupta brothers have been allowed to run roughshod over South Africa for way too long.

ANN7: CAR-CRASH VIEWING, BUT NO LAUGHING MATTER

What do you get when you combine Gupta money, supposedly cutting-edge technology and a bunch of beautiful young models acting as news anchors? The omnishambles that is ANN7. At least, that's what the first few days of its broadcast life suggested.

REBECCA DAVIS, AUGUST 2013

Here at Daily Maverick, we're huge believers in admitting our mistakes and apologising for them. Consequently, we'd like to say sorry for the mixed review we recently gave to the SABC's new 24-hour channel. Because the arrival of 'Gupta TV', as ANN7 has predictably been dubbed, makes the SABC channel look like the slickest operation ever, and a contender for the Pulitzer.

It's hard to know where to start, really. The blooper videos have already been seen online by thousands. There's the one in which the news anchor repeats exactly the same piece of news, word for word, twice in quick succession. There's the one in which the news anchor announces that racing driver 'Louise' Hamilton has won the 'Grand Pricks'. There's the one in which the weather presenter moves on to 'the mother city, Johannesburg'. There is the explosion of awkwardness that sees two female sports anchors left stranded by a misfiring autocue.

We would have posted links to the videos mentioned above, but most of the videos have disappeared from YouTube and have been replaced by a notice that they were removed for infringing copyright. The notice was posted by Aiplex Software, an Indian company that has attracted controversy in the past for trying to silence unfavourable reports. It's an indication that Infinity Media – ANN7's holding company, a joint venture between India's Essel Media and the Guptas' Oakbay Investments – doesn't seem to be finding the critical savaging of its channel funny. Another indication is that a Twitter parody account operating under the handle @ANN7news was suspended suddenly, while others remained up and running.

We're not ones to bandy the C-word – censorship – about too loosely, but it must be said that this approach is pretty rich for an operation with the slogan 'Truth unfolds'. That's a weird-sounding phrase, grammatically speaking, but if we've learned anything about ANN7 over the past days, it's that they're not 'strictlers' for grammar. It's also weird because it suggests that said process of truth unfolding is organic, and takes place without human intervention. *If the truth is busily unfolding all by itself*, you may well think, *why do we need another 24-hour news channel*?

Still, it was a bit of a relief to discover that 'Truth unfolds' was ANN7's chosen slogan, after Editor-in-Chief Moegsien Williams told reporters on 21 August 2013 that the channel would practice with 'no fear or favour'. As far as we're aware, that's the slogan of a rival channel.

An alternative slogan that ANN7 might consider would be 'Not for the faint-hearted', because the initial viewing experience has been exceedingly nerve-racking. One could never really put one's feet up, so to speak, because the atmosphere was fraught with danger. Mistakes occurred so frequently that if you were to have played the ANN7 drinking game that one commentator suggested, you'd probably have been vomiting by the second hour.

The mind boggles at what the backstage scenes must have been like at the ANN7 offices. The proliferation of technical errors suggests it might have been a bit like the control room at the nuclear reactor where Homer Simpson works. A favoured tactic has been to leave an anchor's mic on while the channel crosses to a package. This has left, for example, a panicked sports anchor clearly audible, hissing, 'Where's my script? What's happening? Where am I going? Where am I going?'

It's a question that must have been on the mind of more than one ANN7 journalist in the channel's early stages. The channel claimed it had over 70 journalists with international broadcast backgrounds, but initially the likes of the experienced and professional Chantal Rutter Dros were decidedly in the minority. On the weekend of 24 and 25 August 2013, at least one experienced journalist was known to have tendered a resignation – fewer than four days after the launch. The remainder of the seasoned hacks must have been sweating, because their colleagues appeared to have been assembled at random from the call list at a Boss Models shoot.

To claim that many of ANN7's news anchors are models is not an attempt at snark. They are. Abigail Visagie is a model and BCom student who recently applied to be a *Top Billing* presenter. Before Lebogang Keagile landed her job at the channel, she was a part-time model and full-time flight attendant. Cleopatra Simelane trained as a 'news compiler' but is also an actress and model, and a former Miss Soweto runner-up. Afrika Gola is a model. Taryn du Plooy is a model. Avumile Qongqa is a model.

At other channels, the prestigious news anchor position is generally filled by a journalist with substantial field experience. What ANN7 proved daily in its initial stages is that there is a gaping chasm between 'being able to read' and 'being able to read the news live on national TV'. No doubt the channel's young women will improve with time, but their delivery has, in some cases, been almost incomprehensible, as if they were reading a recipe in Klingon.

Their weather presenters may need additional tuition in geography: one gave the temperatures for both Polokwane and Pietersburg; another allegedly pointed firmly at Botswana while discussing Mpumalanga. They specialised in gently caressing the weather map in a non-specific sort of way, letting their hands airily drift around about five different provinces at once. Perky Lebogang Molefe proceeded to exhort the burghers of two separate South African cities to capitalise on one day's good weather by having a picnic, which may have been a trenchant observation about unemployment rates.

But it is not these young women's fault, and it's hard not to feel sorry for them. Both eNCA and SABC's 24-hour channels took years of planning, with months of dry runs. ANN7 reportedly had only a few weeks of practice, which suggests either ignorance or massive hubris. Many of their on-camera staff were clearly inexperienced and nervous; they were let down by shoddy technical work, and they were fed to the wolves (that would be us). An 'insider' told the *Sunday Times* that ANN7 had hired models as news anchors because 'they believe that men will enjoy watching the news when they see pretty girls'. In that case, why not dispense with the news element altogether, and simply air a scrolling catalogue of tits and ass? They could call it MANN7.

One of the more irritating aspects of the channel is that in the absence of paid advertising (for now – more on this anon), they screened a succession of boastful promos hyping up ANN7 and taking potshots at the competition. One particularly surreal promo, which featured pictures of scantily clad female celebrities for absolutely no discernible reason, welcomed the viewer to 'our wholesome world of news'. Another complained that other media outlets are continuously 'pushing someone's agenda'. Not us, said the channel that President Zuma secretly visited 48 hours before launch.

These promos were still marginally more bearable than the continuous public service announcements warning about the evils of drugs and corruption, which turned the viewing experience into something like a school assembly. The channel has also run regular reminders to the country to stop abusing women. 'What does the word "women" mean to you?' it asked, and the obvious answer – the plural form of 'woman' – was not one of the multiple-choice options. 'Human', however, was – which is nice.

Among their most-hyped offerings is the talk show hosted by former government spokesperson Jimmy Manyi. The show's slogan is 'No comment is not an option', which is gut-burstingly funny if you've ever had any contact with government spokespeople. (See, for instance, *City Press* of 2 March 2011:

'Manyi has no comment on Manuel's letter'.) Manyi was presumably selected for this position due to his reputation as a 'straight talker', which, in South Africa, is often a euphemism for 'racist'. In his inaugural interview with Minister of Water Affairs Edna Molewa, he certainly gave it to her straight – if by 'gave it to her straight' you mean 'handed her a gilt-edged invitation to parrot government policy without being challenged'. Manyi's opening gambit was a request for the Honourable Minister to 'allay our fears'.

There have been grumblings on social media about the hostility that the 'liberal media', and its representatives, have shown to ANN7. (We hope we're liberal media, since we'd hate to be conservative media.) Yes, as has been said repeatedly, the insular South African media scene is notoriously unfriendly to new entries, and turf is jealously guarded. But when it comes to ANN7, there's more at stake than professional rivalry.

Let's not forget that the Guptas' other media investment, *The New Age*, reportedly bagged over R75 million in government advertising in its first year, despite the fact that the publication doesn't even have any audited circulation figures. We don't yet know if the same will be true of ANN7. But it's certainly a good reason to keep a sceptical eye on the channel. The Guptas have shown that they are not afraid to utilise their friendship with Jacob Zuma for personal benefit, even when such benefit is at odds with due process. Inevitably, particularly since Guptagate, their TV channel will attract some jaundiced glances.

There can also be no sugar-coating the fact that the channel initially experienced some major problems. To point this out is not intrinsically ungenerous; it is merely factual. Perhaps, in time, it will right itself. We hope so, because more good media is better for everyone. But we hope so not for the sake of the Guptas, but for the sake of the journalists who took a chance on them.

2
REPORTER'S NOTEBOOK

THE LESSONS NO JOURNALISM SCHOOL CAN TEACH YOU

There are many things that nobody warns you about when you become a journalist. There are many things that you have no idea how to handle, and don't bother thinking about when you're chasing a deadline. But the death of one man I encountered through Lonmin has changed the way I operate. It has changed how I perceive things and left some acutely painful questions I may never be able to answer.

SIPHO HLONGWANE, OCTOBER 2012

The Swahili have a proverb that says *Ndovu wawili wakisongana, ziumiazo ni nyika*. Roughly translated, it means: When elephants jostle, it is the grass that gets hurt.

There are many variations of this saying on the African continent, but they all mean the same thing – the weak and insignificant are inevitable collateral damage when the mighty vie for power.

One such struggle took place in South Africa in 2012, reaching a crescendo on 16 August when dozens of people were mowed down near Marikana by the police, in full view of television cameras. The struggle for power between the National Union of Mineworkers (NUM) and the Association of Mineworkers and Construction Union (AMCU) has been epic. In our efforts to understand what has been going on, and to communicate our knowledge to the world, we have tended to focus on the big players. It has helped that the government, the unions and the big mining companies involved have (mostly) played seemingly open cards – in many instances, it made reaching deadlines a doddle.

But that does not mean that the grass has not been trampled.

I was at the Oppikoppi Festival when the labour unrest in the mining sector finally began to explode. On the weekend on which I had enjoyed the sounds of Fokofpolisiekar, the BLK JKS and Valiant Swart about an hour's drive north of Marikana, several people were killed when an angry crowd descended upon the NUM offices at Lonmin's Marikana operations. More skirmishes between AMCU and NUM supporters happened between that weekend and the fateful Thursday on which the situation finally tipped over.

Just two days before 112 people were shot, I spoke to Daluvuyo Bongo, the NUM secretary at Lonmin. He sounded absolutely petrified on the phone. His most-repeated phrase was, 'I just don't know what to do any more.' He said he was in hiding because people wanted to kill him. At the time, the gravity of the situation hadn't quite dawned on me yet (Oppikoppi hangovers typically last for up to two weeks) and, while he proved to be a very useful source who could provide accurate information, it didn't occur to me to ask personal questions that would not feature in my stories.

I took leave in the midst of the Marikana mess, and did not so much as open my email accounts or Twitter page for about ten days. When I finally did peek at the news accounts on the interwebs, I was confronted with the news that the 'NUM local secretary [had been] killed in Lonmin's hostels'. It was Mr Bongo.

My immediate thought was that I did not know what his face looked like. I didn't know if he was short or tall. Was he very dark, or light-skinned? Was he bald, or did he have a magnificent Afro? I didn't know how many children he had, or what their names were. Who had his friends been?

I knew absolutely nothing about Mr Bongo the human being, except that he had been a low-level unionist who tried desperately to do his job as best he knew. To me, at that time, he had been just a voice down the phone that had given me vital information so that I could file before deadline.

One of the most difficult things to communicate about the Marikana tragedy has been the fact that it is not a simple conflict between goodies and baddies. There are no clear battle lines. I have personally castigated NUM for the way in which the union dealt with the labour unrest and, indeed, for the way in which it contributed to the toxic situation in the first place.

But there are thousands of people who are connected to NUM because it represented the best way for them to get ahead in life. I have no doubt in my mind that for Mr Bongo, being chosen by his peers to be the branch secretary of the most powerful union within Cosatu, was a major life achievement for him, in the same way as so many graduate students dream of becoming a CEO or young journalists like me dream of running a national newspaper someday.

The timing of his term couldn't have been more catastrophic. He was the local face of a union that was hated by some desperate people. His time was always going to be up too soon.

I read of his death – he had been shot in the hostels – with indescribable anguish.

Mr Bongo died because he had the ambition of getting on in life. I didn't know him well, and perhaps we will learn that he did have some dark hand in this sordid tale, but the impression I was left with was that this man was killed because he had a desire to survive and serve as a prominent member of his community. His ambition put him in the crosshairs of a battle not of his choosing. I spoke to many Cosatu-aligned unionists in the five weeks that followed, and their hatred of AMCU was astonishing. I didn't get that from Mr Bongo. The strongest emotion I got from him was terror.

This is one of the things that nobody told me about journalism – desperate people would put immense trust in my abilities to help them when I truly wouldn't know what to do.

My heart broke when a man came to me in Marikana and said, 'My child is sick. She breathed in the tear gas yesterday. The police were firing tear gas and rubber bullets anywhere. It didn't matter that there were women and children in the shacks. Many children got the gas.' They thought that as a journalist I could do something, yet all I was capable of was driving the man to the nearest clinic so he could get medication – then pissing off to the next area of unrest. I had not wept in many years as I did on that day, on the shoulder of the Platinum Highway, while other cars sped past mine.

I know that I could not have done anything significant to save Mr Bongo's life. But I also know that I cannot fully tell the story of his life and death because I hadn't bothered to find out who he was as a fellow human being when I'd had the chance to do so. It made my encounters with new contacts at different mines so traumatic. I spoke to up to ten people when I went to trouble spots; I had no idea how many of them would be alive the next day.

This is why it absolutely drives me up the wall when people speak of the Marikana miners as if they are mindless animals or dumb savages who must be culled. These people know that they have no political clout to be heard at the negotiating table. They feel that they are just black bodies that mining companies throw into the hole to dig up gold or platinum. They don't see the reward of their labour. The only option they have is downing tools. When the law tells them that they can't, they do it anyway. When that doesn't work, they turn to violence.

Cosatu General Secretary Zwelinzima Vavi dubbed the protests in the townships surrounding Johannesburg 'the ring of fire'. These people also felt that nobody listened to them, so they had to do something spectacular (and often terrible) to be noticed.

They know that we, the press, only showed up in Marikana when people started dying. We know that they know.

I don't know how many children have been orphaned by Mr Bongo's death. I don't know how many friends of family have deep wounds, which nothing will ever heal, resulting from his murder. I don't even know what he looks like. He was just the grass that got trampled when the elephants fought. But his life is no less significant than anyone else's just because he didn't have a corner office and a Jaguar in the garage.

What a horrible bloody mess.

A THIN LINE BETWEEN FEAR AND HATE

Saturday should be the best day of the week. One gets to sleep in. See friends; do some shopping; have a long, slow coffee. But not if you live in the settlement of Nkaneng, a cluster of shacks just a stone's throw from Wonderkop. If you happened to be one of its residents, you spent Saturday 15 September 2012 running away from tear gas, dodging rubber bullets and swinging between fear of and hatred for the police.

BRANKO BRKIC, SEPTEMBER 2012

One can think of few, if any, better companions with whom to enter the township limits of Nkaneng than Greg Marinovich, his fearless wife Leonie and the researcher Thapelo Lekgowa, the one who originally unearthed the murder field of Small Koppie while doing a survey with Professor Peter Alexander of the University of Johannesburg.

The events of the morning of Saturday 15 September, before we arrived, filled the world of Marikana with heavy, dark clouds. Police had raided the miners' hostel and homes overnight, looking for arms and confiscating several. These were not firearms, mind you, but sticks and – at a push – pangas or machetes. As we approached, headline news on the radio was that the police had also broken up a gathering of 200 or so protesters using tear gas and rubber bullets.

Fearful of the police Nyalas returning, residents had erected barricades wherever possible. The already impassable 'roads' of Nkaneng were full of massive rocks; the air was thick with the choking smoke of burning tyres.

As we got deeper into the settlement, the news arrived that during the earlier-morning scuffles, four women had been injured by rubber bullets and were in the Andrew Saffy Memorial Hospital, with some having been taken to the Job Shimankana Tabane Provincial Hospital in Rustenburg. We negotiated our way into the heart of the community, where a little 'plaza' enveloped the community centre – in reality, a single-layer corrugated tin shack. As we arrived, the women gathered and talked about what had happened the previous night. Around us, at the 'plaza' perimeter, spotters were dispatched to inform about the police Nyalas' movements.

The women were angry. Beyond angry: incandescent with rage. One after the other, they informed their friends about the night raids, police arrogance and indifference to their children's plight. The police had been looking for their men, they said, which hadn't stopped them from ordering women to the ground, making rude gestures and laughing at them.

'The children are choking on tear gas because it is being shot into our shacks where we live with our children. Where is safety there? Zuma knows nothing about safety. Zuma and Radebe, when they said they will break this thing, did they mean they will be killing us in our shacks?' said one of the women.

'We hear that they will be coming back tonight. What sleep? Where are we going to sleep? How are you going to sleep? It's all in the hand of God now. Where must we run to now? We have children who go to school – it is impossible to pack our bags and go home at this point; December is far from here. Government announced it and we heard it – "kill them" – [but] this people, even if they are carrying weapons, they are killing no one with them but just protesting. It's their weapons anyway. They are sending back the police who killed some of them. They ask for their weapons, then they shoot at them when [they are] defenceless.'

As the women told their stories, the police surveillance helicopter circled overhead: repeatedly, menacingly. But then the accusations became even more far-reaching, in a way that should chill the blood of every South African who cares for this country: the struggle turned tribal.

(Let us digress here for a second: while Lonmin's Marikana mine is on Tswana land, the overwhelming majority of the miners protesting are of Pondo [Xhosa] and Sotho origin.)

The women's talk suddenly switched to blaming President Zuma. Why do you think no Zulu died in the massacre? Because Zuma organised everything. Inkatha warriors had marched with their traditional arms just a day before; how come no one had attempted to disarm them, but when their husbands – Xhosas – had taken up their traditional arms, they had been shot at and killed?

And then all hell broke loose. The spotters' sign, unseen by us, was made, and every man started running in one direction, away from the 'plaza'. Women started praying, with all the air they had in their lungs, their arms up, as if only the heavens could help them. Being enveloped by the sound of many women praying loudly was both beautiful and frightening; it was powerful in its powerlessness.

I decided to investigate. The police Nyala entered the maze of the little ditches that served as streets and extricated itself towards the outer limits. But police were not gone forever: after moving about 200 metres, the Nyala made a U-turn and went straight back towards the community's heart. Another scattering ensued, the road in front of the heavily armed vehicle suddenly abandoned.

The Nyala approached the barricade that was a mere 20 metres away from me, then turned away, exposing its right flank to the shacks into which people fled.

Then the police started firing rubber bullets.

Bravely hidden in their armoured car, wearing their bulletproof vests and sitting behind their portholes, they fired indiscriminately and with no provocation. As I feverishly photographed, they stood there, untouchable and inscrutable, all-powerful, if only for a moment. And then the Nyala made another U-turn and disappeared into the maze of little lanes.

As people started emerging from their shacks, their faces were tensed with anger. They showed me the rubber bullets that, just moments before, had pierced their shacks. There were plenty of children around. The police had fired rubber bullets without concern for whether they would hit a child, a woman, or anyone else. The heavy instrument of state repression had been used against the underclass – there is no police spin or PR that could work its way around that simple fact. I saw it. All of it.

As our time – and welcome – in the heart of Nkaneng eventually came to the end, we moved back.

From the direction of the settlement, the police loudspeakers were ordering people off the streets, and telling the women that the police wanted their men.

But I couldn't stop thinking about the panicky heavy-handedness that the state had displayed on that Saturday.

Who can order people off the streets? Who can violate people's homes at will and without a court order? And even if they had had the legal right to do so, no court order would ever allow for this kind of intimidation and humiliation during arrest, search or seizure.

There had been a national outcry two weeks earlier when the NPA had used apartheid's 'common purpose' law to charge 270 miners with 34 counts of murder each. And yet, on that Saturday in Nkaneng, we had seen an entire community treated as one criminal, where being a child of five, a girl of 13, a woman of 65, or a man who had had nothing to do with the strike had not been enough to keep you safe from harassment and injury. Common purpose, indeed.

After the police had shot 112 miners on 16 August 2012, killing 34 of them, the state of South Africa could have – should have – shown empathy and care for the people everyone had forgotten for such a long time. Instead, it chose to let NGOs deliver food and care for the hungry and sick while it opted to deliver tear gas, rubber bullets and intimidation.

Make no mistake: what happened on that Saturday just a

stone's throw away from the blood-soaked field of Marikana was nothing but state repression. The government of South Africa decided that it was better for it to be feared than loved. What it achieved was something different: it became hated. And a government hated by its own people has no credibility.

As we travelled back towards our comfortable lives, I remembered Greg Marinovich's words: 'Just like apartheid, man. Just like apartheid.'

THE DAY THE CAPE WINELANDS BURNED

By Wednesday 7 November 2012, the Cape winelands had turned into a battlefield. As fires smouldered across the famously scenic fruit-growing region, in the embers of the ongoing labour dispute we found ordinary people who were tired, angry, injured and frightened.

REBECCA DAVIS, NOVEMBER 2012

The strike that began among grape pickers in the Hex River Valley on 5 November 2012 turned violent on Wednesday 7 November. The Minister of Agriculture at the time, Tina Joemat-Pettersson, called for calm on that Wednesday evening, which appeared to have little effect. Assurances from unions that negotiations over a new minimum wage for the sector were ongoing also did little to stem anger. With unrest initially confined to De Doorns, by 7 November protests had spread across the winelands to Robertson, Wolseley, Ceres, Prince Alfred Hamlet and the surrounding areas.

On the Robertson route, many roads and thoroughfares had been rendered almost impassable by rocks heaped by protestors across the road. Tree branches, lead pipes, barbed wire and even the turn-off sign to a winery further blockaded the motorist's path. A smashed car window was evidence of stones having been thrown at vehicles. Close to Robertson, fires burned on both sides of the road. The vines of the Constitution Road Wine Growers flickered with flame. A signboard outside the winery proclaimed it to be an 'empowerment project endorsed by Robertson Winery'.

A steady stream of farm workers appeared out of the smoke shrouding the town. '*Een-vyftig*!' they shouted, a reference to their wage demand of R150. '*Die boere wil vir ons fokol gee*!' one yelled: the farmers want to give us nothing. On Robertson's main drag, riot police formed a tight line, with protestors slowly retreating from their view. The ground was littered with the casings of blue riot ammunition, a sign of earlier violence. An estimated 500 people had clashed with police in Robertson that morning, but by early afternoon the situation had simmered into a tense calm.

Western Cape police had received a directive on the morning of 7 November instructing them not to speak to the media. Lieutenant Cynthia Mngcele of the Robertson police would provide only the bare bones of the morning's events. 'They were toyi-toying, throwing stones, and they burned tyres,' she said. 'There were arrests, but I can't say how many.' She gestured to Raimondi's, a local wholesaler. 'They were trying to get in there to get food,' she said.

Behind the barbed wire that provided an inadequate fortress on the perimeter of Raimondi's, operations manager Jaco van Wyk kept an uneasy vigil. 'They started at the tyre place next door; they wanted to burn it down,' he said. 'Then they came here. They were throwing stones and they broke down part of the wall.' He said he had taken his own workers home early to ensure their safety. 'There's definitely people here from outside. These aren't people from around here. I saw buses outside Worcester this morning.'

Outside, a group of locals sat on the pavement in apparent anticipation of viewing more action. We asked them whether the people who protested were from local communities. 'Ja,' they said. Were there any buses? *'Daar was geen busse nie* (There were no buses),' they said.

Five minutes outside Robertson, the countryside resumed its peaceful dreaminess, as if nothing had ever happened to disrupt it. But elsewhere, worse violence had already taken place. In the small town of Wolseley, a protestor had died after clashes with police. By mid-afternoon, the town was abandoned. Rocks lay strewn on the road, and little fires burned smokily. Police perched on van bonnets and in an armoured Hippo, tensed for further action.

In Ceres, a crowd of several thousand was addressed by strike leaders and unionists in the early afternoon, and motorists were warned to stay away. A doctor at the Ceres Hospital, who spoke to us on condition of anonymity, said he had treated people on 6 and 7 November for protest-related injuries. He estimated that he had seen five to ten cases of patients coming in with injuries from the police's riot ammunition, including one who had been shot in the tongue. 'I am not blaming the police, but it was clear to me that the way they were shot was very painful,' he said.

He claimed further that he had treated 'two or three' cases of protestors shot with 9-millimetre live ammunition. 'We have also had a number of people who were bystanders and suffered broken ankles and so on while trying to run away,' he said. 'Again, I'm not blaming the police, because it must have been a very difficult situation to handle.'

At the Ceres Golf Estate on the edge of the town, golfers teed off as if completely immune to the goings-on a few kilometres down the road. In the centre of town, all was similarly peaceful, but police warned us that if we drove along to the township of Nduli it would be at our own risk. A ditch had been dug by protestors in the road, they said, and stones were being thrown from shacks.

When we entered the informal settlement on foot, a crowd gathered quickly, eager to give their side of events. Moleboheng Sedidi, 22, showed us an angry bruise on her arm where a rubber bullet had struck her. Gesturing to a nearby shack, she said, 'I was standing there near a photographer yesterday at 3 p.m. People were throwing stones and the police were shooting. I was doing nothing, no fighting.' She pointed to a spot about 10 metres away, from where a policeman had fired on her. 'I don't know why he chose me, I was the only one. I sat down and cried.'

Had the photographer helped her? 'Everyone was fighting for their life!' she said.

A man called Nkosinathi, a 55-year-old striking fruit picker, claimed he had been sitting in his house when police had entered and shot him. He showed us a bullet wound on his side.

Kholisile Ndzakana, 38, displayed multiple wounds on his

stomach and back. 'They took me in front of the house when they came,' he said. 'They held me down and they shot me.'

Startled, we pantomimed his words to make sure we understood. 'Yes!' he said, nodding vigorously. A crowd of onlookers chorused in assent. 'They held me down and they shot me.'

Two mothers came forward with their sons. Andile Manyangaza, 18, had a plaster on his face. He was supposed to have written a matric exam on the previous day, his mother claimed, but he had been assaulted by police and taken to the police station. Lwamkelo Nzondo, 14, showed us what was clearly the mark of a rubber bullet on his arm. 'He did nothing!' his mother insisted furiously.

Most shocking of all was Charmaine Jonkers, 29, who held a cloth against her lower face tearily and removed it to show the injury to which the Ceres doctor had already testified: she had received riot ammunition in the mouth. '*Ek was hier voor my huis en ek was besig om te was* (I was here in front of my house busy washing)', she said, with some difficulty. '*Ek gooi uit die water en toe voel ek iets soos 'n klip* (I throw out the water and then I feel something like a stone).'

She was not sure from what range she had been fired upon, but she was certain about something else: she was no protestor. '*Ek toyi-toyi nie!* (I don't toyi-toyi!)' she said with indignation. Jonkers works on a fruit farm where she makes R80 per day. '*My baas is 'n goeie man, hy's 'n kerklike man* (My boss is a good man, he's a God-fearing man).'

Mpho Methula, 24, said that the windows to his house had been shot at while his girlfriend was sitting at the table. Methula, a peach picker, was one of the few workers we encountered who voiced any kind of political grievance. 'We don't want to fight with [police],' he said. 'Yesterday we were there talking. We don't even finish the conversation. They're just shooting.' He was adamant that they would not return to work without a firm pay increase. Was he angry with his boss or with the government? 'We are angry for our boss, not our government,' he replied without hesitation.

Police watched our interactions from across the road in an armoured vehicle. When we approached them for their account, they cited their gagging order, and refused to give names. 'It was chaos,' was all that one would say. 'We would never shoot anyone unless we had to. They were throwing stones.' Did any of the protestors have any weapons other than stones? 'Not that I know of,' he said.

'Just look around at this place,' he said, sweeping his arm to show the battle debris on the road and the burnt grass verges. 'Look what a mess it is.'

We asked what normal police procedure was in the case of a situation like this, in terms of using weapons. He was silent, and after a word from one of his colleagues inside the van, a man sitting at the wheel turned on his engine so that conversation became impossible.

Local ANC councillor Reginald Badela confirmed via telephone that he had seen many of the people in Nduli shot without provocation. 'We know this is correct,' he said. 'People were sitting there in their own homes. Those people who were affected were just running away. They were trying to get to their houses.' He said that while there had been pressure placed on workers – both male and female – by strike leaders to stay away from work, he had arranged for children to be able to go to school.

At that point, our phone call ended abruptly. About 20 metres down the road, some protestors had gathered at the ditch they had dug. The police van roared into action. 'You must go!' people shouted at us. It was impossible to make out what was going on, but as we drove away the unmistakable crack of a gun being fired several times rang out.

Back in Ceres, at a watering hole, the locals were trying to make sense of what was going on. A man who would not be named – the finance manager of a local farm that was on fire – sat drinking beer to mark the fact that he did not have to go work the next day, or for the foreseeable future. He spoke of a farming community who felt terrified and under siege, with no way of knowing whether the reports they were hearing were accurate. He read us a series of text messages from a hysterical friend, one of which claimed that farmhouses were being taken over by protestors.

'We don't know what's true and what's people riling each other up,' he said. Local farmers had hired private security firms, including helicopters, to guard their property, he said. They were most concerned about protecting their packing crates – worth R250 each – and their packing sheds, with fridges still full of the previous harvest's fruit. 'My boss who owns the farm is a really good guy. His workers always seemed happy. They live on the farm, they have nice houses,' he said, shaking his head to make sense of it. 'If he has to pay them double what they get now, he won't make any profit whatsoever.'

In tiny Prince Alfred Hamlet, fires flickered on the hillside as night fell and we felt the sense of a community battening down the hatches. We spoke on the telephone to Hannes Hanekom, 36, who owned an apple farm in the nearby Witzenberg Valley. He sounded exhausted. 'They set alight one of the sheds and some of the fields,' he said. 'This morning I tried to put out a fire and they chased me away with knives and sticks. I had to drive away in my bakkie with my brother because I would have been in serious danger.'

Hanekom said that it was not his own workers who had set his fields alight. He didn't know who they were. There were two dominant theories doing the rounds in the regions. The first, expressed by Robertson's Jaco van Wyk, hinted at a dark political motive, and claims that people were brought in by buses (even paid, one local suggested) in order to disrupt the region. The second was that they were seasonal workers, mainly from Lesotho, who had no permanent status to damage through their actions, unlike longer-established workers. At the time, there was no evidence for either, which is why speculation ran amok among the frightened winelands locals.

'Most farmers here are very good to the people,' Hanekom says.

This view was contradicted by the Human Rights Watch report released in August 2011, which detailed labour abuses within the sector ranging from inhuman housing to a lack of toilet facilities. NGOs such as the Women On Farms Project continue to deplore the living and working conditions of farm workers generally, and the security challenges facing women and children in particular.

Hanekom didn't see the current wage negotiations as likely to bring about a positive outcome. 'How are you going to restore these relationships? They are shattered.' He said he was trying to get a private security firm to protect his land, but that there were too few of them to meet the needs of all the farmers. Hanekom supported Helen Zille's call to bring in the SANDF. 'It's a war zone,' he said. 'Where do you start to clean up this mess, or protect people?'

Hanekom said that he couldn't estimate the value of the damage to his farm. 'A lot,' he said wearily. He said that a group of families had come together in one house for safety, and that some wives and children had been sent to other towns for protection. 'Otherwise we are just waiting at home,' he said. 'Of course we are scared.'

The only individual in the province permitted to talk on behalf of the police on 7 November was provincial spokesman Andre Traut. He told us via phone that he could provide no specific information about the Ceres policing situation until he had received a report the next morning. What is the usual police procedure for handling a crowd armed with stones? we asked. 'It is to respond to circumstances and use the correct procedure,' he replied enigmatically.

When we cited the cases of people who claimed to have been shot while not engaging in any violent action, he said he could not comment on the specifics of individual cases. 'We are dealing with widespread unrest,' Traut said. 'Our endeavour is to restore order. If there are complaints regarding specific procedure, they must be referred to the Independent Police Investigative Directorate.'

REPORTER'S NOTEBOOK

Late on 7 November, Acting Labour Minister Angie Motshekga announced that an agreement had been reached with workers to return to work the following day and desist from violence in exchange for the minimum wage of farm workers to be renegotiated during the following week. It was unlikely that this news allowed many in the winelands to sleep peacefully, and indeed it wasn't clear how successfully the information had been communicated to those on the ground. As the fire continued to creep up the Prince Alfred Hamlet hillside, the question for many may have been: Where will the sparks ignite next?

JULIUS MALEMA AND THE RALLY THAT ROCKED

Pity the fools stuck in the ANC's Siyanqoba rally, dancing to the same old songs and listening to the same old speeches. In Pretoria's Atteridgeville, Julius Malema threw a party to end all parties. It was an EFF-ing blast, and it should serve as a reminder to the country that Juju is going nowhere, and that he'll be making kings – if not wearing the crown himself – for many, many years to come.
RICHARD POPLAK, MAY 2014

Let's see if we can stop time for a moment and grab some close-ups:

Up above, a chopper circling in a flawless autumn sky. A sign is raised on the concrete balcony of the Lucas 'Masterpieces' Moripe Stadium that reads 'Diepkloof Ward 125'. A wooden coffin is borne aloft by ten dancing Fighters; inside, an effigy of Jacob Zuma. A butternut skewered on a long stick – another representation of the president. (His head is said to resemble this tasty vegetable, which has turned out to be something of a boon for the nation's cartoonists.) A young woman stuffed into EFF coveralls sits on the back of a Triumph Daytona sport bike, staring out at 28 000 red berets. Five large men wearing shades – always the shades – lean against a late-model Range Rover, smoking cigarettes, looking like extras from a large-budget HBO series depicting a liberation movement in an unnamed African country, right before all the white folks are hacked to death and dumped in a pit.

The EFF have arrived on the scene.

But that's a cliché, and an unfair one – they *are* the damn scene. Almost all of the excitement (as opposed to the bitterness, disappointment, boredom and outright despair) generated by the 2014 election has belonged to Julius Malema and his Fighters. If the ANC's closing Siyanqoba rally was enormous and dull, the EFF's rally is medium-sized and cool. If the DA's two weekend productions were slick and empty, the EFF's is pumped up and loony. This is politics on steroids, politics as pageantry, politics as performance art.

'We feel inspired, ready and confident,' EFF Communications Commissar Mbuyiseni Ndlozi tells me as we find a spot away from the noise to chat. Ndlozi is a small young man with a revolutionary goatee and a singing voice that is Boyz II Men jaw-dropping. It fades a little in the low notes, but this is a minor quibble – Ndlozi is a world-class entertainer, a first-class MC, and an ice-cold revolutionary. When he looks you in the eye, he's sizing you up for the frontlines of battle, or the gallows, with no in-betweens.

I'll leave it to you to guess where I'd land.

Both Ndlozi and Alexandra ward organiser Kim Heller tell me that numerous buses have been delayed by the traffic, and that they're waiting for about 30 or so to arrive, even though the 28 000-seat concrete behemoth of a stadium appears to be near capacity. 'We can always have more,' says Ndlozi, as if fire and safety regulations would become meaningless in an EFF-run South Africa. Thirty thousand crushed souls are, after all, but a small price to pay for Revolution. As we finish our conversation, a painted portrait of Julius in the aspect of Mao is paraded by, chased by about 400 photographers, in turn chased by 400 red berets.

'You see that?' asks Andile Mngxitama, the party's ideologue-in-chief. 'That's Mao-lema.' I laugh. Mngxitama doesn't. I shift nervously on my feet. 'Mao-lema is the symbolic concentration of Julius's new project,' he says. 'The biggest mistake the left has made is to be terrified of the Stalinist revolutionary concept. A revolution without ideology turns on itself. We saw that in Egypt. You need a unifying symbol. A unifying leader who serves to bridge the concept and the people. But the left is terrified of this. Capitalism has its symbols, just look at Coca-Cola.'

So can we expect a cult of personality built up around Mao-lema?

'I don't think so,' says Mngxitama. 'Look, I'm not a politician. The foundations of this party are deep. The movement is deep. If the EFF goes to Parliament and we pause, we're fucked. We have to harness this energy after May 7. We're not a political party. We're a revolutionary movement. Expect some disruptions, my friend. Expect trouble. We must not fear leadership, but pursue a politics that holds leaders accountable. Julius is our best gift.'

Is he *really*, though?

Mngxitama looks me in the eye. 'My friend, in 1994, I did not celebrate, I did not cheer. I knew it was a sellout. I have gone through about 20 years of depression. *This* is my 1994. My moment is *this* one.' And Mngxitama waves his hand towards the stands of the stadium, thousands upon thousands dancing in unison.

It's now afternoon, and Gauteng Premier hopeful Dali Mpofu has finally arrived. He gets the crowd riled up, hopping about in his EFF overalls, beret and red designer specs. He can move for a big man, and he's sadly not the only zillionaire lawyer who likes to play at being a workingman on the weekend. 'This is a revolution, this movement,' he says, clapping his hands over his head. And then, predictably, 'Viva, Julius Malema, viva!'

But now, ladies and gentlemen, I must ask you to brace yourself for the single best entrance by a politician in the history of South African democracy.

The security gates swing open, and a line is formed by Fighters in white golf shirts and men in ersatz military uniforms. A Mercedes sedan zooms into the stadium, and then a Mercedes Viano van, followed by about 30 bikers on screaming hogs and sport bikes, red-lining their engines to a slaughtered-pig squeal of mechanical agony. Malema hops out of the van, looking like a Teletubbie in his EFF onesie, and is immediately surrounded by bodyguards and photographers. He walks the length of the oval running track, waving to the screaming Fighters in the crowd, who rear up in the stands and roar as he passes by. The high pitch of the bikes battles with the music and the vuvuzelas and the yelling. The exhaust fumes bathe the whole scene a sort of messianic half-light.

This is the Beatles in America. This is *Thriller*-era Michael Jackson. Somehow, the big woman on the back of the Triumph is poised enough to check her phone through all of this mayhem. 'Juju,' yell the Fighters. And Juju stares back at them as if they've always been there.

When we make it back to the stage, Ndlozi leads us in singing *Nkosi Sikelel'* – '*not* the national anthem,' he reminds us, jettisoning the hoary Mandela-isms 'but *Nkosi*.' Then little kids dance around on stage in T-shirts that read, 'I'm jealous of me.' Dali reads from his regular playbook – 'Down with the regime of Buffalo-man Ramaphosa, down!' and 'We have answered the call of Julius Malema. This is not a Mickey Mouse organisation. It is an idea whose time has come! Don't be told that any organisation liberated you. The people of South Africa liberated themselves.'

A cardboard e-toll gantry is then ripped apart by men in fluorescent vests. The singer Busi asks, between breathless verses of an awful song, 'Who wouldn't love a party that guarantees you jobs?' Juju is dancing his rhythmic non-dance, shuffling around on stage like it's a nightclub, except for the fact that it's daytime, and there are no bottles of Johnny Walker Blue Label being passed around. That I can see.

And while Jacob Zuma has just cleared a stadium of 100 000 people with his oratory, Malema is about to rip it up, throw it down, own it all.

'Remember,' he says, in a voice that is a mixture of cigar smoke, dark Lindt chocolate and raw steel, 'that we were officially launched in October in Marikana. We went from Nkandla to Mitchells Plain to everywhere in South Africa. This is a festival of the poor of the poorest. We want to thank you for being brave. We want to thank you for saying no to the status quo.'

He has the crowd howling in laughter over the course of an hour-plus-long speech. He skewers Zuma. He skewers Zille. 'London must know that we're not scared of the queen. Therefore, we shall not report to London. We will report to the people. The people of South Africa will decide how business is conducted in South Africa. We are taking *everything*.'

Juju strolls through the EFF manifesto, deriding those who call their policies ludicrous, even as he gives away bigger houses, free education, larger child support grants, land, mines and banks, all the while taking credit cards, cars and houses away from politicians. 'We pay you a salary,' he reminds parliamentarians. 'Buy your own cars.' He lays out the manifold differences between his party and the ANC/DA duopoly. 'Where will the monies come from? Nationalisation. And the second monies will come from politicians.' No more middlemen. No more botched tenders. No more houses without a breadwinner earning less than R4 500 a month – a veritable fortune for most of those in the stands.

Mao-lema raises his fist in the air and says, 'They said that we are a joke, but now none of them will sleep without mentioning the EFF. The future looks bright. The future looks bright.'

Indeed, on stage, the future is so bright that the EFF

commissars stare out at their people from behind their shades, lounging in their Big Man love seats. There is, it must be said, a tinge of Mobutu Sese Seko about the proceedings; if Juju hurled a bottle of fake blood into the crowd, à la Mengistu during the Red Terror, I'd remain unsurprised. After a while, the enormous sunglasses start to tell their own story, and one doesn't need to be a psychologist to parse their meaning: these people are not what they say they are. Sure, if this *is* a revolutionary movement – and one that manages to stay untamed by Parliament and power – then it will not be pleasant for many in the country, and that's fair, because the pain will eventually need to be shared. But the policies that Julius Malema is promising the crowd have never, *ever*, worked before, and there is nothing to suggest that this bunch will render them workable. Because none of them has actually *done* anything.

There's a bit too much noise. A bit too much red. A bit too much bling. We know how this HBO series ends.

'Victory is certain,' continues Juju. 'No one will defeat EFF. Let us deliver victory on the seventh of May.' But whatever happens, Malema has already won. Six months ago this party was a punch line. Now, it's the only party that can throw a party.

Minutes later, Malema is back in his van, breathing deeply, wiped. The bikes roar to life. The security converges around the vehicle. And the revolution sweeps off, into the future.

3

A HOMESTEAD IN THE HILLS

AN UNCONTROLLED CREEP: ZUMA, BUSTED BY MADONSELA

Surprise! Jacob Zuma wielded his signature lack of integrity in order to spend R246 million on a home renovation. Which would be hilarious if you hadn't paid for it. The findings of Public Protector Thuli Madonsela's 'Secure in comfort' report are devastating, even if the results will be benign.
RICHARD POPLAK, MAY 2013

In a review of non-fiction writer Janet Malcolm's story collection *Forty-One False Starts*, Gideon Lewis-Kraus wrote that 'Malcolm has always seen rooms as psychological stages, full of props'. One wonders, then, what Malcolm would make of the frontispiece of a document called 'Secure in comfort: Report on an investigation into allegations of impropriety and unethical conduct relating to the installation and implementation of security measures by the Department of Public Works at and in respect of the private residence of President Jacob Zuma at Nkandla in the KwaZulu-Natal province.'

Above this necessarily unpoetic title squats an image of a

Zulu kraal that could function as an exclusive game park in a science fiction movie – one expects to see unicorn zebras with lasers for eyes stalking the perimeter fence. Instead, dozens of thatch-roofed structures huddle in languid groups, interrupted by a pool, a cattle kraal, an amphitheatre, a helipad and several late-Roman-Empire adornments.

What would Malcolm make of the man who, according to 'Secure in comfort', used public funds to build this expression of his id and ego? Perhaps she would consider him a typical president of a typical kleptocracy. The Ukrainians who walked through Viktor Yanukovych's blinged-up, taxpayer-funded shag pad would certainly agree. Perhaps she would identify his handiwork as another example of the Big Man mentality – the need for a chump to behave like a chief and use the money belonging to those he ostensibly leads to create an architectural manifestation of his power and status. Maybe she'd just see the homestead of a tasteless asshole with access to a bottomless supply of money, and no access to a Woolworths lifestyle magazine.

Regardless, the nature of non-fiction storytelling has always been Malcolm's beat – principally, that there is no such thing as a story that demands to be told in one way, in the *right* way. The slant of the story reveals the soul of the author, and not some granite factual underpinning. Likewise, I suspect that 'Secure in comfort' will prove to be one of the more malleable documents in South Africa's malleable history – pushed and pulled and yanked like the last piece of toffee at a nursery-school graduation party. Public Protector Thuli Madonsela, who was responsible for compiling the report, surely sees it as a devastating indictment of Jacob Zuma's behaviour. The government, on the other hand, sees it as toilet paper. The ANC refuses to see it at all. And whether it will have any impact on our collective future is a question for those unicorn zebras to answer.

In other words, we are well into a stage in this country in which there are no such things as facts – when there is nothing to agree upon, no underpinning, no centre. Let us merely say that 'Secure in comfort' – and spend a moment with that title, roll it around in your mind for just a second – is full of *findings*. Pounded into the hardscrabble earth of rural KZN, then, we *find* a president's homestead that was legally in need of a security upgrade. (In August 2010, it was deemed a national key point, and anyone who owns a national key point is responsible for securing it. Therefore, Zuma was off the hook for ringing Nkandla with a fence and some cameras, for which the Minister of Public Works was legally entitled to front him the cash.)

Over the course of several years, Zuma – or rather, a toxic admixture of sycophants, henchmen, Guptas and taxpayers – has dropped a mind-blowing R246 million on the 'upgrades'. The report, 433 pages of not-so-awesomeness, physically flops open on page 188, which reveals a graph that rips through all that remains of this country's soul. Here, we see a continuum of five presidents, beginning with PW Botha and ending with Jacob Zuma, and a rendering of how much their respective estate upgrades have cost. First of all, it's a bummer to see a scumbag like Botha used as precedent for the current leader of a free Mzansi but, hey, one commander-in-thief is as good as another. Second of all, Zuma's graph is an inestimable number of times larger than Botha's when the latter's is adjusted for inflation. On the page, the rendering looks as priapic and swaggering as Zuma himself, or like a huge middle finger pointed at the South African taxpayer in lieu of a thank-you note.

By gum, the stupidity! It takes a village to build a village, and Zuma has acquired a troupe of drooling morons to facilitate his worst instincts. Take Nkandla's architect, Minenhle Makhanya, who, in a classic case of conflict of interest, was working for both the state as a security upgrader and for Zuma as a home improver. Thing is, while he knew how to overcharge for wallpaper and towel racks, he knew absolutely nothing about fencing. Never should have been there, never should have been hired. According to the report, 'There is no evidence that Mr Makhanya had any experience in the design of security related projects. The argument presented that being an architect qualifies him to design security installations has the same implication as arguing that just because I'm a lawyer I'm an expert at any area of the law. That cannot be logical.' When Thuli Madonsela, whose sensibility most resembles that of Data from *Star Trek: Next Generation*, is driven to drollness, you know the country is fucked.

Madonsela notes how none of the institutions that have been created to care for South Africans cared how much money was being blown on Nkandla – not the Department of Defence, not the South African Police Service, not the Department of Public Works. According to the Public Protector, 'they took no interest in the extent and outrageous escalation of the cost of the Nkandla Project'.

And scheme this: 'It has already been indicated that no

specific documents were provided that expressly authorise the building of a clinic.' Or this: 'It is obvious that the state has made a major contribution to the president's estate at the expense of the taxpayer.' Or this: 'Clearly, items such as the Visitor's Centre, swimming pool and terrace, amphitheatre, elaborate paved roads, terraces and walkways and the building of the kraal, with an aesthetically pleasing structure, a culvert with a remote controlled gate and chicken run, added substantial value to the property.'

Chickens wielding remote controls? Yes, South Africans, welcome to Nkandla.

You will find in this document the usual examples of crooked tendering (or non-tendering), and much cronyism and straight-up idiocy. No plans for the design were ever handed in to the Department of Public Works, which has a Scrutiny Committee to deal with exactly this sort of thing. Bulletproof glass cost R3 million when it didn't need to; no one asked for competing bids on R3 million worth of lifts. Zuma lied to Parliament about taking out a mortgage to pay for some of the joint; he didn't bitch about shoddy work in 'a timely manner', and therefore, 'the president allowed or caused extensive and excessive upgrades that go beyond necessary security measures to his private residence, at state expense'. The man doesn't only blow our money illegally, he is incapable of saving a few of the bucks he is not entitled to blow.

So, what's next? Madonsela has told Zuma that he has to pay back a reasonable portion of the overspending, which means his handlers will be writing a cheque. She's told him to discipline his ministers, which means less than nothing in this country. She's provided his enemies with a cudgel, but he doesn't seem to notice their beatings.

But Madonsela has certainly nailed Zuma to history's grimiest post – he will be forever remembered as a thief, a fool and a Zulu man who was incapable of managing the affairs of his kraal. Even in Janet Malcolm's factless world, where the defenders of truth are mere storytellers, Jacob Zuma will not escape his fate as one of this country's more reprehensible figures. And Nkandla will be the crown he wears as he slithers into historical ignominy.

MADONSELA: IT'S *ANIMAL FARM*, AND THE PIGS ARE FEEDING

Public Protector Thuli Madonsela went to Wits to talk about her Nkandla report (is anybody talking about anything else?). To a hall of adoring students, she used the power of metaphor to say all the things she can't say directly. Comrade Napoleon, get that snout out of the trough.

SIMON ALLISON, MARCH 2014

Thuli Madonesela is a careful, fastidious woman. 'I am cowardly,' she told the 350-odd students who gathered to hear her talk at Wits University (there were another few hundred in a hastily arranged overflow venue). 'We can't work in any way we can't explain ... we try to stay within the law and within the facts. That way we don't worry about how we will explain ourselves, if we are taken to account.'

She doesn't, in other words, say anything that she can't prove. This methodology is evident throughout her report, and in all her subsequent utterances, where she has refrained from making any conclusions that are not supported by documentary evidence. This is why she is so reluctant to put too much blame squarely on Jacob Zuma's shoulders. A typical example: 'I didn't say the president lied … I simply said the information he gave to Parliament was incorrect,' she said.

This doesn't mean that the Public Protector does not have her own opinions on the issue, opinions she found a way to make abundantly clear. 'Metaphors have a way of holding the most truth in the least space,' observed author Orson Scott Card, and rarely has he been proved more accurate.

Madonsela fell back on a classic metaphor that no one in her well-educated audience could fail to understand.

'George Orwell tells us about a community, pretty much like ours, but it's a community of animals. These animals were enslaved by humans, and the humans made those animals work very hard. The humans never produced anything for themselves … but the humans ate all of the food and gave the animals very little. Over time, among the animals, leaders emerged that started to tell the animals that it's not right to be oppressed by humans. We deserve not to starve while they are eating all the food. Those conversations kept happening over time in little circles until they reached a critical mass … one day the animals revolted and kicked the humans out of the farm.

'When the animals then decided to govern their own farm, they created rules for themselves. These rules included all animals are equal, no animal should eat milk or eggs, no animal should sleep in a bed with sheets. It was going to be to each according to their ability, and each according to their needs. After a little while everyone was happy. The humans were gone.

'The animals that liberated most of the other animals were the pigs. After a period of time, the pigs started to feel that we liberated you, we deserve better, and after time the pigs started to eat more than the others ... [the pigs] do all of the thinking, they do all of the co-ordination, they liberated the animals, they deserve to be fed better. And the rules started changing, imperceptibly overnight ... It used to say all animals are equal, then suddenly, it said some are more equal than others.'

The *Animal Farm* reference was devastatingly applicable to South Africa's current polity, with liberators-turned-tyrants and Comrade Napoleon, chief of the pigs, with his snout firmly in the trough. As for the rest of us – well, we're the other animals, wondering what happened to our glorious liberation.

As she told her story, the jam-packed Senate Hall – students crowding the aisles, hanging on every word – went deathly quiet. Everyone understood exactly what she was saying – and that there was no other way she could say it.

After her speech, the Public Protector was mobbed by students asking questions and taking photographs. If she was looking for a little bit of moral support, she didn't struggle to find it here.

In answer to one of the questions, Madonsela offered a few words of advice for her future successor, whoever that may be. 'Make decisions that are owned by you and your team. Also make decisions that will make you sleep well at night. You should never try to please everyone. You should just make sure that what you do is something you can live with.'

On the evidence in her report – given the strength of the moral conviction that she clearly demonstrated – Thuli Madonsela has no trouble sleeping at night. Unlike Comrade Napoleon, we suspect.

OPEN LETTER TO PRESIDENT
JACOB GEDLEYIHLEKISA ZUMA

Mr President, neither the most sycophantic member of the press nor the most protective layer of the government should convince you that South Africa is doing well under your stewardship. It is not. The question is, do you care?
STEPHEN GROOTES, APRIL 2014

～～～～～～～～～～～～～～～～

Dear Mr President
Re: Your presidency

As someone privileged and arrogant enough to talk and write about politics for a living, it's been a busy time for me. And wherever I go these days, I hear one word; it's a geographic place-name in KwaZulu-Natal, the place where you're from. And at every social function, family event or braai I go to, I get asked the same question. Will you survive? Will you really last your entire second term? And how on earth is that at all possible?

I must admit, I find myself conflicted in my answers.

There's my emotional answer, my white middle-class frustration, my anger about how the taxpayer's money is being used and misused, and how devastating that must be for the party.

And then I try to get away from the anger we see all over the media and the national discussion; there's my other-side-of-the-brain response, a rational, sober look at the structure of the ANC, your place within it and the reality that it is truly unlikely that anything will change, not while you are in such tight, total control.

I simply cannot marry the two.

As a middle-class man, there are moments when I just want to point and shout 'liar liar' at you. I want to tell my children that this is the man whose example you should not follow. I simply cannot turn my eyes away from the letters and correspondence that appear to show how you must have known everything.

For goodness' sake, Mr President, it's your home, you've been there many times, you are (presumably) in contact with your wives, who live there. You must have known what was going on.

And how could someone as rational as you go on TV and say that you simply 'didn't ask for it and therefore [you] won't pay for it'? It's insulting. It insults every South African, female and male, young and old, poor and rich, well-read and illiterate, citizen and peasant, black, white, Indian, coloured. It insults our intelligence. It insults our sense of decency.

And, Mr President, as a voting citizen, I ask that you please show me at least some respect, and refrain from laughing in your response.

From anyone else this would all be bad enough. From

you, Sir, it's piled on the top of your appointment of Menzi Simelane as National Prosecuting Authority boss, the damage you did to the National Prosecuting Authority when you had your charges 'withdrawn', your post-coital shower, your protection of Richard Mdluli, the fact that every time you act, it seems only to be in self-interest, and never in the interests of the nation. Your security apparatus turned their arms against your own people when they massacred 34 miners in Marikana and their families and communities are harassed daily. (You kept your Minister of State Security when his spouse became a convicted drug trafficker?) Your friends use South African military airports as their private landing strips. You made us fear for our freedom of expression. I could go on, for hours.

There is a part of me that wishes I could turn the clock back to that rainy day at the FNB stadium so that I could boo you too.

But that is anger and frustration speaking.

In my less irrational moments, I try to step back a bit.

If, as is the case here, the majority of the country backs you, Sir, then obviously you must stay. Isn't that what democracy is about?

As a journalist, I am also acutely aware that media organisations, here and in many other democracies, can hunt as packs, that often they can't be satisfied by anything other than the taste of blood. In South Africa, the media can hardly claim to hold the moral high ground: it is mostly a middle-class morality, or a certain strand of it, that dominates this space. So, then, I have to ask: Are you being treated fairly? Well, you may feel that you are not. After all, you have always treated most of our media as an opposing force, as an enemy. But why, then, have you given them such a big weapon to use against you? Because there are so many almost-smoking guns that it's impossible for reporters to stop these stories coming.

There's simply too much data showing that you don't seem fit to be the president.

At the same time, I also understand that you hold the reins of power within the ANC, after a free and fair democratic leadership election. It's because of this that Gwede Mantashe could quite truthfully say that Nkandla was the shortest discussion at this weekend's National Executive Committee meeting. You have too much support for anyone to take you on. It would be pointless even to try. Then again, those who want to speak in your favour may have found it quite difficult to find something to say. As a result, neither your supporters nor your critics had anything to say.

Funny, that – isn't it?

Mr President, there is a strange near-silence from many of the ANC structures. While the ANC and your alliance partners have obviously come out in your favour and sort of against the Public Protector, it's not like those heady days in the run-up to Polokwane in 2007. We haven't had provincial structure after provincial structure releasing statements in your favour; maybe that's still to come. But there is part of me that's reminded of a similar silence during what appeared to be the height of Thabo Mbeki's power.

During that time he could do almost anything and no one would dare criticise him. NEC meetings were quiet affairs – again, like the one this weekend. But resentment was building up. Anger and frustration were mounting, more and more people were dying of HIV/Aids, more and more people were rumbling about Mbeki's dictatorial tendencies. In the end, when the reaction came, it was brutal. Partly because you allowed it be.

Of course, I realise things are different in 2014. But after the ANC's 2017 congress, when you may no longer control the NEC, things could be different. If there will be a whirlwind, you will be the one to reap it.

But I do want to ask you this. Do you ever think about how people will talk of your time in your office? Of what your 'legacy' will be? Do you ever think that when children ask their parents about the Zuma years, those mothers and fathers won't just hush them and talk about something else – about Nelson Mandela, and maybe even Thabo Mbeki, instead? Do you ever wonder what you have done for this country as president? Sure, there's the progress on HIV/Aids. Things were so bad under Mbeki that these were relatively easy policies to change. But what have you, Jacob Gedleyihlekisa Zuma, done as the most powerful person in the country?

How did you make sure that your people, the people of South Africa, wake up every morning in a country that is better than the one in which they fell asleep on the previous night? Do they feel inspired by you? Do they feel the country is doing well under your stewardship? Are they – especially the youth – looking forward to their future?

Mr President, no sycophantic member of the press or protective layers of the government officials around you should convince you that South Africa is doing well these days. It is not. Do you care?

Unless you give people a reason to fight for you, maybe they will one day just stop. Maybe they will just look at the next guy; maybe they will want to forget you as quickly as possible once you're gone.

Yours,
Stephen Grootes
(Registered voter)

GOODBYE, DEMOCRACY; SO LONG, ACCOUNTABILITY; HELLO, ZUMOCRACY

It was no big surprise that President Jacob Zuma chose not to respond in detail to the serious findings that Public Protector Thuli Madonsela made against him and his government relating to the security upgrades at his Nkandla residence. It is quite clear that the president treats constitutional institutions, Parliament and the people of South Africa with disdain. A March 2014 move showed that he did not even care about the impact of this scandal on his own party.

RANJENI MUNUSAMY, APRIL 2014

When the corruption charges were finally withdrawn against President Jacob Zuma in 2009, a few weeks before the national elections, an alliance leader made a remark that was quite chilling. 'After the rape case and this, nobody will ever believe any charge against Baba. He can actually shoot someone and he will never go to jail,' the leader exuberantly proclaimed.

The remark exposed that leader's fundamental misunderstanding of the rule of law and political invincibility. The fact that it was said by someone in Zuma's inner circle is possibly an indicator of the thinking of people who have influence over the president. Such sentiments, along with Zuma's own predilection for deferring responsibility to others, could explain why the president is under the impression that he is accountable to nobody, no matter what he does.

During the two weeks that Zuma had to contemplate the report by Public Protector Thuli Madonsela, we wondered whether he or anyone in his legal or government entourage considered that it was the worst indictment of the head of state in democratic South Africa. If they did, they surely would have realised that a nonchalant letter to the Speaker of Parliament suspending a full response to the Public Protector's report was an inadequate reaction.

On 2 April, Zuma met Madonsela's deadline to respond to her report through Parliament. She had asked that the president report to the National Assembly 'on his comments and actions' regarding her report within 14 days. Zuma, however, simply wrote to Speaker Max Sisulu saying he was aware he was accountable to Parliament, and noted that there were 'stark' differences between the reports of the government task team and that of the Public Protector.

In the letter to Sisulu, Zuma stated that the Special Investigating Unit (SIU) was also investigating the Nkandla upgrades and that he had written to the unit's head, Vas Soni, for an update on that probe. Zuma said he would therefore give full and proper consideration to the matter once he received a report from the SIU.

The SIU indicated to the media on 2 April that it expected to complete the investigation by the end of May. If all went according to the presidency's plan, this would neatly take the Nkandla matter off the formal agenda until after the elections and establishment of a new government.

The problem, though, is that it did not expunge the matter from national discourse. In fact, Zuma's response only added fuel to a raging fire. There was no relationship between the SIU investigation and the Public Protector's report. In fact, with Zuma pointing to an 'anomaly' between the government task team and Madonsela's report, it is almost as if there was an expectation that the SIU investigation could reconcile the contradictions. It could not. And the SIU definitely could not deal with Madonsela's findings of ethical breaches by the president.

There was, in fact, no need for Zuma to delay responding to Madonsela's findings against him. If he had any appreciation of the seriousness of her conclusions and respect for the Public Protector's office – a constitutional institution – and for Parliament, the president would have been eager to clarify these findings. More than that, if he took his own constitutional obligations as president and his image seriously, he would immediately have wanted to give an explanation to the nation.

But it seemed that Zuma was unruffled and happy to let the matter ride for as long as possible.

What about the damage to the ANC and its election

campaign? Zuma seemed just as unperturbed about that. ANC Secretary General Gwede Mantashe made it clear that the ANC had had a 'short' discussion about Nkandla at its National Executive Committee meeting that weekend, and that the party had decided it would not demand an explanation from the president or interfere with government processes.

Why the ANC feels it cannot hold its presidential deployee accountable is worrying. But the fact that Zuma did not feel the need to take his own party into his confidence and also relieve some of the pressure and negative publicity in the heat of the election campaign showed that his only concern was his own protection. Had Zuma provided some reasonable explanation for his role in the Nkandla upgrades, the ANC would not have been in the untenable position in which it found itself, trying to justify the unconscionable and indefensible.

But Zuma failed the 'reasonableness' test long ago.

From the moment the *Mail & Guardian* broke the story in December 2009 that the president's Nkandla home was to undergo a multimillion-rand face-lift, alarm bells should have rung in the Zuma household and in government that this project would be under constant scrutiny. It should have alerted everyone involved that any potential wrongdoing would be exposed. Yet neither Zuma nor any of the ministers and officials involved exercised any caution. On the contrary, processes and prescripts were manipulated and violated.

Madonsela noted this in her report: 'The earliest concerns regarding opulent or excessive expenditure at the private residence of President Zuma were expressed on 4 December 2009 by the *Mail & Guardian* in an article titled "Zuma's R65-million

Nkandla splurge". Apart from the release of a statement by the Presidency on 3 December 2009, denying that government was footing the bill, nothing seems to have been done by government to verify the 2009 allegations or attempt to arrest the costs which the article predicted would continue to rise.'

It is on this basis that Madonsela made the grave findings against the president that he had violated the Executive Ethics Code and acted inconsistently with the Constitution. 'It is also not unreasonable to expect that when news broke in December 2009 of alleged exorbitant amounts, at the time R65 million on questioned security installations at his private residence, the dictates of sections 96 and 237 of the Constitution and the Executive Ethics Code required of President Zuma to take reasonable steps to order an immediate inquiry into the situation and immediate correction of any irregularities and excesses,' the Public Protector's report states.

But Zuma did not think it was necessary to take these 'reasonable' steps. And for the same reason, he did not find it necessary to explain to the Public Protector during her investigation, to Parliament, to the nation or to his own party why he allowed his home to become a national scandal.

Zuma is set to be re-elected as president of South Africa in May 2014. He will stand in the Nelson Mandela Amphitheatre at the Union Buildings, hold up his right hand and take the oath of office. In the oath he will swear to 'be faithful to the Republic of South Africa, and [to] obey, observe, uphold and maintain the Constitution and all other laws of the Republic'.

He will also 'solemnly and sincerely promise' to 'discharge [his] duties with all [his] strength and talents to the best of

[his] knowledge and ability and true to the dictates of [his] conscience'. Zuma will do all this while there are findings hanging over him that he violated the Executive Ethics Code and acted inconsistently with the Constitution.

The situation would be almost comical if it were not so serious. The most solemn of moments in any democracy – the presidential oath of office – will be a pre-violated farce. The institutions that uphold our democracy, such as Parliament and the Office of the Public Protector, are being undermined by the one person who takes a solemn oath to 'devote [himself] to the well-being of the Republic and all of its people'.

And then, for the five years that follow, this same person will continue to preside over South Africa, in all likelihood still accountable to nobody. It is the redefinition of democracy before our eyes. Brace yourself, South Africa, for the Age of Zumocracy.

REQUIEM FOR A DREAM:
ON LOVING AND LEAVING THE ANC

Born in exile, when I came home to South Africa in 2004 a song played a constant loop in my head as I struggled through a torturous break-up. Later, that song was to become emblematic of my complex relationship with the faltering political party I had once loved, my own requiem for a political dream.
SISONKE MSIMANG, MARCH 2014

I put it on when I got up in the morning, I brushed my teeth to it, I pressed Play in my car and it came on, I got to work and played it on my headphones as I clicked away at my computer.

I fell asleep to it each night. I lived in a fog, wrapped in a delicate blanket of misery, and this song was my soundtrack:

> *It could all be so simple*
> *But you'd rather make it hard*
> *Loving you is like a battle*
> *And we both end up with scars*
> *Tell me who I have to be*
> *To get some reciprocity*
> *No one loves you more than me*
> *And no one ever will.*

I was in love, and in the throes of a horrible break-up with a boy who was impossibly good-looking and hopelessly complicated. It was a torturous back-and-forth process (as break-ups tend to be when you are 23) and this song was my solace.

And because we have all been there and all understand the pain of it, I will risk melodrama and say that as I have grappled with events in South Africa, and with the conduct of the ruling party, I have often looked back at my 23-year-old self. I have felt on some days, as I have scanned the headlines, as though I am walking away from a dramatic love affair in order to save myself even as I am uncertain about what I am walking towards.

So, forgive me, but it does feel like I'm breaking up with the boy I love; the one who has loved me the most and for the longest, the one who has intoxicated me with his brilliance and his pathos. It's hard to imagine life without him, even as it has become impossible to live with him.

This contradictory impulse is most acutely apparent among

South Africans who feel both betrayed by and indebted to the African National Congress.

I was born in exile and spent my earliest years as part of an ANC community. Maybe this is why it feels so raw. The ANC put food in my belly, a pen in my hand and paper on my desk. The ANC gave me the tools I have used to make my way in this world.

So the long, slow slide into a moment on the cusp of elections, 20 years into democracy, has felt heart-wrenching and deeply hurtful. I don't think that this feeling is exceptional. Indeed, my story is the story of many, many South Africans – not just those who left the country. The ANC clothed us and raised us. No one loved us more than the ANC, and we can't imagine that any party ever will. In South Africa, history is not distant, so we remain torturously in love with the idea of the ANC and what it did for us, even as we bemoan what it has become.

> *Is this just a silly game*
> *That forces you to act this way?*
> *Forces you to scream my name*
> *Then pretend that you can't stay?*
> *Tell me who I have to be*
> *To get some reciprocity*
> *No one loves you more than me*
> *And no one ever will.*

Thuli Madonsela opens the Nkandla press conference by gazing at the camera and reminding us, in her whispery voice, that she is the Makhadzi: the aunt who serves as a buffer between the ruler and the ruled. She says that the Makhadzi 'enhances the voice of the people while serving as the king's eyes, ears and conscience'. He ignores her 'at his own peril', she intones.

She is saying, patiently and with steely eloquence, that she is still in love. Her voice shakes. This is hard. She is asking who she has to be to get some reciprocity. No one loves the ANC more than she does, and no one ever will. I watch her throughout the gruelling session, alternately composed and shaken, angry and hurt. It occurs to me that we are all Thuli.

We are all standing on the edge of a pool of tears, fighting fiercely for what we love. Wondering when we are going to get it, wondering why we still try, wondering how it would ever be possible to stop trying.

I watch her and wish that the miners who were shot down at Marikana had her persistence on their side. I wish they had her savvy and her determination working for them. Instead, the Commission happens somewhere in the middle distance. Cyril is the deputy president of the party that oversaw their killing. He was the chairman who sent the 'dastardly' email. He walks atop their corpses and we watch in quiet shame.

Oscar and Reeva and Nkandla and the state of the nation bury the ghosts of dead miners under a pile of headlines. But the memory of the wailing of widows will not leave us. There are some crimes that demand justice.

There is no peace without justice. No reconciliation without truth. We know this from our bitter war against racism. In Marikana there has been no justice, no truth, no peace.

I keep letting you back in
How can I explain myself?
As painful as this thing has been
I just can't be with no one else.

The *City Press* reports that in Bekkersdal, a 61-year-old woman 'who claimed to be a staunch ANC member said the ANC had fooled people for too long and was reaping what it had sowed'. She claims to be a staunch ANC member because she is one. She loves the ANC and because of this, she can't stand the sight of its face any more. The people are saying, 'We love you, but don't come around here any more'.

See I know what we got to do
You let go and I'll let go too
'Cause no one's hurt me more than you
And no one ever will.

There are taxi ranks and squatter camps that bear the names of our national shame. Monuments to Marikana are scrawled into the soul of our nation. They take their place next to Chris Hani, Solomon Mahlangu, Andries Tatane – all of them killed shamefully.

The ANC has hurt us and we are remembering our pain as we always have. But there will be no RDP settlements called Nkandla. The people will not even joke like that. The people are on Makhadzi's side on this one.

There was a time when the only hurt that we could collectively remember had been inflicted upon us by the apartheid regime. Perhaps what we needed was someone to remind us – Makhadzi, in her whisper-soft voice of steel – that we have new wounds to tend to, and that our pain lies not only in the past, but also in the present.

Perhaps this admission is the beginning of letting go.

4

THIRTY-FOUR HUMAN BEINGS DIED THAT NIGHT

THE COLD MURDER FIELDS OF MARIKANA

Some of the miners killed in the 16 August 2012 massacre at Marikana appear to have been shot at close range or crushed by police vehicles. They were not caught in a fusillade of gunfire from police defending themselves, as the official account would have it.
GREG MARINOVICH, SEPTEMBER 2012

Of the 34 miners killed at Marikana, no more than a dozen of the dead were captured in news footage shot at the scene. Most of those who died, according to surviving strikers and researchers, were killed beyond the view of cameras at a nondescript collection of boulders some 300 metres behind Wonderkop.

On one of these rocks, encompassed closely on all sides by solid granite boulders, is the letter N, the 14th letter of the alphabet. Here, N represents the 14th body of a striking miner to be found by a police forensics team in this isolated place. These letters are used by forensics to detail where the corpses lay.

There is a thick spread of blood deep into the dry soil,

showing that N was shot and killed on the spot. There is no trail of blood leading to where N died – the blood saturates one spot only, indicating no further movement. (It would have been outside of the scope of the human body to crawl here bleeding so profusely.)

Approaching N from all possible angles, observing the local geography, it is clear that to shoot N, the shooter would have to have been close. Very close – in fact, almost within touching distance. (After having spent days here at the bloody massacre site, it does not take too much imagination for me to believe that N might have begged for his life on that winter afternoon.)

At sites like N, all four sides are hemmed in by rock. Photo credit: Greg Marinovich

And on that deadly Thursday afternoon, N's murderer could only have been a policeman. I say 'murderer' because there is not a single report of an injured policeman from that day. I say 'murderer' because there seems to have been no attempt to uphold our citizens' right to life and fair recourse to justice. It is hard to imagine that N would have resisted being taken into custody when thus cornered. There is no chance of escape from a ring of police.

Other letters denote equally morbid scenarios. J and H died alongside each other. They, too, had no route of escape and had to have been shot at close range.

J and H died alongside each other. Photo credit: Greg Marinovich

Other letters mark the rocks nearby. A bloody handprint stains a vertical rock surface where someone tried to support himself standing up; many other rocks are splattered with blood as miners died on the afternoon of 16 August.

None of these events was witnessed by media or captured on camera. The events were only reported on as component parts of the greater tragedy.

One of the striking miners caught up in the mayhem – let's call him Themba, though his name is known to Daily Maverick – recalled what he saw once he escaped the killing fields around Wonderkop.

'Most people then called for us to get off the mountain, and as we were coming down, the shooting began. Most people who were shot near the kraal were trying to get into the settlement; the blood we saw is theirs. We ran in the other direction, as it was impossible now to make it through the bullets.

'We ran until we got to the meeting spot and watched the incidents at the koppie. Two helicopters landed; soldiers and police surrounded the area. We never saw anyone coming out of the koppie.'

The soldiers he refers to were, in fact, part of the police task team dressed in camouflage uniforms, brought to the scene in a brown military vehicle. Asked about this, Themba said he believed people were hiding at the koppie, and police went in and killed them.

In the days after the shooting, Themba visited friends at the nearby mine hospital. 'Most people who are in hospital were shot at the back. The ones I saw in hospital had clear signs of being run over by the Nyalas,' he said. 'I never got to go to the mortuary, but most people who went there told me that they couldn't recognise the faces of the dead (they were so damaged by either bullets or from having been driven over).'

It is becoming clear to this reporter that heavily armed police hunted down and killed the miners in cold blood. A minority was killed in the filmed event in which police claim they acted in self-defence. The rest was murder on a massive scale.

Peter Alexander, chair of social change and Professor of Sociology at the University of Johannesburg, and two researchers interviewed witnesses in the days after the massacre. Researcher Botsong Mmope spoke to a miner, Tsepo (not his real name), on Monday 20 August. Tsepo witnessed some of the events that occurred off camera.

'Tsepo said many people had been killed at the small koppie and it had never been covered (by the media). He agreed to take us to the small koppie, because that is where many, many people died,' Mmope said.

After the shooting began, Tsepo said, he was among many who ran towards the small koppie. As the police chased them, someone among them said, 'Let us lie down, comrades, they will not shoot us then.'

'At that time, there were bullets coming from a helicopter above them. Tsepo then lay down. A number of fellow strikers also lay down. He says he watched Nyalas driving over the prostrate, living miners,' Mmope said. 'Other miners ran to the koppie, and that was where they were shot by police and the army with machine guns.' (The witnesses and speakers at the miners' gathering who refer to the army, or *amajoni*, refer to the same police task team unit, in camouflage uniforms and armed with R5 semi-automatic rifles, as the one mentioned above.)

When the firing finally ceased, Tsepo managed to escape across the veld to the north.

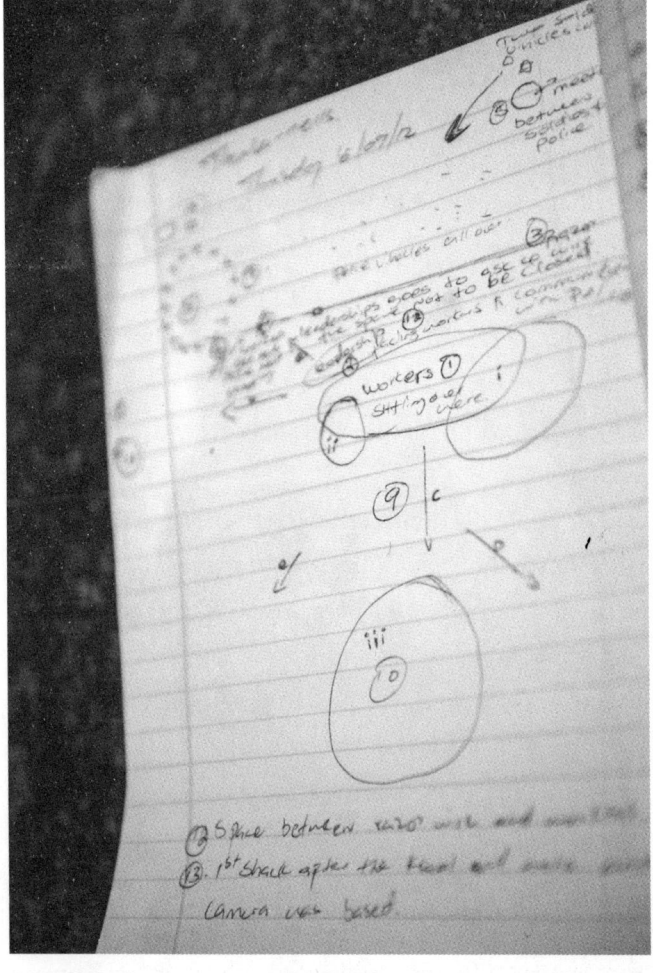

A map drawn by an eyewitness and a researcher shows the spatial context of the events of 16 August, as well as their sequence. Photo credit: Greg Marinovich

It took several days for police to release the number of those killed. The number 34 surprised most of us. With only about a dozen bodies recorded by the media, where had the remaining miners been killed, and how had they died?

Most journalists and others did not interrogate this properly. The violence of the deaths we could see, again and again, was enough to contend with. The police certainly did not mention what had happened outside of the view of the cameras.

The toll of 112 mineworkers (34 dead and 78 wounded) at Marikana is one of those few bitter moments in our bloody history that has been captured by the unblinking eye of the lens. Several lenses, in fact, and from various viewpoints. This has allowed the actions and reactions of both the strikers and the police to be scrutinised in ways that undocumented tragedies can never be. Therefore, while the motives and rationale of both parties will never be completely clear, their deeds are quite apparent.

Thus developed a dominant narrative within the public discourse. Facts fed by the police, various state entities and the media suggested that the strikers provoked their own deaths by charging and shooting at the forces of law and order. Indeed, the images and footage can be read to support this claim.

The contrary view is that the striking miners were trying to escape police rubber bullets and tear gas when they ran at the heavily armed police task team (our version of SWAT). The result was the horrific images of a dozen or so men gunned down in a fusillade of semi-automatic fire.

From the outside the jumble of granite at Small Koppie, the weathered remains of a prehistoric hill, it would appear that nothing more brutal than the felling of the straggly indigenous trees for firewood occurred here.

Once within the outer perimeter, narrow passages between the weathered bushveld rocks lead into dead ends. Scattered piles of human faeces and toilet paper mark the area as the communal toilet for those in the miners' shack community without pit toilets.

It is inside here, hidden from casual view, that the rocks bear the yellow letters methodically sprayed by the forensic team to denote where they found the miners' bodies. The letter N appears to take the death toll at this site to 14. Some of the other letters are difficult to discern, especially where they were sprayed on the dry grass and sand.

The yellow letters speak as if they are the voices of the dead. The position of the letters, denoting the remains of once sweating, panting, cursing, pleading men, tells a story of policemen hunting men like beasts. They tell of tens of murders at close range, in places hidden from sight.

N, for example, died in a narrow redoubt surrounded on four sides by solid rock. His killer could not have been further than 2 metres from him – the geography forbids any other possibility.

Why did this happen?

Let us look back at the events of Monday 13 August, three days prior to these events.

Themba, a second-generation miner from the Eastern Cape, was present then too. He was part of a group of some 30 strikers who were delegated to cross the veld that separated them from another Lonmin platinum mine, Karee.

It was at Karee mine that other rock drill operators led a wildcat strike to demand better wages. The National Union of Mineworkers (NUM) did not support them, and management took a tough line. The strike was unsuccessful, with many of the strikers losing their jobs. The Marikana miners figured there were many miners there who were still angry enough to join them on Wonderkop.

The Marikana strikers never reached their fellow workers; instead, mine security turned them back and told them to return by a route different from the one by which they had come.

On this road, they met a contingent of police. Themba said there were some ten Nyalas and one or two police trucks or vans. The police barred their way and told them to lay down their weapons. The workers refused, saying they needed the pangas to cut wood, as they lived in the bush – and, more honestly, that they needed them to defend themselves.

On the previous Friday, they said, three of their number had been killed by people wearing red NUM T-shirts.

The police line parted and they were allowed to continue, but once they were about 10 metres past, the police opened fire on them.

The miners turned and took on the police.

It was here, he said, that they killed two policemen and injured another. The police killed two miners and injured a third severely, from helicopter gunfire, Themba said. The miners carried the wounded man back to Wonderkop, where he was taken to hospital in a car. His fate is unknown.

Police spokesman Captain Dennis Adriao, when asked

about the incident by telephone, said public order policing officers had been attacked by miners who had hacked two policemen to death and critically injured another. He said eight people had been arrested for that incident and for the ten deaths prior to 16 August. 'Two are in custody in hospital who were injured in the attack on the police.'

The police version of how this event took place is quite different from that of Themba's, but what is clear is that the police had already arrested people for the murders committed thus far.

Why, then, the urgency to confront those among the thousands camped on Wonderkop in the days leading up to the massacre on 16 August?

But let us, in this article, not get too distracted by this obvious question, and return to the events of 16 August itself.

The South African Government website still carried this statement – dated 16 August 2012, the day of the Marikana massacre – on 8 September 2012:

'Following extensive and unsuccessful negotiations by SAPS members to disarm and disperse a heavily armed group of illegal gatherers at a hilltop close to Lonmin Mine, near Rustenburg in the North West Province, the South African Police Service was viciously attacked by the group, using a variety of weapons, including firearms. The Police, in order to protect their own lives and in self-defence, were forced to engage the group with force. This resulted in several individuals being fatally wounded, and others injured.'

This police statement clearly states that the police acted in self-defence, despite the fact that not a single policeman suffered any injury on 16 August.

And as we discussed earlier, it is possible to interpret what happened in the filmed events as an overreaction by the police to a threat. What happened afterwards, 400 metres away at Small Koppie, is quite different. That police armoured vehicles drove over prostrate miners cannot be described as self-defence or as any kind of public order policing.

The geography of those yellow spray-painted letters tells a chilling and damning story and lends greater credence to what the strikers have been saying.

One miner, on the morning after the massacre, told Daily Maverick that '[w]hen one of our miners passed a Nyala, there was a homeboy of his from the Eastern Cape inside, and he told him that today was D-day, that they were to come and shoot. He said there was a paper signed allowing them to shoot us.'

The language reportedly used by the policeman is strikingly similar to that used by Adriao early on 16 August and quoted on MineWeb: 'We have tried over a number of days to negotiate with the leaders and with the gathering here at the mine, our objective is to get the people to surrender their weapons and to disperse peacefully.

'Today is D-day in terms of if they don't comply then we will have to act … we will have to take steps,' he said.

A little later, Adriao commented: 'Today is unfortunately D-day. It is an illegal gathering. We've tried to negotiate and we'll try again, but if that fails, we'll obviously have to go to a tactical phase.'

Speaking to the possible intention of the police, let us look at how the deployed police were armed. The weapons used by the majority of the more than 400 police on the scene were

R5 (a licenced replica of the Israeli Galil SAR) or LM5 assault rifles, designed for infantry and tactical police use. These weapons cannot fire rubber bullets. The police were clearly deployed in a military manner – to take lives, not to deflect possible riotous behaviour.

The death of their comrades three days previously set the stage for the police, who have been increasingly accused of brutality, torture and death in detention, to exact their revenge. What is unclear is how high up the chain of command this desire went.

There has been police obfuscation and selective silence in a democratic society in which the police are, theoretically, accountable to the citizenry and to its elected representatives. We live in a country in which people are assumed innocent until proven guilty, where summary executions are not within the police's discretion.

Let us be under no illusions. The striking miners are no angels. They can be as violent as anyone else in our society. And in an inflamed setting such as at Marikana, probably more so. They are angry, disempowered; they feel cheated and want more than a subsistence wage. Whatever the merits of their argument, and the crimes of some individuals among them, more than 3 000 people gathering at Wonderkop did not merit being vulnerable to summary and entirely arbitrary execution at the hands of a paramilitary police unit.

In light of this, we could look at the events of 16 August as the murder of 34 and the attempted murder of a further 78, who survived despite the police's apparent intention to kill them.

Back at the rocks the locals dubbed Small Koppie, a wild

pear flowers among the debris of the carnage and human excrement – a place of horror that has until now remained *terra incognita* to the public. It could also be the place at which the Constitution of South Africa was dealt a mortal blow.

A FILM EVERY SOUTH AFRICAN SHOULD SEE, AND NEVER FORGET

> *Rehad Desai's documentary,* Miners Shot Down, *is about so much more than the Marikana killings in August 2012. The film offers a unique prism through which to view contemporary power relations in 'democratic' South Africa (and perhaps globally) where the unholy trinity of capital, politics and security were (and are) pitted against labour – poorly paid, badly educated and exploited workers.*
> MARIANNE THAMM, JUNE 2014

There is much that is disturbing and shameful in Rehad Desai's tender 86-minute filmic exploration of events over six days in August 2012 leading up to what has become known globally as the Marikana massacre, one of the most disgraceful events to have taken place in post-apartheid, 'free' and democratic South Africa.

So significant were the tensions that played themselves out on the ochre koppies of Marikana that winter that they feature in the opening lines of the first chapter of Thomas Piketty's book *du jour*, the international bestseller *Capital in the Twenty-First Century*.

After describing the massacre, Piketty writes that 'this episode reminds us, if we need reminding, that the question of what share of output should go to wages and what share to profits – in other words, how should the income from production be divided between labour and capital? – has always been at the heart of distributional conflict.'

So, on one level, what happened at Marikana was not just a tragedy for South Africa, but emblematic of the potential for state-sanctioned violence in the face of increasing inequality and impoverishment triggered by the 2008 collapse of global financial markets.

In *Miners Shot Down*, Desai has crafted an intimate, claustrophobic and deeply moving film using footage taken at the scene over the course of the strike and interwoven with SAPS and Lonmin security videos. The narrative trajectory is driven by interviews with key players in the saga, including union and strike leaders, politicians and legal representatives of families at the Farlam Commission of Inquiry.

The director's own voiceover from the start uncompromisingly establishes and situates his sympathies with the workers, their struggles, their working conditions and their role, as young black men, in the continuing unhappy history of the mining industry in South Africa. Philip Miller's haunting score threads throughout the film, lending it a fitting funereal gravitas.

What is disturbingly evident from the start of Desai's film is the view of the striking workers as being somehow outside of the 'system' or the 'normal' or usual 'channels' of control and coercion – that is, NUM and Lonmin management.

It is clear that in refusing to allow NUM to negotiate on their behalf, joining the rival union AMCU or opting to attempt to bargain with Lonmin management themselves, the striking miners of Marikana changed the rules of the game – perhaps forever.

Desai sets up the general viewpoint of the striking workers as 'other' or 'outsiders' using footage filmed by Lonmin's security guards early in the strike as disgruntled rock drill operators initially gather at the mining house's headquarters. The banal running commentary about what the camera is witnessing sets up the 'us and them' narrative that begins to take shape around the issue of the R12 500 wage demand.

A second ludicrous encounter occurs when police send in a 'hostage negotiator' to talk to the miners who have gathered at the infamous koppie. A police armoured vehicle, its engine straining, drives up to the crowd. The police, and the Afrikaans-speaking negotiator, simply refuse to get out of the vehicle and talk to the miners face to face, human to human.

Instead, they order the unarmed spokesmen for the miners to approach their vehicle and force one of them to stand on tiptoes on the grille in order to try and negotiate over the loud diesel rattle of the SAPS vehicle.

The third encounter in which the 'us–them' divide once again becomes evident is when provincial police commissioner, Major General William Mpembe, confronts a group of miners, armed with spears and sticks, as they attempt to walk home through the veld. Mpembe explains that he is not going to arrest the strikers but has been ordered disarm them. One of the miners stands up and respectfully tells Mpembe that they have no quarrel with the police, that they will not cause trouble, but that they will not surrender their weapons.

The speaker then verbalises what so far has remained unsaid.

'You are black like us,' says the miner, casting his eyes over the jumpy police officers gathered around the major general while the workers softly begin to sing '*basiyazi we…we, basiyazi thina…* (they do know us)'.

For a brief moment, it appears that Mpembe and the older striking miner with whom he is negotiating are making headway – both men are speaking respectfully to each other using the term 'elder'. Then the major general's phone rings. He takes the call and returns with an entirely different and much more confrontational mindset.

And it is as this group of cowering workers rises up to begin walking home through the parched veld against police orders that the tragic events that will soon end in 34 deaths and at least 70 injuries are set in motion, Desai sweeping the viewer through each horrific moment.

In the most shocking display of apparent dissociation, Desai shows how – after that awful crack of lethal live ammunition that has been fired at the fleeing strikers – police callously move among the dead and the dying, overturning bloody bodies, putting a boot firmly on a chest to search for a weapon, simply ignoring the death rattle of a wounded man or the panicked gaze of another.

These are scenes disturbingly reminiscent of documentary film-maker Lindy Wilson's *Gugulethu Seven*, about seven ANC operatives who were lured to Gugulethu and assassinated by apartheid police in 1986. At the TRC, footage was shown of police manhandling the bodies of the dead men in a similar fashion. Desai knows that South Africans who survived the violence of apartheid will make those visual connections and be horrified and outraged.

In this regard, *Miners Shot Down* follows a great tradition of films that have helped to change the course of South African history over the past 50 years. Documentaries such as Chris Curling and Pascoe MacFarlane's influential *Last Grave at Dimbaza* (1974) helped to galvanise global opinion against the apartheid government, as did many others such as Betty Wolpert's *Awake from Mourning* (1981) and Lindy Wilson's acclaimed documentary *Last Supper at Horstley Street* (1983), about the District Six forced removals.

From this perspective it is only fitting, then, that the current regime would not – as was the case with its political predecessor – be too keen for ordinary citizens to see this important and courageous film, which is why it will not be screened by the SABC.

It is enlightening to watch ANC Deputy President Cyril Ramaphosa, whom Desai has beautifully captured in both pre- and post-democracy incarnations. The juxtaposition of the young, thin, bearded firebrand who established NUM and the fat, shiny, bemused tycoon speaks entirely for itself.

The absences in the film – the list of those who refused to be interviewed, including President Jacob Zuma, former Minister of Police Nathi Mthetwa, Police Commissioner Riah Phiyega, NUM Secretary General Frans Baleni or anyone from the Lonmin executive – also speak volumes.

Desai's ability to reconnect the dead miners – the working men whom the mines so often view as disposable or replaceable (as the workers themselves tell the camera) – brings to the film a human solidarity that is so lacking in the response from politicians, officials, the SAPS and Lonmin executives.

It is worth asking why the Marikana massacre and what it represents played such a minor role in the 2014 general election. Julius Malema's EFF was the only party that understood the greater significance of the underlying currents that led to the massacre in August 2012, and that bothered to address the underlying issues that are not going to go away soon.

That the majority of South Africans did not take to the street in outrage is testimony the effectiveness of the state media and ruling party's ability to dazzle voters with singing, dancing, rhetoric and big promises.

Miners Shot Down reveals the nexus of power in this country, and no amount of officialese or political jargon can disguise it.

Rehad Desai is an accomplished film-maker and, in time, *Miners Shot Down* will come to be seen as one of the most important physical remembrances, not only of the lives of the men who were killed, but also of a shameful and cowardly chapter of our recent history. It will show that liberation credentials mean nothing if true and meaningful transformation does not take place.

TWELVE-POINT-BLOODY-FIVE

As AMCU's platinum strikes edge towards five months, I despair about what's going on and how it came to this. The historians, however, will know that this period is significant on the road from repression to democracy.

GREG NICOLSON, JUNE 2014

The air is thick with analysis and I don't know what's going on.

10 June 2014. Press conference, Department of Mineral Resources, Pretoria, Minister Ramatlhodi. Colleagues (other people from other media organisations) trade in comment interpretation and source discrepancies. The minister is no longer involved in negotiations. He makes his official announcement on one of the biggest boardroom tables I've ever seen. On his appointment, he had said that nothing could be done in mining without solving the strikes. Now, he says the union and platinum companies need to know he has other work to do.

I raise my hand for a question. What to ask? I'm not sure, but I raise my hand. The spokesperson doesn't choose me and I lower my hand, listen to the discrepancies between foreign and local news angles.

Who in the room has seen *Miners Shot Down* (the documentary by Rehad Desai – film-maker, activist, sometimes contact and all-round interesting-ish guy), I wonder. 'Respectable' is one of the words that sticks with me since seeing the film on Friday.

In the six days leading up to the massacre in Marikana, the miners appear respectable, I would say. Yep, they kill a handful of people, set off by two incidents – NUM shooting at them and cops deciding to fire tear gas on 13 August 2012. But they appear respectable. Old-school values. Old-school marching techniques – from Eastern Cape? There's also old-school respect in dealing with authorities. Of course, 34 of them were killed on 16 August 2012 and more have been killed in the battle since. Anyone who watches *Game of Thrones* knows that unjust deaths lead to more (just or unjust?) deaths.

Desai tries to convey the failure of post-apartheid leaders to stay committed to improving the life of miners (extrapolate: ANC and black working class). Cyril Ramaphosa was a NUM leader. He's now rich enough to buy any of the houses in those real-estate guides that cater to the rich, selling McDonald's burgers, shakes and a whole lot of other crap for a profit.

Yes, miners' lives have improved since '94, but remember the Ernest Cole picture of the mine recruits, naked, being searched, hands in the air, in front of a black background in a white room? Pre-1994 isn't the best base from which to start. Today, we see more pay, still lots of deaths on the job but supposedly (surely?) better safety standards. But look at the settlements in Marikana: that's where many of Lonmin's miners live. I'll tell you: they suck. Nkaneng is perhaps a level or two above the worst I've seen in the country. And those places are so *kak* they beggar description.

Yes, the platinum miners already earn decent wages by South African standards. But, unlike most people who earn the same, they live like *this*. Something's wrong, no? What? Why? How will it change? Their ability to strike for so long shows that things have changed. But if things have changed beyond legislation, why the need to strike for so long?

It's the South African story. Things are better. But if we have such a good story to tell, why the fuck do we have so many problems? Cue the line, 'It's apartheid's fault.'

I digress. Let me tell you my thoughts on the platinum strike. The problem *was* created by colonialism and apartheid. The blood and humiliation of black workers flowed from one system into another, supporting the system of inequality – subjects and citizens. The rhetoric that gave talented leaders like Ramaphosa the ammunition to rise to prominent positions was true. For black migrant workers, life was hard, and their hardship directly boosted the bank accounts of some white South Africans, and indirectly benefited others.

Minister Ramatlhodi seems like a decent guy. His decision to intervene in the strike reflected many people's views, just like his comments on the sunset clauses in the negotiations for democracy reflected many people's views that they were bullshit. Those agreements ushered in a reasonably peaceful democracy, but let's be honest – in light of the ongoing poverty, unemployment and inequality, you have to wonder whether wealth accumulated on the rack of racist, oppressive, degrading laws should be wealth respected.

That's where the miners are.

But the chief concern isn't how screwed white rule was. It's an enormous factor contributing to the current situation, but there's more. What has happened since 1994? AMCU leadership is proving ever harder to reach, but when Joseph Mathunjwa answered my calls he always spoke with incredulity about how little has changed. How can we have the same system – a system that ... the system that ... the same system that ...

A system in which workers on strike can end up being massacred by police and turning on each other. For twelve-point-bloody-five.

The withdrawal of the government task team is significant beyond these wage negotiations. I like individuals within the mining companies. But the companies themselves? They're exploitative, leeching entities trying to benefit their shareholders. But, as frustrating as they may be, they need to stick within the law.

Those laws are created by the state, which, since democracy, has been run by the ANC. One of the best pieces of research from the platinum strikes came out of Wits. The study looked at the huge profits the mining companies made before the 2008 global financial crisis and at how little of that money went to workers. It recommended a resources rent tax, which could ensure that some of that money is invested in South Africa's future.

For now, however – in June 2014 – the platinum boom is gone. We've missed the boat for turning mining profit into local development and no platinum producer can claim it has done enough for its workers in the last 20 years. The ANC has managed to enrich a few talented and connected leaders while leaving the overall system of the past intact. The party's fabric has been interwoven with that of the mining bosses so that when someone outside of its alliance tries to tear it apart, like AMCU, it wants no part in the destruction.

The mineworkers on strike are stuck in a zero-sum game. If they reach their demand of a R12 500 basic wage – which, really, is unlikely – there'll be job losses and mine closures. The platinum price just isn't where it needs to be. If they settle for less, it still could be a substantial gain for workers, but what could pacify the cries of their exploited ancestors, the dead of Marikana and the failed hopes of those who believed that 1994 would lead to a better life, something different from the experience of their fathers?

The post-apartheid story, whether you believe it's a good story to tell or a narrative of ongoing repression, can be seen in the platinum strikers. Future historians on the path from tyranny and segregation to democracy will note what happens here.

WE'RE NOT IN EDEN
ANY MORE, SOUTH AFRICA

> *The deaths at Marikana have been called the end of innocence for post-apartheid South Africa. Perhaps the spate of unexpected downgrades of the country's sovereign debt and state-owned enterprises, and the reverberations from a startling* The Economist *cover story, is South Africa's expulsion from the delights of its geopolitical and economic Eden.*
> J BROOKS SPECTOR, OCTOBER 2012

Immediately after a pair of scathing articles on the state of South Africa was published in *The Economist*, two warring tribes staked out the turf of their views of the South African experiment – and of the world's judgement of it.

Prophets of doom inside and outside South Africa showed a kind of smug satisfaction, a palpable 'I told you so' *Schadenfreude*, over the signs of South Africa's imminent collapse, as adumbrated by *The Economist*. On the other side, the country's ever-shrinking roster of cheerleaders – including some, but not even all, of the members of the governing party's political class – took umbrage at this international public insult unfairly sullying a nation that had inherited a savagely distorted economy, social structure and political system and that has since moved vigorously and aggressively to right these many wrongs.

In fact, neither of these extremes has hit the nail on the head. The critique in *The Economist* of South Africa's circumstances was offered in sorrow and distress – the magazine clearly took little joy in this review of current circumstances. Its commentary was not an 'Ah ha! Gotcha! You've been found out, the emperor has no clothes!' exposé of a nation in which everything has gone wrong and the precipice is close at hand. In fact, *The Economist*'s writers went to great pains to place the country's current problems in their historical context and to identify the challenges from South Africa's history that have produced its current circumstances.

At the same time, it noted the real advancement that has happened in housing, growing electrification, the expansion of basic education – and a general rise in income (much of it attributable to the extension of social welfare systems that provide support grants to about a third of the country). This real progress is acknowledged and applauded for what it is.

However, this country's circumstances are now being measured against a continent whose larger circumstances and likely future are very different from what was true a decade or so earlier. Back in 2000, *The Economist* had despaired of Africa as the hopeless continent.

At that time, in sharp contrast, South Africa was the continent's one great shining beacon. It was energised by a new democratic tradition and abundant income from its extraordinary endowment of natural resources, whose production and revenue had just entered the long-cycle commodity boom. This almost guaranteed growing wealth for doing ever more good.

But, in contrast, during 2012 *The Economist* reversed the order. The rest of the continent – except, perhaps, for war zones like Mali, Somalia or the eastern Congo – has a region of 'go-go' possibilities. Even Nigeria, sometimes seemingly perched on the lip of a social and political volcano, was viewed as a likely candidate to surpass South Africa's GDP within a few years. South Africa was the place in which the future had gone sour.

Government and other cheerleaders were quick to reply with anger or in pain that *The Economist* had got it all wrong. South Africa has problems, yes, but there is a will to deal with them, resources to address them and the international respect (its BRICS membership, the UN Security Council role, a South African as head of the AU Commission) to bolster such efforts. The country's economy is basically sound, there is an appetite for new infrastructure and plans to put it in place, and its sovereign debt has been included in a world bond index as a mark of respect for what has been achieved here. And besides, this South Afro-pessimism is really – at its heart – envy for what has already been achieved by an African nation.

But some things can't be ignored or wished away. And that is the crux of things. The country continues to bleed manufacturing, mining and agricultural jobs as its economy shifts increasingly into a service economy, but its education system has not kept up in quality or quantity to respond to the new challenges. In the absence of such an effort, the foundation for real economic growth is forever weakened. And in fact, the critics say, South Africa is falling behind, despite a major contribution from the national budget to education. It is slipping in comparison with other African nations, let alone with putative competitors in South Asia, Southeast Asia or Latin America.

As South Africa entered its 2012 year-end examination period, some cruel facts bore noting. Out of a learner cohort of a little over one million who had entered Grade 10, fewer than 400 000 would pass the school-leaving exam in 2014, with an aggregate-level pass being just 30–40%. Moreover, fewer than 150 000 would receive a minimum university-acceptance-level passing grade. And, of that shrunken subtotal, only about 50 000 would achieve a 50% pass in mathematics; fewer than 10 000 will achieve 80% in that subject. But this is the very subject that is the core of capability in so many of the fields that make up the new economy. This level of achievement is not the mark of a society prepared for the challenges of a 21st-century economy.

Even putting aside garden-variety issues – like service delivery protests, increasingly obvious systemic corruption and glaring inefficiencies in government, rentier economic gatekeeping, a growing disengagement with the contemporary political landscape by disaffected citizens, rising and increasingly violent labour unrest and a lack of sustained investment in infrastructure that leaves a huge catch-up gap – the problem is not just a lack of social, educational and economic preparedness for the future for many members of South Africa's most poorly equipped population.

The looming problem is that the rest of world is in fierce,

unrelenting competition for whatever investment capital is available. While places like China, India or Brazil continue to suck in such investment capital, South Africa has now begun to stagnate – or worse – on this front.

More than a decade ago, in his book *The Lexus and the Olive Tree*, *New York Times* columnist Thomas Friedman observed the new global liquidity of investment capital in combination with growing electronic capabilities to move money around almost instantaneously and coined the phrase 'the electronic herd'. This electronic herd behaves like springbok or herring – the slightest threatening movement, shadow or noise is enough to send the herd slewing off in an entirely different direction at a moment's notice. Sometimes the trigger is a false alarm, sometimes not. But the intense mobility of capital mimics the behaviour of all those frightened fish that don't wish to get eaten by other fish.

As if to prove this point, the news in the week of 26 October 2012 contained the startling information that foreign direct investment (FDI) in South Africa had dropped by an astonishing 43% year on year, and that much of the drop seemed to have been connected to signals South Africa was unfriendly towards FDI. This unfriendliness was a combination of the tussle between different government departments over who owns national investment policy; a sense that the country has truly restrictive labour mobility; a fight over the conditions under which big-box retailer Wal-Mart Stores, Inc. could enter this country's retail and wholesale markets; and the negative impact on potential investors of continuing turmoil – and – worse in the mining sector.

The long-cycle commodity boom seemed to be over, and even the mining sector would have to fight much harder with increasingly less success to gain any traction with that increasingly skittish electronic herd of potential investors. This would put a real crimp on future growth in production or revenues.

And so, having been expelled from a blissful paradise of the world's admiration and love, perhaps South Africa, in October 2012, was entering a time in which observers would look carefully at virtually any writing that may have appeared on the wall to foretell the future. The problem was that it seemed less and less likely that the words would read 'This way to the promised land' and more likely that they would say '*Mene, mene, tekel, upharsin*', those mysterious words Daniel was summoned to interpret for Babylonian King Belshazzar.

After entering the king's chamber, Daniel told Belshazzar that the words meant that he had been weighed, measured and found wanting, that his kingdom would be divided and given over to the Medes and Persians. For South Africa, the question for the current crop of political leaders who stay up late contemplating the fate of the country's undereducated, unemployed, disaffected and unemployable will almost certainly be: Who are our Medes and Persians, riding down from the distant hills – and what will they want when they arrive?

5
PEOPLE IN THE NEWS

MY FRIEND, THE WAR PHOTOGRAPHER

The early 1990s in South Africa were a turbulent time, perhaps best documented by the band of fearless photographers named the Bang-Bang Club. Only two of the team, Greg Marinovich and João Silva, made it out of the era alive. But this didn't deter them from continuing to risk their lives to capture images of war.
GREG MARINOVICH, OCTOBER 2010

Afghanistan is a placc I automatically associate with João Silva. Not just because he has spent several months every year there for the *New York Times*, covering the war, but because it seems that he and that fated country were destined to share a small slice of history.

During our momentous 1994, João was in a bad emotional and psychological place. South Africa had successfully thrown off the bonds of apartheid, but at a hefty price. The violent sideshow of the Hostel War, as we had called it, had been devastating for township residents and migrants alike.

Even for us occasional interlopers, cameras at the ready and an easy escape at the end of the day, there was a price to be paid. For João, it was survivors' guilt – he had lived through his best friends getting killed, wounded and committing suicide in the space of a few months. In addition, he felt bad that, as he said, the last thing he did for his friend Ken (Oosterbroek) was to take pictures of him dead.

Without regard for his own safety, he had pulled me into cover after I had been shot, and had then run to help Ken. He had shot only a few images (let's say some 20 images with an exposure time of 1/250th of a second) over a period of ten minutes, which means he had taken pictures for less than 1% of that time. Nonetheless, the perception that stuck in the public mind was of João having taken pictures of his dead friend. It haunted him.

Later that year, our friend and colleague, Kevin Carter, committed suicide. João then went to Afghanistan on assignment and, while there, witnessed an artillery attack on a residential neighbourhood in Kabul. João recalled that, as his car had approached the site, he had seen an amazing scene, with a pillar of smoke in the background and a distraught father carrying his wounded toddler, running towards them, calling for help.

João had had a choice: shoot or help. He had chosen to bundle the father and child into the car, and to race to the hospital. Only at the hospital had João taken pictures of the fatally wounded child in his father's arms.

In 1999, João returned to Afghanistan with me in tow. We were going in on the side of the Northern Alliance, the only forces stopping the Taliban from overrunning the whole country. We spent a week in neighbouring Tajikistan trying to get in, but the Pakistani military were weighing in on the side of their proxy, the Taliban. Flights in were grounded.

Finally, one day – while eating the sweetest melons and tastiest *shashlik* – we got the message to get to the helicopter: we could fly! We were very excited, and so lulled by the delights of Dushanbe that we settled into the stinky, patched-up, Russian-made helicopter and, cavalierly, used our flak vests as cushions.

It was a nervy flight, the chopper hugging contours to avoid exposure. Our fellow passengers invoked Allah repeatedly. We landed without incident but as we alighted we realised we were taking fire. Everybody was running. A Pakistani MiG was strafing us and dropping cluster bombs. We ran, our flak vests left behind in the chopper.

João and I took shelter in a disused airport building, lying flat as the cluster bombs exploded all around us and the earthen roof crumbled alarmingly. Suddenly, bees were attacking us – a hive in the room had been hit and the bees were insane with rage. João and I looked at each other as the little buggers attacked and, reading each others' minds, laughed and said 'Run!' We made it to a better shelter without injury, but several civilians lay dead and wounded.

We should have read the portents. Several days letter, I got hit by flying debris from a mortar attack and João had the dubious pleasure of photographing me being stitched up, without anaesthetic, by a self-trained village medic. We got through that one too, and other tricky situations, yet João returned to Afghanistan time and again.

He is, without doubt, the best war photographer in the world: fearless, tactical, calm under stress and compassionate.

He was also quite phlegmatic about the possibility that something might one day happen to him. Not that he was resigned to becoming a casualty, but with each return trip, the odds mounted.

On Saturday 23 October, João was on an embed with US troops, and went out with a minesweeping team. He followed them as they cleared the way, but they missed a mine.

Just 300 metres from the base, he stepped on it.

Three medics attended him within seconds, and he lost hardly any blood, which is what enabled him to survive. João being João, he asked for his camera and a cigarette while they were working on him, telling them to get the Marlboros out of his trouser pocket. While the medics toiled on him, he took pictures.

For me, that says everything about João.

THE BEAUTIFUL
MIND OF JONATHAN JANSEN

When Jonathan Jansen arrived at the University of the Free State (UFS) in 2009, it was an institution with deep divisions haunted by the spectre of the Reitz Four. With a transcendent recipe of listening, unwavering moral fortitude, servant leadership and love, by 2011 Jansen and his team were well on their way to turning the university into a model of integration worth emulating.
MANDY DE WAAL, MARCH 2011

It is surprising that Jonathan Jansen says the remarkable and rapid change that has taken place at the University of the Free State is something he's still trying to figure out. Although he denies being personally responsible for the change, hearing the heart of Jansen one intuitively knows he had a big part in its turnaround.

Jansen was appointed in May 2009 and took up his position in July of that year, inheriting a campus that had been humiliated by the Reitz Four. Named after the residence in which they lived, the four male students had filmed a globally infamous initiation video showing five workers being subjected to demeaning tasks. These included drinking beer and doing athletics, as well as being made to consume a concoction in which one student had appeared to urinate and that made the middle-aged university staff vomit.

'I went in June one afternoon to try to figure out the place,' says Jansen, explaining how he had been mentored to listen. 'I was trained by someone who himself was trained by Milton Friedman and Theodore Schultz, Nobel Prize winners of economics.' As part of his instruction, Jansen was advised not to speak when moving into a new organisation, but rather just to listen, taste, hear and feel for the first six months.

'I thought, let me get down there first because the place was in pain. White and black students would walk past me and not greet. They would see you coming and they would look down. People were literally sitting with their fists clenched. I had never seen this before.'

On a wintery day in June 2009, he saw two huge guys sitting outside the chemistry building, eating sandwiches out of Tupperware lunchboxes. 'Their body language said: "Don't even think of disturbing us", which, if you know me, is an invitation to conversation. They clearly didn't know who I was and were sitting on a concrete slab. So I went to sit down and forced myself between these two guys, like I did when I was a kid in the third-class train to Mowbray. I remember one of them going really red in the face.'

Jansen sat without saying anything, and when it was clear that the one huge lug of a boy was getting antsy, the new vice chancellor thought he'd better introduce himself. 'Their response was: "*Meneer, vat maar 'n toebroodjie* (Sir, please have a sandwich)". And there were these three huge guys eating sandwiches. I didn't say anything for a while to see what was going to happen.'

Eventually Jansen, whose notion of leadership is servant leadership, asked them a question that he would continue asking students, staff, alumni and the community surrounding the university for six months. The question was: 'What do you want me to do for you?'

'Even before I asked the question I ran through a list in my head of the possible things they might come up with. Things students all over the world tend to ask. More parking spaces, to fix up the science lab, that lecturer who can't teach economics … the food, that's always a big deal. I thought one of these things would come up. But I will never forget they spoke as if they had rehearsed their answer, which of course they couldn't have done. With one voice they said: "Please don't force us to racially integrate".'

Now, these students weren't a product of apartheid. They had grown up in an era in which Nelson Mandela was free and in which they witnessed the first democratic elections. 'They didn't even live through the crap, but they were behaving as if they were there.' Fortunately, Jansen's experience at the University of Pretoria (known by its nickname Tukkies), which is written into a seminal book on racism and integration called *Knowledge in the Blood*, had prepared him for these strange South African scenarios.

Knowledge in the Blood centres on Jansen's experiences as the first black dean at Tukkies and how white South Africans have chosen to deal with apartheid by denying and avoiding history. Silence and the rejection of pre-1994 atrocities realise a 'knowledge in the blood', in which generations pass down prejudice and ignorance instead of wisdom and healing. The result is the continual re-enactment of an apartheid past, which Jansen had witnessed at Tukkies and again at UFS.

What's remarkable about Jansen's stories is that, unlike a Trevor Manuel, he doesn't come from the moral high ground, but from a place of extreme humility with the acknowledgement that he, too, is wounded. 'Like all of us I too am wounded, I too carry racial pride and I work daily to try to break it down. I am embarrassed, and I say this everywhere I go, at one stage I hated white people. I hated them for turning my grandfather blind. I hated them for taking our property in Montagu and giving it to white folk and then destroying the property. I hated white people for so long it is a deep, deep embarrassment to me that I could be so incredibly foolish.

'And yet this is a path of transformation, not the ANC's view of transformation, but a deep human transformation through which all of us have to pass. The pretence that we are okay is the problem.' South Africa is caught in a trap of political correctness underpinned by racial quotas in an attempt to correct an apartheid past. Yet its people, says Jansen, are trapped in stereotypes of 'perpetrator' or 'victim'. This exists in a vacuum of dialogue that is burst open when a Manyi, Botes, Hofmeyr, Roberts or Malema happens. Then South Africa is all righteous rage and aggression and is further polarised instead of taking tentative steps towards healing.

But back to Jansen's story. He was in his third month at UFS and students were choosing leaders for their 23 residences for the next year. 'I went to this huge room where these students were choosing house committee members. And there were all these black kids and white kids looking at me strangely. The white kids were *die moer in* (spitting mad) and I said to them: "Listen, I have been around the residences and I see you are completely segregated, at our university it is as if 1994 never happened, and I just want to tell you guys, irrespective of what you think, and I love you very much" – my staff will tell you if I use the phrase "I love you very much" there is bad news in the next sentence – "this is how it is going to be, we are going to integrate the residences."

'Up jumped this beautiful student and said to me: "*Wie de fok is jy*? (Who the fuck are you?)" Let me tell you about Afrikaans-speaking kids, when an Afrikaans-speaking kid speaks to an adult, a rector of the place like that, then the stress is enormous. "*Wie de fok is jy? My ouma was in Roosmaryn. My ma was in Roosmaryn. Jy is nie eers van hierdie provinsie nie. Wie de fok is jy om vir ons te sê hoe ons moet leef?* (Who the fuck are you? My grandmother was in this residence. My mother was in this residence. You are not even from this province. Who the fuck are you to say how we should live?)"'

This was a new and highly traumatic event for Jansen, but he maintained his composure, saying that because of his experience at Tukkies, he knew where the trauma was coming from, but that he was also deeply conscious of everyone watching him. 'And how I act is absolutely crucial to the resolution of this girl's trauma. So my body language is completely neutral. I stood smiling there as if nothing was going on, but meanwhile she was ranting on and on.'

Three weeks later, during an open-door session, Jansen would meet this young woman again. 'We have open-door sessions where anyone can come and speak to me about what is going on and in walks this kid, and I think: Here we go again. But she says to me: "Professor, do you remember me?" I say: "Yes, my child, I remember you and I am scared. Please have a seat." She looks at me and this child begins to cry. She says: "I just want to ask your forgiveness for what I did and I am going back to that group of students and I am going to tell them what I am going to tell you." Then she says: "I made a terrible mistake. Please make me a part of the solution."'

Jansen says since that day he has had encounters with students, white and black, in which they don't display anger, or ask about the terrible happenings at Reitz. They don't elicit memories of inclusion or exclusion. Instead, the question they ask is how they can be part of the solution.

'What's the secret? How did this happen? You don't overturn 300 years of colonialism and apartheid in a weekend, so I am very aware of the fact that transformation is not an arrival, it is a journey. I understand that backsliding will happen. I understand very clearly that things we see every day are not guaranteed to always be beautiful. That's the nature of organisational change, and that's the nature of social change in a country with our history.

'If you want to change an organisation, if you want to change young people, whether you are the parent or the director of a company, you just have to know two things. One, you have to be firm in making decisions about difficult things. Prevarication is the end of you. Clear moral choices are what Jim Collins called it in *Good to Great*. The second is that you have to love the people you lead unconditionally.'

Jansen goes silent for a while and then changes his mind. 'Actually it is in the reverse, because the love comes first. When young people sense that you will walk through fire for them, when your employees have the sense that the job is not about you, it is about them, when they have a sense that this man or woman will do anything for you in a crisis, they will do anything for you.'

I looked around the large audience at an EE Publishers event, as Jansen was speaking. There was hardly a dry eye in the room.

Fast-forward to 2011, and the university has a new problem. The big problem, Jansen says, is interracial love affairs. 'With young people, when you remove the barriers to human interaction they tend to fall in love.' Jansen has to counsel fearful sons and daughters who are scared of going home because their white fathers might kill them if they find out that they are in an interracial love affair.

So, why did this miracle of integration happen at UFS and not at the more liberal campuses of Cape Town or Wits?

'Universities like Cape Town and Wits cannot change fundamentally. When black people moved into the residences at Wits, the white kids fled to Parktown and Rosebank. When UCT started to integrate its residences, the white kids fled to Observatory, Mowbray and Rondebosch. I saw that with my own eyes. And these are the so-called liberal universities, but don't believe that crap. The assumption of innocence is what you still have to work through.'

In the historically Afrikaans universities like UFS, the students stay in the residences and they fight, and then they meet their fears head-on. When they do, the miracle happens. That is where change happens and people can begin to reconcile the past – and, perhaps, even fall in love.

BAD COPS, ASSASSINS, CZECH FUGITIVES: THE MEANING OF PAUL O'SULLIVAN

Forensic consultant Paul O'Sullivan spent eight years relentlessly investigating former police chief Jackie Selebi. As Selebi's trial drew to a close in 2010, the apparently indefatigable Irish expat began focusing on his next project – toppling the extensive criminal empire of one of the most dangerous criminals in the country, Czech-born fugitive Radovan Krejcir.

MARIANNE THAMM, JANUARY 2014

On 10 September 2010 at about 6.30 p.m., Paul O'Sullivan was in Dublin when he received a call on his cell phone. He answered in his usual manner: 'O'Sullivan, good day.' The caller at the other end paused momentarily before speaking.

The man, recalls O'Sullivan, had an Eastern European

accent and said, 'Hello, clown. You want to fuck with me? I will show you who is Radovan. When you will come back to South Africa, I will make you suck my cock, then I will kill you, to show you you fucked with the wrong guy.'

The caller then hung up.

On 18 September 2010, Paul O'Sullivan made a sworn statement at the Bramley police station, providing a phone log of the threatening phone call as well as other details. In the statement, he reminded police of another sworn statement he had taken from a source who had said that Radovan Krejcir had asked him to procure a '.30-06 sniper rifle for the purpose of killing [him]'. O'Sullivan also provided police with information and a photograph of an illegal elephant's tusk that hung on the wall of the bar of Krejcir's house at the Vaal River.

'I request urgent police intervention to prevent the conspiracy to murder me from becoming a reality,' O'Sullivan ended the statement back then.

Fast-forward to the afternoon of 9 January 2014, and the arrest of Siboniso Miya (32), Jacob Nare (28), Owen Serero (32) and a woman, Zodumiso Biyele (23), after a planned assassination attempt on O'Sullivan and Colonel Nkosana Ximba (who arrested Krejcir in December), as well as other members of a Hawks specialised unit, was thwarted in Johannesburg.

Two weapons, including an R5 assault rifle (believed to have been used in the drive-by killing of Lebanese businessman Bassam Issa in October 2013), blue lights, balaclavas and several number plates were confiscated from the would-be assassins. Several telephones and iPads were also recovered, and these were investigated for encrypted communications that would lead to the mastermind behind the assassination plot, believed by many to be Radovan Krejcir.

Shortly after the arrests, O'Sullivan sent a characteristically provocative email (which he copied to select journalists) to Krejcir's lawyer, Eddie Classen.

In the mail, O'Sullivan suggests that Classen tells his client 'that I will do all that I can lawfully do to strip him of everything he or his crooked family members have acquired through his criminal conduct, and see that he rots in jail FOREVER'.

O'Sullivan told Classen that he believed that Krejcir had issued the instruction for the assassination to take place at noon on Thursday 9 January so that he could claim that he had had nothing to do with it, as he would have been behind bars in C-Max.

'They walked straight into a trap and Krejcir's attempt was thwarted. Again!' said O'Sullivan.

O'Sullivan suggested that if Classen appealed the court's decision not to grant Krejcir bail, he would 'legally intervene … as it is not in the interests of justice to have that gangster on the streets. However, after the chaos of his failed hit on me and the colonel that was behind his arrest late last year, you may wish to reconsider your futile attempts at trying to get him out of jail.'

The investigator ended the mail with a cheerful 'Thinking of suing me for defamation? Go ahead, bring it on, I will wipe the floor with you and bring a counter-claim that will make your claim pale into insignificance.'

Jackie Selebi had felt the full wrath of O'Sullivan after

'pissing in an Irishman's beer'. Imagine the shit-storm Krejcir could have expected from the investigator after threatening to have him suck cock before killing him.

Paul O'Sullivan has been on Radovan Krejcir's tail since 2010, when the Czech fugitive's name first popped up on the radar while the private investigator was hunting down Jackie Selebi.

Since starting his investigation into Krejcir, O'Sullivan has handed 12 to 15 damning sworn statements (some of which I read during the course of researching *To Catch a Cop: The Paul O'Sullivan Story*) to police from a range of people implicating Radovan Krejcir in a string of serious crimes including money laundering, smuggling drugs, smuggling contraband cigarettes and much more. Meanwhile, at least 12 bodies have piled up around Krejcir who has, until now, managed to escape police dragnets and the coils of justice.

It was O'Sullivan who submitted an extensive and detailed affidavit – with attached sworn statements – of the various crimes linked to Krejcir, including the murder of former apartheid police operative turned 'private investigator' Kevin Trytsman, Teazer's strip club boss Lolly Jackson, and German luxury car convertor, Uwe Gemballa, to the refugee appeals tribunal requesting the Czech not to be granted asylum in South Africa.

'I do not believe our system is perverted. I have faith in South Africa and its government, its people and this honourable tribunal. I do not believe Krejcir's claim that he has paid all the right people in the right places to ensure he gets to stay in South Africa. I have faith that you will do the right thing and send this gangster back to the Seychelles, where he belongs, or any country that will take him,' O'Sullivan wrote to the tribunal in January 2011.

In his short sojourn in South Africa (he arrived in 2007), Krejcir has managed ruthlessly to infiltrate and destabilise established crime networks while police appeared to look on helplessly, at times appearing to aid and abet him. O'Sullivan says the question is not how many cops are on Krejcir's payroll but how high up the corruption goes.

Krejcir has been allowed to operate – and, indeed, flourish – partly because of the corruption of police criminal intelligence by rogue elements. In 2011, before his arrest after the murder of one of his associates, Cyril Beeka, in Cape Town, Krejcir was given access to illegally taped conversations about him between O'Sullivan and Major General Shadrack Sibiya, the head of the Hawks in Gauteng.

A faction within police intelligence, loyal to controversial suspended crime intelligence head Richard Mdluli, has been consistently accused of working against Sibiya in an attempt to discredit him.

In 2011 General Joey Mabasa was asked to leave the police service (but not without receiving a golden handshake) for his close connections with Krejcir. Mabasa had driven with Krejcir to the house of Lolly Jackson on the night he was murdered. Not only that, Jackson had been shot with Mabasa's gun that had allegedly been stolen the day before but only reported afterwards. Apart from this, Mabasa's wife, Dorcas, had gone into business with Krejcir's wife, Katerina Krejcirova.

When I first met Paul O'Sullivan in April 2013 to research

a book on his role in the investigation and conviction of Jackie Selebi, I was aware that his was one of four names on a hit list found by the Hawks during a dramatic raid on Krejcir's R30-million Bedfordview home in 2011.

The other three names on the list were Cyril Beeka, the notorious Cape Town former bouncer and underworld crime boss who was cultivated by both security agents of the former regime as well as underground ANC operatives; state prosecutor Riegel du Toit; and Krejcir's former doctor, Marian Tupy.

Du Toit had been investigating Krejcir's link to the murder of German supercar conversion specialist, Uwe Gemballa, who disappeared shortly after arriving in Johannesburg in February 2010. Gemballa was found eight months later in a shallow grave, a plastic bag over his head, his hands tied behind his back, having been shot at close range in the head. Three men were subsequently arrested for the murder.

Gemballa acted as a sort of Secret Santa for murdered Teazers' boss Lolly Jackson and Krejcir, stuffing wads of fresh Euros in the panels of converted luxury vehicles he shipped to South Africa. Jackson and Krejcir both shared a love of exotic vehicles and at the time of his death the Teazers' boss had around R90 million worth of cars in his garage.

Krejcir had reportedly argued with Gemballa during a phone call made or received at the Harbour Café in 2010 after money that was meant to have been stashed inside a Porsche delivered in September that year had gone missing.

Beeka was dead by the time I met Paul, so he had clearly moved up a slot on the list. Friends and family were concerned for my safety but for some reason – foolishness, perhaps – I was not worried. I had worked as a crime reporter for the *Cape Times* for over eight years and had been exposed to human beings at their worst.

Besides, if I were going to be hanging around with someone whose name was No. 1 on a hit list compiled by one of the country's most ruthless criminals, I was glad that was Paul O'Sullivan, and not someone else. I spent a week with him in Jo'burg, where we sped through the streets and highways, O'Sullivan driving like a man accustomed to avoiding a bullet (he has been shot at several times in this country).

Playing back my interviews, I can often hear myself gasping as O'Sullivan's car engine suddenly roars as he takes a gap in traffic, making sure always to be on the move – never, ever stationary.

People warned me about the investigator. Some had said he was mad, crazy, an agent, a brusque man. But I liked him.

O'Sullivan is someone accustomed to keeping secrets and even though he had officially approved me to write the account of his role in Selebi's downfall, I could not dig out more than he wanted to reveal. Much of the research had to be done poring over thousands of pages of court records, emails, affidavits, sworn statements, letters and taped phone calls.

In the end it proved to be a sprawling narrative that featured a cast of thousands, including petty thugs and criminals, crooked businessmen and cops, and that rippled all the way to the Union Buildings.

The thing about the Selebi and the Krejcir narrative and the intersection between organised crime, police and even politics is that it is so deep, wide and complicated that it is almost impossible for someone outside of it to fathom just how much *kak* we are in.

I like Paul O'Sullivan because of the way he speaks to those he deems his enemies – criminals and the lawyers who represent them. I want to do an air punch when I read his emails to corrupt cops; I want to shout 'Yessssss!' when he fearlessly tells Selebi that he is going to take him down. I like Paul O'Sullivan because in spite of it all, he believes that there are more good cops than bad and that in the end the bad guys always get their comeuppance. And if he can believe it, why shouldn't you and I?

In a world where crime series like *The Wire* or *CSI* have become the most-watched TV, and crime fiction has become the most widely read genre, it is important to bear in mind that Paul O'Sullivan and the crooked cops and criminals who occupy his world are not fictional characters. They are frighteningly real.

'Sounds like the plot of a Bond movie,' people say about O'Sullivan and his life. The point is that this is not a movie; this is the cold, chilling reality of organised crime and the deep and urgent threat it poses to our young democracy.

It was Sam Sole – managing partner of amaBhungane, the *Mail & Guardian*'s Centre for Investigative Journalism – who, in April 2011, published a compelling piece titled 'The Meaning of Radovan Krejcir'. Sole wrote: 'The Czech fugitive is a connoisseur of weak states. His choice of SA as a refuge is symptomatic of the country's deepening moral malaise. There's not really a single point at which a country suddenly becomes a failed state. States exist across a continuum of dysfunction.

Some things still work in Zimbabwe, in Swaziland, after all. And in Italy, for instance, some things don't. In war the collapse of law and order happens so fast we can see it and it is usually mirrored by physical destruction, which underlines the impact. Organised crime and corruption are more like slow biological warfare or radiation. The infrastructure seems to remain intact – there are just bodies that accumulate haphazardly – until you realise the infrastructure (or the institution) has become so contaminated, it is no longer functional; indeed, it has become a threat itself and must be abandoned or destroyed.'

For that reason alone I'm glad that Paul O'Sullivan, as unorthodox as he may be, is on our side.

TALKING 'BOUT A REVOLUTION

Julius Malema, his sidekick Floyd Shivambu and a few of their mates have decided to form a group called the Economic Freedom Fighters. In an interview Malema reveals more about his economic freedom campaign, how his expulsion from the ANC served as a blow to the 'Forces of Change' within the ANC and his intentions for a 'revolution' in South Africa.

RANJENI MUNUSAMY, JUNE 2013

It surprises Julius Malema that some people are scared of him and think he is a monster of sorts. I ask him how is he going to attract people to come on board his economic freedom campaign when he has built himself as an aggressive radical, spewing bile and instilling fear.

He grins coyly and says he doesn't know why people are

scared of him. As with the local and international radio and television interviews Malema has done during his stint as South Africa's most controversial political figure, he is soft-spoken, polite, articulate and deliberate, answering everything asked of him. It is difficult to amalgamate this image with the persona on a political podium – fiery, audacious, belting out war talk.

Malema says that when he addresses rallies and public meetings, he has to use language that is different from when he speaks to people face to face. 'You have to agitate and get the message across in a short space of time. It is the language of mobilisation and agitation.'

'I'm Julius throughout,' he says, bemused, as if the contradictions between his two personas should not be disconcerting.

He relays an anecdote of how even he gets shocked by people's perceptions of him. Malema says he and a handful of friends attended the launch of a new cruise ship in Durban. The function was in a cinema on board the ship and the lights were turned off. When the lights were eventually turned on, the mostly white crowd was stunned to discover Malema sitting among them. When the initial shock had worn off, many rushed over to take pictures with him.

'I couldn't understand it. It was as if I was some big TV personality; they were behaving like I was a celebrity,' Malema says.

So, how did it come about that Malema decided to re-emerge from the political wilderness and dive back into the game? He says he has continued to address public meetings and 'engage with the masses' away from the media spotlight. He took a two-month break to study – he is doing a BA degree in politics and citizenship through Unisa – and recently finished his exams. It was then that he, former ANC Youth League (ANCYL) spokesman Floyd Shivambu and a 'few comrades' decided that the time was right to launch a process of consultation to decide how to advance their economic freedom campaign.

The campaign, as it was when Malema and Shivambu were still in the ANCYL, advocates for a radical economic policy shift in South Africa, including through expropriation of land without compensation and the nationalisation of mines. Malema says he and 'a few young people' decided to form the group, calling themselves 'Economic Freedom Fighters' to refloat their old campaign by holding consultation forums around the country.

He says they have not yet decided whether to form a political party. There were three options on the table: an independent political platform 'agitating' for economic policy change but not affiliated to any political organisation; contesting the elections and then pushing for change through Parliament; or remaining loyal to the ANC and hoping that it would 'self-correct' some time in the future. Malema says the public forums and submissions would culminate in a national consultative meeting that would ultimately decide which option to take.

Malema says his announcement upset some of his former allies in the ANC and ANCYL, who felt affronted that he had not consulted with them about the idea before going public. But he says he did not want anyone else to control his agenda. 'Every generation has its own mission. This is ours.'

But if he could not succeed with the nationalisation

campaign from within the ruling party, how does he hope to make any policy impact from outside? 'The 1976 Soweto uprising was not an ANC initiative,' Malema responds. 'In fact the ANC criticised those kids until they were overtaken by events. So it doesn't need to come from inside the ANC, they will join later.'

So, you want an uprising then, Julius? Malema does not blink and answers instantly: 'We are agitating for a revolution. We want a radical policy shift. The ANC can only be forced into it by the masses.'

Throughout the interview, Malema weaves in his views of Zuma's failures as ANC leader and president. He claims his expulsion was 'a well-calculated move' to ensure that Zuma was re-elected at the ANC's national conference at Mangaung last December. He also claims that his charges of racketeering and money laundering, and the seizure and sale of his properties by the South African Revenue Service (SARS), were all politically motivated to destroy him.

Malema says he thinks the outcome of the Mangaung conference could have been different had he still been in the ANC, as his expulsion 'served as a blow to the Forces of Change'. He says that after he was expelled, those who were running the Forces of Change campaign to remove Zuma as ANC president were 'advancing their own names' and were 'inspired by self-interest', which further damaged the campaign.

Malema was in Mangaung during the conference and monitored the events throughout. 'I knew we were going to lose, there was too much manipulation.' He says he knew there was 'something fishy' when ANC membership figures in

KwaZulu-Natal escalated rapidly ahead of the conference so that support would sway in favour of Zuma.

Malema says he nonetheless 'admired the spirit of comrades' in the Forces of Change camp. 'No matter the consequences and the hardships, they fought until the conclusion, including Comrade Kgalema. I felt very bad for the comrades who were inside (the conference tent) and kept soldiering on.'

Asked whether, with the benefit of hindsight, he could have done things differently to remain in the ANC and perhaps still be living the high life he once enjoyed, Malema says he believes he acted according to his political beliefs and would not change anything he had done. He said he was punished for speaking out against Zuma and had no regrets about that.

However, he says he and his colleagues who were subjected to disciplinary procedures by the ANC had made approaches to try to broker a settlement, but these were snubbed. Malema's written request to the Mangaung conference to reconsider his expulsion was also rejected.

At first, Malema says he was not bitter about losing his possessions and homes because he understood it to be politically motivated. 'I don't feel angry, I know it is part of the game.' But later, he admits that he was cross about the sale of his cabbage farm.

'I did get angry seeing that the land of an African child was bought by a white Afrikaner male, presided over by the ANC government on the eve of the 100-year anniversary of the 1913 Land Act. The Afrikaner males ganged up there to secure the land.'

Asked what he has been doing with himself since being

expelled from the ANC, Malema says he is in business but is reluctant to say what exactly this is. He says his business only deals with the private sector so that the state does not interfere with it. 'I live in Limpopo and survive through family and friends.' He had to return the swish black Mercedes Benz Viano in which he used to travel around to a friend who had loaned it to him, as he says SARS kept asking questions about it and state agencies were harassing the owner.

So, where would the resources come from to run a countrywide consultation process? 'You don't need much resources, you need political will,' Malema says. 'If it means we use public transport to reach the masses so be it.'

Perhaps the biggest obstacle to Malema's new political career is his pending corruption trial. But he does not see it as such.

'The economic freedom campaign is not a personal project. The Economic Freedom Fighters will lead it whether I am there or not.'

If Malema is there, leading the campaign, it is guaranteed to run interference against the ANC and the state. Malema agitating for change inside the ANC caused unprecedented turbulence. Now he wants a revolution and has no restraints.

The prospect of Julius Malema talking directly to the forgotten people of South Africa will keep many an ANC politician awake at night.

Add things together and Malema 2.0 may be a terrifying opponent to the very organisation that spawned him. His impulsive, maverick move should make the inhabitants of Luthuli House extremely nervous. They have been warned.

WALKING WITH KATHRADA: A JOURNEY TO ROBBEN ISLAND

To mark Ahmed Kathrada's 85th birthday, the Ahmed Kathrada Foundation is producing a coffee-table book capturing about 300 tours he has conducted on Robben Island with presidents, royalty, celebrities and other notables. Accompanying a giant of the liberation struggle to the place at which he had been held captive for 18 of his 26 years of incarceration was a testing and emotional journey.

RANJENI MUNUSAMY, JUNE 2014

Ahmed Kathrada is standing on the ramp of the Clock Tower building at the Victoria & Alfred Waterfront, from which the ferry to Robben Island leaves. He is clutching his tour ticket, waiting in the queue behind buzzing tourists who are eager to see one of the South Africa's most historic places. You would think that a renowned former inmate and previous chairman of the Robben Island Museum Council would have special passage or privileges. But no, he is standing in the queue.

It appears that none of the tourists knows who he is, mostly because he tries to go unnoticed in his simple clothes and insistence on no special treatment in everything he does.

I am standing further behind in the queue, stealing glances at him. He looks so fragile. Cape Town's weather is being temperamental, with clouds overhead. I worry whether he will be warm enough in the wintery breeze. He shuffles restlessly on the ramp; the ferry is late and he is eager to go.

With us is photojournalist Benny Gool, who chronicled the life of Nelson Mandela through his pictures. A camera crew from Videovision Entertainment, the producers of the biographical film *Mandela: Long Walk To Freedom*, is taking the footage of our tour. Zaakirah Vadi, a communications officer at the Ahmed Kathrada Foundation, and Mahomed Seedat, Kathrada's former aide and driver, complete our posse. The camera crew has filmed Kathrada before and knows the island from the filming of *Long Walk*. They're not fussed about the day's assignment – just let it happen naturally, they say.

I am, however, apprehensive. I have never before interviewed Uncle Kathy. There is something about his manner, his gait and his self-effacing character that always makes me tear up. I have sat in audiences to which he had spoken, drinking in his wonderful anecdotes about his life and experiences. I have been in his presence many times but have never had a one-on-one conversation with him.

The invitation to interview him on the island is a great honour, but one I knew would be an uphill climb. It is something you get to do once in a lifetime – journey with a legend to the place of his torment, and walk him through the experiences of a legion of icons, most of whom are now gone. It needs respect and gentleness and, at the same time, the ability to probe an old man's memory for what is buried deep within.

I am mindful of all this as we cross the gangplank to board the ferry. Uncle Kathy is shuffling slowly, taking small steps, a sign showing that the youngest Rivonia treason trialist now has eight and a half decades of life behind him. In my mind flashes an image of him and Govan Mbeki shackled together in leg irons, shuffling towards their long imprisonment.

My mission is to get through the day without crying.

He sits beside me, explaining that the ferry we are using that day had been hired as the Robben Island boat was being serviced. As the boat chugs across the harbour towards the open sea, he starts talking about his first trip to the island 50 years ago when he and six of his comrades were flown in by military plane on an icy morning in June 1964. He has told the story hundreds of times, but he relates it with emotion, pausing to recall little details, as if he is telling it for the first time.

The boat is now bouncing on the waves and my insides are starting to churn. Uncle Kathy is sitting calmly next to me as if he is on his couch watching television. If he notices that I have broken out into a cold sweat and am battling not to heave, he doesn't say anything. The journey to the island takes 35 minutes and I feel every one of them. Eventually Uncle Kathy sticks out his finger to the left: 'There's the island!'

He and I get miked, so everything we say from the time we disembark is recorded. We are passing a wall of iconic pictures running along the harbour. The crew is filming. I start asking questions about the arrival of the Rivonia trialists on the island so that this time his answers are captured. Uncle Kathy is, however, dealing with the logistics of getting us around the island, as he has done close to 300 times when he escorted luminaries from US presidents Barack Obama and Bill Clinton to Fidel Castro, Yasser Arafat, Oprah and Beyoncé.

We are driven to B-Section, where Mandela, Kathrada, Walter Sisulu, Govan Mbeki, Raymond Mhlaba and others were imprisoned. When we get to the courtyard where pictures of the prisoners are mounted, Uncle Kathy switches into tour-guide mode, explaining the layout, some of the experiences, the hardships. In his hand is a huge key that he is using to gesture and point.

He tells the crew not to waste too much time taking pictures because we will be late for the ferry back. He says there is never enough time to get through everything so it's best that we keep moving. It then dawns on me that Uncle Kathy doesn't realise that the purpose of the visit is to capture him, not the island. The island has been recorded hundreds of times and will be there forever for future generations to visit. We are there to ensure future generations will have the benefit of hearing and seeing the island's most famous tour guide telling the story.

I am asking questions but he wants to keep moving, telling me we'll be able to talk properly inside. The crew rushes ahead so they can capture Uncle Kathy walking through the prison doors. He ruins the shot because he is too much of a gentleman. He wants me to walk in first.

The passage in B-Section is deadly silent. I look for signs of the heroes who once traversed it. There are none.

Uncle Kathy is shuffling towards the Mandela cell, holding the key. I have been here before, 17 years ago, but not inside the cell. Uncle Kathy and I go in, and he points out the mat on the floor where Madiba slept, the bucket that was used as a toilet, and explains that in later years, there was a desk in the cell. I disregard the pang in my chest and start asking about the famous people who came there to pay homage and what they asked Uncle Kathy when they were inside.

But he wants to move on. He says not everyone can come inside the cell and we need to get moving so he can give the key back. I go to the bars and try to look out, to see what Tata saw every day. I am too short and can't see anything.

It would make precious footage to capture Uncle Kathy speaking inside the Mandela cell, but we are herded out and down the passage. 'This is my cell,' he points ahead. 'I know it because of this red thing,' he says, gesturing to a tag on the wall. I try to ask questions at the entrance to his cell, but it's not working. He doesn't seem to think it's that big a deal.

We get to the recreation room where benches are lined up facing a screen on the wall. A bird is trapped inside and making a racket against the bars, trying to get out. 'Now we can talk,' Uncle Kathy says, sitting down against the wall. This will not make the best pictures and footage, but, well, we need to let it happen naturally.

We talk about the best and worst of their stay on the island, the deep bonds of comradeship, his longing to see children, the one and only time they saw the night sky, an incident when drunken warders forced them to stand naked against the wall and Govan Mbeki collapsed.

I ask him how he can keep coming back here, a place of so much pain and torment. He says he had made it his home. I probe why he applied to come back to the island after they were transferred to Pollsmoor Prison in 1982. He explains that when prison conditions were relaxed, he enjoyed the company and discussions with his peers. Only the senior leaders were transferred to Pollsmoor and you could not swear and make jokes in front of them. So he missed being in this horrible maximum-security prison on an island secluded from the rest of humanity.

My bewilderment must not be that visible because he goes on to say that he wants to get a house in the village on the island, one of the houses that were previously the warders' houses. Only a few are now occupied by island staff. Why on earth would he want to stay there? 'Oh, I like the peace and quiet. And it is nice to walk around in the mornings.' He explains that he would not stay there full-time if he does get a house, just when he wants to.

I get to his relationship with Madiba. He explains the one clash they had in 1950 when Madiba was in the ANC Youth League. They never fought again through all their years of friendship. Uncle Kathy was Madiba's parliamentary counsellor when he was president and their relationship remained close after their retirement.

I stray from the brief of the interview. 'When did you really say goodbye to him?' Uncle Kathy tells of going to see Madiba during his last stay in hospital. It is the intensive care unit, there are pipes in his nose and mouth, he cannot speak. The look on his face shows he is reliving the moment. 'It was a one-sided conversation,' he says. 'But he held my hand.'

'That was the last time I saw him. Before then, when he could speak, he sent Zelda [la Grange] to me. He wanted to know if I was okay, if I needed anything.' The pain in his eyes is now profound. Nobody else in the room seemed to be breathing. Even the hapless bird has fallen silent and is listening. I wish away the tear threatening to fall out of my right eye, mercifully away from the cameras.

I say it must be hard to let them all go, and be the one left behind to tell the world of their greatness. He tells how difficult it was to speak at Sisulu's funeral and then at Mandela's. I remark about how his tribute at Madiba's funeral made the world cry. He repeats the sentiment he expressed then: When Sisulu died, he lost a father; Madiba was his brother.

The bird starts squawking. It is time to go. We are back to tour-guide mode as we make our way to the limestone quarry, where the B-Section prisoners did hard labour for 13 years. But being outside also gave them a chance to have political debates and teach each other. One not-so-political debate was about the reproductive patterns of chameleons after one appeared and then came back some time later with babies.

Their former warder, Christo Brand – who now works for the Robben Island Museum – joins us. Uncle Kathy and Brand are chuckling together, talking animatedly. Brand joins in with the anecdotes, telling how he was informed that he would be guarding dangerous terrorists and his shock when he saw the gentle old men in the cells. Brand allowed them special privileges and favours on the island, and went with them to Pollsmoor when they were transferred. Uncle Kathy tells me that Brand's wife bakes him delicious cakes for his birthday and Christmas.

One of the things I ask Uncle Kathy is why he retired from politics in 1999. 'I didn't think I was making a difference,' he says. I want to laugh, wondering if anybody in politics has such considerations any more.

Our last stop is the Alpha 1 Officers' Club, on a cliff from which there is a magnificent view of Cape Town with the dramatic backdrop of Table Mountain. Uncle Kathy tells us that this is a favourite spot for photographers. We are unlucky: there is a heavy cloud over the mountain and the city is hardly visible. Zaakirah tells Uncle Kathy we should take the pictures anyway for the book. He thinks we want pictures of the view. He pauses only briefly for the picture before shuffling us into the shop, asking us if we want water or chocolates.

We now have to hurry back to get the ferry. Uncle Kathy thinks it will waste time if we stop to take more pictures at the landmark arch at the entrance. We do it anyway but there are tourists in the way and he is shuffling forward, anxious because the ferry's hooter is bleating.

Just before we board, I clutch his arm and thank him for all he shared and for the surreal experience. 'Oh, that's all right,' he says.

We are bouncing our way back to the mainland, now unmiked, so we are just chatting. Uncle Kathy is telling me how he shunned all the privileges he had been offered for drivers and bodyguards. Mahomed Seedat was the only aide he needed during the time he was in the presidency as Mandela's parliamentary counsellor. Uncle Kathy says he had tried to drive once after his release from prison in 1989, and got such a fright with the new roads and fast cars that he never drove again. Mahomed has been driving him since and, even though he is no longer employed by Uncle Kathy, helps when Uncle Kathy needs to get around Cape Town.

Uncle Kathy says he prefers to go around without drawing attention to himself. But when people do recognise him, he never declines requests for pictures. One of the odder requests was a woman who wanted a close-up picture with him and wanted her dimple in her cheek to show. 'She was moving my head this way and that so that her dimple was visible in the picture,' he chuckles.

I try to ask about his perceptions of current politics. He is too wily to fall into the trap and dodges skilfully. We are back on the mainland and in the bustle of the Waterfront. I miss having him to myself already.

Mahomed is to drop Uncle Kathy off at his flat before driving us to the airport. I try to prolong the time with Uncle Kathy by trying to motivate that he come along for the ride to the airport. But this will inconvenience Mahomed and we pull up outside Uncle Kathy's flat. I get out of the car and run around to hug him. I hold on for longer than I should, feeling as if he is the link to those onto whom we can no longer hold.

'It was nice being with you,' he says into my hair. Then he turns and disappears through the gate, shuffling slowly in that way of his.

6

PRINCESS THULI AND CO.

To get Daily Maverick ready every day, the editorial process takes our production late into the night and early hours of each morning. To combat the fatigue that these long, dedicated hours of wordsmithing bring (and, of course, to have some fun), we sometimes play with our main photos, courtesy of Photoshop and some extra imagination. These are some of our better efforts, although some of the protagonists depicted might not agree with this statement.

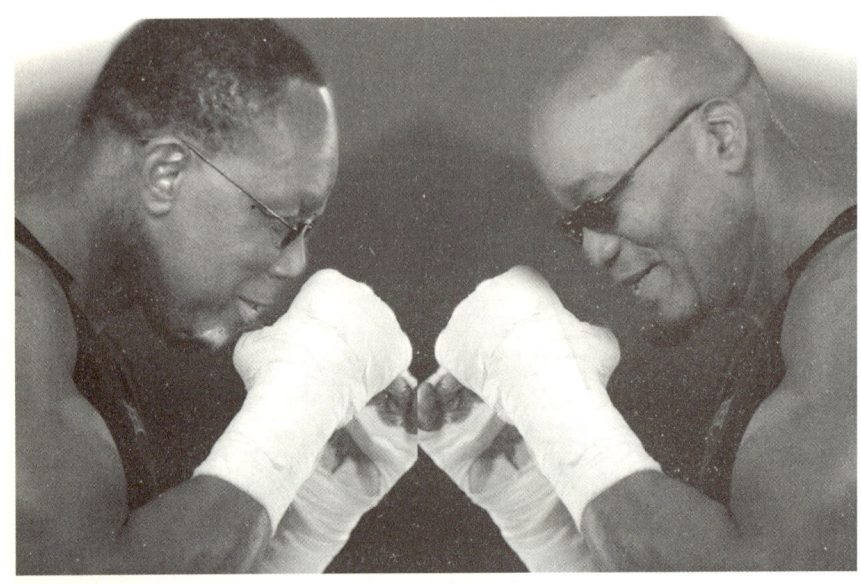

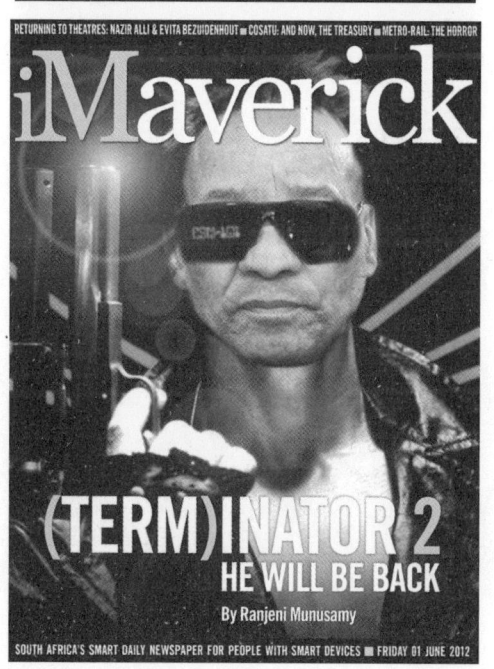

7
THINK AGEIN

KAROO FRACKING SCANDAL EXPOSED

At first, it seemed concerned environmentalists might have a point about Shell's plans to explore for deep shale gas in the Karoo. Everyone else believed them; I, too, was inclined to give them the benefit of the doubt, reserving my opinion pending more reading on the subject. Closer inspection, however, revealed the green arguments about hydraulic fracturing to be riddled with cracks.

IVO VEGTER, APRIL 2011

Lewis Pugh was rousing. He invoked Mandela and Gandhi and the brave people who fought and died for freedom. The propaganda was spectacular and alarming. There would be war over water, he warned, if we permit Shell to prospect for shale gas in the Karoo.

This is about our children's future, and that of our children's children, he preached. Shell is proposing to destroy our environment, he said, launching into stirring rhetoric about the ravages of global warming. Then he invoked the political tyrants being toppled in North Africa, and deftly juxtaposed 'corporate tyranny' as if it was the same thing.

It was grand oratory, concluding in Churchillian fashion with a call to arms and a vow to fight on, so that 'good will triumph over evil'. Yes, he actually used those words.

It was a slick performance, full of emotive appeal and rhetorical hyperbole. Dutifully, the mainstream media – whose sympathies I may have mentioned before – cheered this green David, standing up against the corporate Goliath.

But just because a little guy is facing up to a big guy doesn't make the little guy right.

Even David, when he slew Goliath, was attacking a man whose only crime was defending his country from an aggressive invasion. When Goliath fell, and the Philistines fled before the marauding invaders, they were pursued and mercilessly killed. David's only claim to virtue appears to have been that he was a little guy, backed by a big God.

Likewise, Pugh might strike a heroic pose, worthy of grand theatre. However, at the heart of his argument lies a false dichotomy.

He represents the Treasure the Karoo Action Group (TKAG), whose very name is meant to imply that treasuring this region is incompatible with permitting shale gas exploration. This is simply not true, and most of the claims advanced in opposition to Shell's proposed exploration hold little water (if you'll forgive the pun).

Let's consider water, since this is a big part of the argument.

The TKAG claims that Shell's exploration will require between 7.2 million and 144 million litres of water. Millions always sound like a lot, and that is undoubtedly why they chose not to use cubic metres, the more usual unit in which large-scale water use is measured. However, once you do the arithmetic, it turns out the worst-case scenario is a drop in the ocean compared to, for example, the projected water consumption of the Medupi power station – which, at 14 million cubic metres, is 100 times more. Eskom as a whole consumes about 2 000 times what TKAG expects Shell to use for exploration. Eskom accounts for 1,5% of South Africa's water use. Fully 75% goes to irrigation. Shell will hardly make any impact at all.

Still, energy companies are well aware of public sensitivity to such issues, and Shell has long since agreed to ensure that it will not compete with local residents or farmers for water. If necessary, it will go as far as the sea to find water nobody else wants. It knows it cannot afford to give the public genuine cause for complaints, because the legal and regulatory implications would severely threaten its business.

A study commissioned for the TKAG from Haveman, a firm of 'specialist energy attorneys', tries to cite international precedent about the dangers of hydraulic fracturing.

Hydraulic fracturing is a technique commonly used worldwide to extract shale gas or prolong the lives of oil and gas wells. For example, it is used extensively in gas fields in the Netherlands, underneath an extremely densely populated, environmentally conscious and highly regulated society. Worldwide, the precedent for fearing hydraulic fracturing is weak, at best.

Indeed, the Haveman report quite openly bemoans the 'real paucity of information' about environmental or health impacts, and the 'considerable uncertainty surrounding the environmental impacts of shale gas extraction'.

In short, they have no real evidence of negative effects. Witness recent testimony before Congress in the US.

'In recent months, the states have become aware of press reports and websites alleging that six states have documented over one thousand incidents of groundwater contamination resulting from the practice of hydraulic fracturing,' submits Scott Kell, the president of the Ground Water Protection Council (GWPC). Such reports are not accurate. Attached to my testimony are signed statements from state officials representing Ohio, Pennsylvania, New Mexico, Alabama and Texas, responding to these allegations. As a result of our regulatory review and analysis, the GWPC concluded that state oil and gas regulations are adequately designed to directly protect water resources.'

A report funded by the US Department of Energy, entitled 'Modern Shale Gas Development in the United States: A Primer', states: 'Groundwater is protected during the shale gas fracturing process by a combination of the casing and cement that is installed when the well is drilled and the thousands of feet of rock between the fracture zone and any fresh or treatable aquifers.'

Ordinary boreholes are seldom more than 100 metres deep. Major water supply boreholes may go to 300 metres. Drinkable water aquifers may occur as deep as 500 metres but, below this, the water is typically brackish. These shallow water supplies contrast starkly with typical shale gas operations at depths of 2 500 metres or more.

Yet the maker of a documentary that claims to show drinking water contamination as a result of hydraulic fracturing,

Josh Fox, is unable to explain how, exactly, it occurs. 'That target layers of fracking are far below underground drinking water sources was never contested by Gasland,' he admits. 'We don't know why fracking chemicals and fugitive natural gas are getting into water supplies, we just know that they are.'

Might that be because regulators are correct in their findings that methane contamination in water supplies comes, in fact, from decomposing biological matter at shallow depths, rather than from deep pockets of shale gas?

Fox further admits that contamination by shale gas has never been 'proven', claiming that this is because it has 'never been investigated'.

Does this not seem odd, in a sophisticated and litigious place like the United States? And does it not seem odd that a raft of state officials are willing to put their signatures to Congressional testimony that says investigations were, in fact, conducted, whenever they received claims of damage or contamination after hydraulic fracturing?

Perhaps Fox doesn't want to draw attention to these investigations, because whenever causes were found, even if they were related to oil or gas drilling activity, it turns out they were not related to the hydraulic fracturing process.

'After 25 years of investigating citizen complaints of contamination, [Ohio] geologists have not documented a single incident involving contamination of groundwater attributed to hydraulic fracturing,' swore John Husted, head of the Division of Mineral Resources Management of Ohio.

'While we do currently list approximately 421 groundwater contamination cases caused by pits and approximately an equal number caused by other contamination mechanisms, we have found no example of contamination of usable water where the cause was claimed to be hydraulic fracturing,' wrote Mark Fesmire of the New Mexico Energy, Minerals and Natural Resources Department.

'After review of [our] complaint database and interviews with regional staff that investigate groundwater contamination related to oil and gas activities, no groundwater pollution or disruption of underground sources of drinking water has been attributed to hydraulic fracturing of deep gas formations,' testified Joseph J Lee Jr, head of the Source Protection Section of the Division of Water Use Planning of the Pennsylvania Department of Environmental Protection.

'I can state with authority that there have been no documented cases of drinking water contamination caused by such hydraulic fracturing operations in our State,' concurs David E Bolin, deputy director at the State Oil and Gas Board of Alabama.

'I sincerely hope that you [Scott Kell of the GWPC, in testifying before Congress] will clear up the misconception that there are "thousands" of contamination cases in Texas and other states resulting from hydraulic fracturing. The Railroad Commission of Texas is the chief regulatory agency over oil and gas activities in this state. Though hydraulic fracturing has been used for over 50 years in Texas, our records do not indicate a single documented contamination case associated with hydraulic fracturing,' wrote Victor G Carrillo, chairman of that august body.

He is worth quoting further: 'The Texas Groundwater

Protection Committee (TGPC) tracks groundwater pollution in Texas. All Texas water protection agencies, including the Railroad Commission, are members. Each year, the TGPC publishes a "Joint Groundwater Monitoring and Contamination Report". The 2007 report cites a total of 354 active groundwater cases attributed to oil and gas activity – this in a state with over 255 000 active oil and gas wells [11 000 of which use hydraulic fracturing]. The majority of these cases are associated with previous practices that are no longer allowed, or result from activity now prohibited by our existing regulations. A few cases were due to blowouts that primarily occur during drilling activity. Not one of these cases was caused by hydraulic fracturing activity.'

Colorado? Nada. Alaska? Nope. Kentucky, Louisiana, Colorado, South Dakota, Tennessee? Nothing.

According to Michigan's Office of Geological Survey (OGS), '[t]here is no indication that hydraulic fracturing has ever caused damage to groundwater or other resources in Michigan. In fact, the OGS has never received a complaint or allegation that hydraulic fracturing has impacted groundwater in any way.'

The same thing as well in Indiana and Oklahoma: no harm was ever found to have resulted from hydraulic fracturing, because they had never even received any reports of such a thing.

Not one instance. Not a single one, over more than half a century, covering hundreds of thousands of wells.

Now one may grant that politicians and civil servants are open to corruption and simple incompetence. They may be under-resourced, or averse to attacking industrial interests that provide many jobs in their respective states.

However, it stretches credulity that having been asked such direct questions, they all either say that no allegations were ever made, or can produce reports of investigations that disproved hydraulic fracturing to be at fault. It is hard to believe that every single one of these people perjured themselves in regulatory statements or sworn testimony.

Yet either they all lied, or the hysteria about groundwater contamination caused by hydraulic fracturing is misplaced and there is some other explanation for what our intrepid filmmaker admits he simply doesn't know.

It is true that isolated incidents of pollution do occur. Some have been cited above. They do not, however, occur as a result of hydraulic fracturing, but in the normal course of drilling.

The same risks occur during one of environmentalists' favourite activities: carbon sequestration. The same goes for another fashionable green pursuit: geothermal energy. Why would it 'destroy the environment' to permit drilling for shale gas, when drilling for other purposes is celebrated?

It is also true that the Karoo consists largely of unspoilt wilderness. If one (generously) concedes that such wilderness is worth preserving for its own sake, it should be noted that far from destroying the environment, as Pugh claims, the impact of drilling will be fairly minor in contrast with the vastness of this area.

Better yet, hydraulic fracturing reduces the usual impact of drilling, since multiple horizontal shafts can be drilled from a single vertical well, dramatically reducing the footprint of drilling operations on the surface. By that standard, hydraulic fracturing is the most environmentally friendly means of drilling and is perfectly suited to a relatively unspoilt wilderness such as the Karoo.

It seems that Pugh and the TKAG hold the radical and unrealistic view that even low-impact activities are taboo, and our lives and activity ought to have no impact on the environment at all.

To be fair, some of the concerns raised by green propaganda films such as *Gasland* merit holding exploration companies to high standards of responsibility and accountability. It is perfectly possible to mitigate the impact, minimise the risk and ensure adequate recourse for any accidents that might occur. For that reason, environmental impact assessments and environmental management plans will be required of anyone who prospects for shale gas in the Karoo. All of this is reasonable, but none of this is what those who challenge shale gas exploration plans want.

The TKAG lobbyists should just be honest. It's not hydraulic fracturing that annoys them. It is drilling for any oil, gas or coal that gets their goat. They have an ideological bias against fossil fuels, and will do anything, anywhere, for any reason, to stop fossil fuel exploitation.

Let's return to the Haveman report. Point 16 states that the hand-picked subject experts were asked to provide information under 'very severe time constraints'. In contrast with this rush job, the US Environmental Protection Agency's study only produced preliminary results in late 2012.

To help them, even in the face of the aforementioned

paucity of information, they were asked to respond 'in accordance with' a predetermined set of arguments. It is no surprise, then, to discover that this sham of a report – despite the rush and the lack of information – concludes exceptionally strongly: 'The underlying argument of this Critical Review is that an immediate halt should be imposed on Shell's application for an exploration right as well as on any other application for any other form of permit, right or authorisation that, if successful, may bring the advent of fracking in South Africa a step closer to fruition.'

It helps to have your conclusions written before you draft the report itself. It is not honest, however, and it destroys the credibility of any valid concerns you might have raised. Why believe another word of what this bunch is peddling?

Regardless, the TKAG promptly ran with it, and now demands an outright ban, even on any future exploration. It wants no discussion, no debate, no waiting for environmental impact assessments and environmental management reports, nothing. It wants to make it illegal to drill for gas, finish and *klaar*.

Another spokesperson for the lobby group, Jonathan Deal, is quoted in *Mining Weekly* as saying that the 'unsustainable nature of the resource' is the core concern. That contradicts the claim that it's all about the perils of hydraulic fracturing, or the heavy demand for water.

If true, however, this merely means he disagrees with energy company investors about what resources are sustainable and profitably exploitable. In an open market, in which everyone enjoys the freedom Pugh so warmly extolled, Deal's argument would be a perfect rationale for starting a competing wind or wave or solar outfit and putting Shell out of business. It is not, however, a rationale to prevent Shell from pursuing potentially lucrative exploration.

A News24 columnist, Andreas Späth, makes the case clear: 'Note to Shell: Even in the extremely unlikely event of you being able to convince us that you are capable of producing gas in the Karoo without wasting and polluting our water, we wouldn't want you to. We don't even want you to explore for it. We want you to leave the gas in the ground. The age of carbon-based fossil fuels – of coal, oil and natural gas – is coming to a close and until you propose to help us develop our abundant, clean, green and truly sustainable renewable energy sources, including solar and wind power, stay out of the Karoo.'

This preconceived goal must be why lobby groups like the TKAG think it's okay to lie about the impact of hydraulic fracturing. The end justifies the means, and they can only rouse sufficient objection if people are terrified of the consequences of this nasty-sounding process, ominously called 'fracking the Karoo'.

They aim to make it so expensive to drill for oil or gas that exploration companies will simply give up.

It's true. They will. But here's the problem with their view. These people aren't harmless greenies, concerned only with pretty pictures of pristine landscapes and protecting endangered fluffy bunnies.

While they can afford expensive fuel and other such self-indulgent eco-luxury, most of us cannot. While they can wax lyrical about the age of fossil fuels being over, the rest of us depend – for 95% of our electricity and 100% of our transport – on fossil fuels.

Ordinary South Africans will feel the impacts in the rising price of food and transport, and in the number of us who are employed. When millions remain mired in poverty in South Africa, it isn't harmless to lie about gas drilling. It is a cold and callous denial of people's basic rights: to benefit from economic development.

Just the exploration phase of this project is said to be worth over a billion rand. This will create employment, raise GDP, increase tax income and stimulate a great deal of secondary economic activity. Who knows how much wealth and employment might be created if the exploration proves successful, and the gas proves to be abundant?

It will reduce the cost and increase the supply of energy of a sort that South Africa undoubtedly needs, quite aside from the fact that gas is cleaner than dirty coal. It is ironic that no environmentalist seems to want to permit feasible alternatives to let us get away from our 95% dependence on coal at a price we can afford.

Who is this 'we' that Späth talks about? Does it include the thousands of potential employees of a successful gas drilling operation? Does it include the consumers of electricity who, far from seeing abundance in his charming 'clean, green' waffle, are faced with rolling blackouts and rising electricity prices?

When big industrial projects don't come to South Africa, whether because of inadequate infrastructure or the obstructionism of angry greens, this harms the country in a very real way. The ecomentalists, with their 4×4s and bicycles and hemp handbags and enough free time to organise petitions, protests and PR campaigns, might not care. However, millions of poor or unemployed people do.

Oh, and one other thing. Ditch the word 'fracking'. It is a barbarous bastardisation of a perfectly good English term. Using it has only one purpose: spin.

It is designed to make people who don't know better fear a perfectly ordinary industrial technique that has been in used safely and successfully around the world for many decades. It permits cute, but crude, phrases like 'Fracking up the Karoo'. It should be beneath any self-respecting journalist.

One keeps hearing how Big Oil lobbyists are evil spinmeisters and insidious manipulators of public opinion. Don't forget that Big Green lobbyists can deceive the public with the best of them.

Green subterfuge in this campaign is the real scandal about 'fracking the Karoo'.

**MAMPHELA RAMPHELE,
THE FUTURE FOR SOUTH AFRICA? NOPE**

Dr Mamphela Ramphele didn't have to wait long for her first bitter taste of the realities of active politics. It came when she finally launched, well, her intention to launch the 'consultative process' that would eventually launch her party. And, if the launch was any yardstick, life outside her academic and corporate cocoons was not going to get any sweeter.

VUKANI MDE, FEBRUARY 2013

When it first emerged in January 2013, through the helpful offices of one Mr Tony Leon, that Dr Mamphela Ramphele would soon launch a new political party into our already crowded surrounds, the reaction from politicians was welcoming, if somewhat cautious. The exception was Gwede Mantashe, the secretary general of the African National Congress and the ruling party's most dependable battering ram.

Labelling her a 'biased academic', Mantashe said Ramphele had used her critiques of the ruling party as a launch pad for her impending political career. Now that she was about to come out of her academic cocoon and 'unmask' herself as the opposition politician she had always been, the ANC and South Africans would be able, finally, to take her for what she is and 'deal' with her in those terms.

You can interpret this typically over-the-top reaction in two ways: generously, as a timely – if unsolicited – reminder of the unforgiving rough-and-tumble of active politics, with its deficit of honesty and integrity, its estrangement from munificence, its abundance of petty enmity and the disdain with which ordinary people regard all who engage in it for a living. Or you could see if for what it is – a warning that the gloves were off from undoubtedly the most accomplished bully in South African politics since those who forced the retirement of Thabo Mbeki.

But if one looks beyond the Mantashe in the statement, it is easy enough to appreciate its useful grains of truth and the few lessons in it, and Ramphele didn't have to wait long for her first bitter taste of the realities of active politics. It came on Monday 18 February, when she finally launched, well, her intention to launch the 'consultative process' that would eventually launch her party.

The first point to make is that unless you are Jacob Zuma, indecisiveness is not a winning strategy. You either have a political party with a programme for changing the country, ready to be taken to the electorate at the earliest opportunity, or you have a broad societal forum for articulating and discussing our problems, a platform around which interested political parties could coalesce, leading – eventually – to wherever its internal momentum takes it. On 18 February, Ramphele attempted to do both, with frustratingly messy results.

These internal inconsistencies about what Agang (the name of her 'party political platform') was led to the next painful lesson that Ramphele would need to absorb quickly: the media would see her differently; there would be no more free rides. At the launch there was already a palpable sense of frustration from many journalists as they battled to extract straight answers from Ramphele about the political stance of her organisation (too strong a word?), its specific programmes, and even the process going forward. Rolling eyes, despairing sighs, groans and moans accompanied each question skirted, each rhetorical flourish to avoid a direct answer – in other words, every instance of her acting like a politician.

The South African political press corps is a particularly jaded bunch. After the launch, they would approach everything she does – as they did the press conference – with a sense of 'we've been here before', because they had. The older journalists in the room on 18 February would have been veterans of the launch of Bantu Holomisa's United Democratic Movement in 1999, Patricia de Lille's Independent Democrats in 2004 and Mosiuoa Lekota's (assuming it is legally established as his) Congress of the People (COPE) in 2009. They know it will be someone else's something else in 2019. They are increasingly disinclined to mollycoddle the perpetual succession of chancers who are conceited enough to posit themselves as saviours every time an election is around the corner.

Dr Mamphela Ramphele, the former academic and civic advocate, had enjoyed a positive public profile and could generally rely on the media to pitch up at every event and hang on her every word. Being profiled as 'an intellectual' helps, of course. (Most journalists fear the very mention of the word. They think it's a sign of some mystical qualification that they have no hope of obtaining for themselves. They would rather quote you verbatim, no matter how long-winded you are, than paraphrase you; they won't dare to question your facts, let alone your conclusions; they defer to your knowledge of everything, because you're 'an intellectual'.)

Dr Mamphela Ramphele the politician will find the going tougher. Suddenly, people who used to be keen to report your views on invasive plant species in suburban gardens no longer diligently record everything you say. They ignore even your most important outpourings on matters of clear public interest. They now believe you have 'an agenda', a flaw that presumably did not exist before your entry into formal politics. Henceforth, everything you do will be seen and reported through the prism of politics, power and power's pursuit. If you contest an election and come out on the other side with nothing but a handful of seats, you will promptly be deposited into the file marked 'small parties' and forgotten about. From then on, only the junior reporters will be sent to cover your press conferences, and even that's not guaranteed. ('Sorry, the kid's at the magistrate's court this afternoon, we'll pick it up off Sapa.')

And this leads inexorably to a third lesson: the need to recalibrate her relationship with the fourth estate, acknowledging and engaging with the fact that the power dynamic between her and them had shifted. Someone with her background and her obvious hubris would struggle with this adjustment. She didn't have the most promising start either. Within days, she'd already threatened one newspaper editor in a fit of anger (menacingly telling him she 'reserved' her rights), and snapped at his correspondent for having the audacity to pose questions she didn't feel ready to answer. She'd chastised the media about daring to write and speculate about her initiative before she'd made a formal announcement, seemingly believing that she had a right not only to control her own story (doubtful) but *their* news agenda as well (fanciful). On 18 February, she attempted several put-downs of people who were asking question she didn't like, instead of engaging (or, if possible, you know, answering) them. She berated the room for repeating questions, oblivious to the fairly simple reality that if people feel you haven't answered a question they think is important, they'll repeat it.

In one revealing exchange, a young female reporter asked her what she planned to do about the fact that she wasn't 'known in Soweto', used as shorthand for all similar locales. The doctor was visibly irritated by the suggestion, and pointed to one of her supporters seated in the front row, who hailed from Soweto and 'knows me'. The whole interaction was a study in evasion and missed opportunity.

Of course there are people in Soweto who know Ramphele. There are even people there who will follow and support her. The formulation of the question may have been clumsy, but at its core was a query about the very real gap between Ramphele's media-driven public profile on one hand, and her links (or lack thereof) to ordinary rural and urban township folk on the other. By fixating on how many people 'know' her (how does demonstrating that some people in Soweto are aware of your existence, which is how the term 'know' is being used in this instance, even begin to answer the question posed?) in 'Soweto' (which was only the symbol for a greater whole), she missed the opportunity to put to rest the fears of many who may be inclined to support her, but fear being led into another wilderness by yet another one-wo/man movement with no organic links to the only constituency capable of sustaining a viable opposition political party, the working class and the poor. As a general rule, if you intend to launch yourself into the venal mud bath of electoral politics, the last thing you want to do is squander the goodwill and favour of the press. Once lost, it is rarely ever regained.

Which brings us, through that circuitous offer of unsolicited counsel, back to the main question. The question that all of us should be asking is really: What the hell is this? Why had Ramphele not just launched a political party and given it an ideological (or at least programmatic) identity and been done with it? It's clear that this is what she wanted in the end. Why make a show of consulting South Africans (*all* South Africans, not just the prominent ones, mind) if you have a fairly set idea about what you want in the end? What if, after all the diligent consultations with *everyone*, their overwhelming view is, 'No thank you, we have enough snouts at that particular trough. We don't need another party in Parliament'?

What then? Would she go back into her box? Would Gold Fields even take her back? The answer, of course, is that ultimately Ramphele wanted more than just a political party. She wanted the ultimate political movement outside of the ANC at her fingertips, and she wanted it to land there on her own terms. Ramphele, it seems to me, imagined Agang (or whatever results from it eventually) less as a political party than as the amalgamation of all the unfortunates who had spent the two decades preceding its launch sniping at the heels of the ANC. She heard the talk and saw the frantic moves towards a 'realignment' of opposition politics, and she wanted in. She wanted, simultaneously, to be a part of it and above it. She did not want to join the opposition coalition; she wanted the opposition to coalesce around her. Why had she not joined the DA, which espouses all the values and aims she articulated on 18 February and which, according to reports, had been wooing her to the point of guaranteeing her the party leadership at the next electoral congress of the party? She was well aware of the party's desire to unite the disparate opposition, mainly around the same constitutionalist platform that she claimed to champion. Yet she eschewed the DA, behaving as if the party carried some taint she was keen to avoid.

In fact, the political rumour mill was abuzz with the story

of how she told DA leader Helen Zille that she wouldn't join the DA, but that she'd be happy for the DA to 'join' her!

Now, one need not like the DA to perceive just what an outrageous slight that is to the party. Nor does one need to be a fan of the Bantustan general from Umtata to acknowledge that he has, since 1999, worked tirelessly (with only modest success) to build the UDM. By what logic should he, the man who had trouble following Mandela, follow Ramphele? As for Lekota, he took a real risk when he tore COPE out of the ribcage of the ANC and showed evidence that perhaps, under the exterior of rotund buffoonery, there still beats the heart of a UDF warrior. Nothing was guaranteed when COPE broke away from the ruling party; however badly they've since squandered their momentum, it took real understanding and efficient use of the political ground operation to poll as well as they did in 2009. Add to this the slick political machinery of the DA, and ask why any of that accumulated know-how should be handed over as a gift to someone who hadn't demonstrated any ability to organise communities politically in the 21st century.

Dr Ramphele's behaviour is hubris of the most breathtaking kind, and personally I'm not sure how the opposition parties could stand for it. Are they so desperate, so unsure of their own ability to articulate an alternative vision to the people of this country that they could fall for Ramphele's obvious trick? Is everyone so desperate for a black messiah who ticks all the boxes (African woman: check; struggle credentials: check; PhD: check; media darling: check) that anyone with a half-decent CV and a history that stretches back to before 1994 will do? There is absolutely no basis for the deference with which the opposition parties treated Ramphele, and they will pay a heavy price for their seeming indulgence of her self-delusion. Even if one accepts, for argument's sake, the wholly dubious notion that South Africa is in danger of 'failing' and needs saving, it takes a leap of credulity to believe that the saviour is the chairwoman of a mining company board and ex-World Bank bureaucrat with no political constituency.

On 18 February Ramphele made a few astounding claims for herself and her new 'party political platform' that suggested any number of unflattering things about her as a politician and a potential leader. Asked why anyone should care about Agang and whether she had a political programme that went beyond the statement of middle-class grievances she had just read, her answers were a hodgepodge mixture of half-truths and obvious fabrications, inventions and complete rewrites of our recent history:

She claimed that her movement was 'declaring a war' on corruption (she genuinely seemed to believe this would be the first one), with nary an acknowledgement of anyone else's efforts or stance on the matter. Corruption's easy, and being 'against' it is not a distinguisher. Contrary to the frenzy of moral panic the middle classes have worked themselves into about Zuma and the ANC, virtually no one in the country is *pro*-corruption, and it's possible to think of more convincing anti-corruption crusaders than one who sat on the board of a mining company accused of doing a dodgy BEE deal.

She claimed that among the extensive consultations she had done about forming a party, she had included Equal

Education (EE), a well-regarded NGO, and also made gratuitous mention of Corruption Watch, the Cosatu NGO. For its part, EE has denied any involvement.

She claimed that she was launching a million-signature campaign to put election reform 'on the table', suggesting, again, that no one else had done this before her. Calls for election reform are as old as our post-apartheid electoral system. Every opposition party has a policy stance in favour of it (even though constituency-based elections would be disastrous for most of them). Parliament itself has appointed a panel, the Independent Panel of Assessment of Parliament, to look at the institution's functioning. Its chapter on Parliament's oversight mandate is a ringing call for electoral reform to boost MPs' accountability to voters and strengthen the institution's ability to oversee the government. The panel included politicians and other prominent people from across the spectrum, including leading lights in the ANC such as National Assembly speaker at the time, Max Sisulu; former Public Protector Selby Baqwa; and ex-MP Pregs Govender.

She made a lot of the fact that Agang has 'an indigenous African name', claiming that none of the other parties in our politics have African names. This is quite obviously false. Of the 208 parties registered with the Independent Electoral Commission, probably as many as one-third have African names, from Ahanang People's Organisation and Afrika Borwa Kgutlisa Botho, through Dabalorivhuwa Patriotic Front, to Ximoko Party. And that is only parties registered nationally; if you go further down, and look at the parties and movements registered to operate locally and provincially, the proportion of African-named parties rises. And that is not to include the parties whose names are in Afrikaans, a South African language. Did she perhaps mean only the major parties, the ones represented in Parliament (if so, it's a curious qualification given that Agang was neither)? If she did, she was obviously ignorant of the 40-year existence of the Inkatha Freedom Party.

But why tell this fib at all? There is nothing to be gained by falsely claiming to be the only political party with an indigenous African name, so what could be gained from it if it were true? The answer is to be found in another grandiose self-delusion: Ramphele's apparent belief that she is the last great disciple of Black Consciousness and the responsibility falls upon her to remind us of our African-ness. This is a strange one, considering that nothing in her post-apartheid career suggests she gives a fig about Black Consciousness. In fact, on the key BC question of identity, her stance is a DA-like post-racial fantasy. At least on one occasion she sanctimoniously declared there was only one race, 'the human race'. Pat yourself on the back all you like for making that observation; it is still a wholly unsatisfactory answer to the vexed question of race in South Africa, and those who claim the ability and intent to deliver us into a future without race are little more than false prophets.

I said earlier that the idea that this country is on the brink of collapse and needs to be rescued is itself disputable, and is usually advanced by its advocates for completely self-serving purposes. This remains so despite that view being espoused by *The Economist*. And even if you acknowledge, as I do, that there is a lot that has gone – and is going – wrong with our post-apartheid direction, it is dishonest to pretend that the causes can be located exclusively in the political arena, and that a change in 'leadership' can deliver us to the country of our dreams.

Are South Africans, even those who steadfastly support the ANC, entirely satisfied with the ruling party's stewardship? I would say no. What is their attitude to Zuma and their assessment of his time as head of state? I would say sceptical at best. But the ordinary people for whom Ramphele and others claim to speak have a more comprehensive view of their country's problems. They have been betrayed by politicians, no doubt, but they have also been taken advantage of by greedy corporates and executives. They know the causes of their poverty and inequality are systemic, and not the result of a recent 'failure of leadership' that Ramphele could miraculously cure.

To them, she offers no real solutions other than general platitudes about 'restructuring' our economy so it 'can serve everyone'.

I remain, like them, cautiously pessimistic.

TO MY GENERATION:
LISTEN. LISTEN VERY CAREFULLY

Nelson Mandela famously said that the day the ANC does to us what the apartheid government did, we should do to the ANC what we did to the apartheid government. Corruption, greed and the rising discontent in our society should have us very concerned indeed – and more so, the ANC.

JAY NAIDOO, DECEMBER 2012

Having lived through the brutal repression of the apartheid state, I have developed more than a healthy mistrust of securocrats of any political colour, including the current crop who seem intent on taking away a number of our constitutional rights.

And what a short memory our leaders have. The preamble to our Constitution calls for 'a society based on democratic values, social justice and fundamental human rights' and '[lays] the foundations for a democratic and open society in which government is based on the will of the people and every citizen is equally protected by law'.

The South Africa I fought for, alongside millions of fellow citizens, and that Nelson Mandela personified as our founding father, was at the forefront of freedom of expression, enshrining it in its Constitution, ostensibly for eternity. Freedom of expression is not a neo-liberal principle. It is the embodiment of the democracy for which we fought.

The security cluster's rise has been a steady trend, from the cowboy behaviour of shooting to kill to the increasing militarisation of the police force. I, you, we all, should be very afraid of the increasing influence of intelligence sectors that are being subordinated to political agendas, intent on drawing a veil of secrecy across our country.

In its essence, this process has little to do with the media, which is purely a soft target and stalking horse. It is first and foremost an assault on the very essence of the citizens' rights for which we fought. The endgame is a delivering a battering ram of political enforcement against the people. It comes close to a rise of populist authoritarianism that will crush dissent and our ability to expose the corruption and maladministration of predatory elites in our country. Our covenant with our people in 1994 to deliver a better life to all will have all but disappeared.

It is therefore disingenuous to argue that the secrecy laws are needed in the interests of national security. One cannot deny that every state, even a democratic one, has secrets whose compromising constitutes a national security threat. But we have a right to question our ANC government or, for that matter, any public leader. Citizens have a right to demand accountability for, and transparency about, the expenditure of taxpayers' money, and to hold the feet of public representatives to the fire on the issues of service delivery.

Mandela, in his address to the 1993 Cosatu congress, said to thunderous applause, 'If the ANC does to you what the apartheid government did to you, then you must do to the ANC what you did to the apartheid government.' I, as general secretary of Cosatu alongside 19 other comrades, was hoisted high as we were elected to go onto an ANC ticket for our first democratic election.

Our mandate was to advance the fundamental human rights of which apartheid had robbed our parents and generations before them – the right to a better life, the right of our children to quality education and health, and a government that would be democratic, accountable and transparent. I cannot imagine that the founding Parliament of 1994 would have passed the secrecy laws that we have before us in 2012.

On a second front, I see the rise of a dangerous demagoguery in civil society. I am aghast when I hear the SADTU general secretary, Mugwena Maluleke, say to the *Mail & Guardian* that '[s]ome NGOs are working with other political parties and there will come a time when we will identify all of them. They are driving an agenda that education is a national crisis [and] using education to destroy the confidence of the public [in the government].'

I come from a family of teachers. They were proud, dedicated public servants who believed, like the majority of teachers today, that quality education is the right of learners in our schools. As Nelson Mandela said, 'Education is the most powerful tool we have to change the world.'

I see the work that these NGOs are doing as being as honourable and essential as what we did in our struggle for freedom against apartheid. I believe that we have a deepening crisis in education, that the state is failing in its obligations, and that its denialism is destroying the most important pathways out of poverty. I, alongside the founders of SADTU and Nelson Mandela, vowed at SADTU's launch in 1990 that never again would our children sit under trees or in mud schools, or attend schools without textbooks, libraries, laboratories, proper toilets and clean drinking water and electricity. In 2012 – 22 years later, and in the 19th year of ANC rule – the reality of millions of our children in our poorest communities in our townships and rural areas still contains the same problems.

I am outraged by the epidemic of rape of girl children in our schools. I do not believe that teachers, where substantive evidence exists against them of sexual assaults, are entitled to representation by any union. The very fact of sexual relations between teachers and learners, even consensual, should be made illegal. These measures should be accompanied with a public blacklist that ensures that these sexual predators who pose as teachers are rooted out of the education system forever.

Now, if any union or political leader wants to describe the group of NGOs that works with parents, learners and communities as part of an 'ideological third force', let me enlighten you that I am proud to be associated with such an NGO. I fully endorse the work of Section27, the LRC, Equal Education and the Centre for Child Law to ensure accountability in the education sector.

The last time we saw such denialism was in relation to HIV/Aids, and it is what led to the needless deaths of over 350 000 innocent citizens. We cannot allow such blind politics today to destroy the future of our country. The challenges we experience today are happening on our watch. Let us have the courage to face that fact. And act.

The world-famous economist, Amartya Sen, made a fascinating link between freedom of expression and famine. In fact, a free press and the right to freedom of expression stirs public debate about food shortages, corruption and maladministration, resulting in public pressure that brings changes. In the bad days of apartheid it was global public reporting and the work of a small but fearless independent media in South Africa that often meant the difference between life and death for many of us as activists in the resistance movement. A free press and robust civil society is not a neo-liberal middle-class issue. It is about human rights and the struggle of the poor for constitutional rights to quality education, healthcare and service delivery.

As the students in Soweto in 1976 said, 'Our parents are prepared to suffer under the white man's rule. They have been living for years under these laws and they have become immune to them. But we strongly refuse to swallow an education that is designed to make us slaves in the country of our birth.'

Today I again hear that refrain, but in the streets, slums and villages across the world. My advice to my generation – those who control the levers of economic and political power and dominate even civil society: listen, listen very carefully, and be afraid of the drums of discontent as they gather in the restless anger that will one day drown the privilege you enjoy today at the expense of the majority.

PALIN, MALEMA AND
THE RISE OF THE UNREAD

He's a reactionary who's hated as much by conservatives as he is by liberals, which is why the theories of John Lukacs are so edifying to read. As a profile of Sarah Palin in the October 2010 issue of Vanity Fair *seems to suggest, the politics of proudly unschooled nationalist populism are back in ascendancy in America. Sound familiar?*

KEVIN BLOOM, SEPTEMBER 2010

In his 2005 book *Democracy and Populism: Fear and Hatred*, the Hungarian-born American historian John Lukacs puts forward the argument that the greatest threat to 'our civilisation' is the backwards slide of liberal democracy into national populism. The primary target of Lukacs in the polemic is the

US's Republican Right. He claims that US conservatives have abandoned their founding principles of order, tradition and stability in favour of a political strategy that invokes external and internal enemies, and he cites leaders who manipulate the masses by appealing to 'the myth of the people'. There's nothing particularly new in this, except the fact that Lukacs is a self-confessed reactionary who despises liberals as much as he despises conservatives. His only allegiance is to a clear-eyed analysis of politics in the current age.

Also, during the course of his long career, Lukacs has served as a visiting professor at John Hopkins University, Columbia University, Princeton University and the University of Budapest, so even if he is despised by Americans on both the left and right, he presumably knows what he's talking about. He has written over 30 books, one of the most significant of which – *The End of the Twentieth Century and the End of the Modern Age* (published in 1992) – points to nationalism as the world's most dangerous political force.

'Populist nationalism,' writes Lukacs in the book, 'as distinct from the now almost extinct variety of the liberal nationalisms of the 19th century, is a modern and democratic phenomenon. Populist nationalists are self-conscious rather than self-confident, extroverted, essentially aggressive and humorless, suspicious of other people within the same nation who do not seem to agree with some of their populist and nationalist ideology. Hence they assign them to the status of minorities, suggesting – and at times emphasising – that such minorities do not and cannot belong within the authentic body of the national people.'

The book, when it was published, got mixed reviews. Michiko Kakutani of the *New York Times* called it 'naïve' in parts, specifically for its neglect of the US's role in the Gulf War and its focus on America and Europe at the expense of the rest of the world. But it's possible that Kakutani might hold a different view now – she was, of course, writing before 9/11 and the phenomenon of George W Bush. By 2005, when *Democracy and Populism: Fear and Hatred* was published, the views of Lukacs seemed to inspire much more sympathy among critics.

In 2010, applying the phenomenon of Sarah Palin to his theories, Lukacs can tend to come across as something of a prophet. The rise of populism and the decline of classical democracy are reflected, for him, in the vulgarity and debasing effects of modern mass culture. The $150 000 worth of clothing and accessories bought by the Republican National Committee for the vice-presidential candidate and her family in 2008 might be a case in point, symbolising as it does a crude attempt to pander to the material values and consumerist heart of her constituency.

But it's in the way that Palin silences dissent within the ranks that her character as a populist would appear to come through most stridently, at least according to the criteria of Lukacs. A profile in *Vanity Fair* that ran in the October 2010 issue describes how 'Palin's connection with her audience is complete,' and how those who don't adore her – because, unlike the others, they don't see themselves as 'just like her' – have almost no way of deciphering the person behind the carefully constructed facade.

'Her on-the-record statements about herself amount to

a litany of untruths and half-truths. With few exceptions – mostly Palin antagonists in journalism and politics whose beefs with her have long been out in the open – virtually no one who knows Palin well is willing to talk about her on the record, whether because they are loyal and want to protect her (a small and shrinking number), or because they expect her prominence to grow and intend to keep their options open, or because they fear she will exact revenge, as she has been known to do. It is an astonishing phenomenon. Colleagues and acquaintances by the hundreds went on the record to reveal what they knew, for good or ill, about prospective national candidates as diverse as Bill Clinton, George W Bush, Al Gore, and Barack Obama. When it comes to Palin, people button their lips and slink away.'

Self-conscious rather than self-confident? Extroverted? Essentially aggressive and humourless? Palin would appear to tick all the Lukacs boxes, along with just about any other populist of the modern era – Juan Peron, Hugo Chaves and Benito Mussolini are names that come to mind – and along with many from early history, too. Not that Palin is a Mussolini in the making, of course, but she exhibits the core characteristics of this political caste that, again, essentially draws its power by setting up the masses ('us') against the elites ('them').

There's an obvious comparison to be made locally, and it's one that's been made before – by the columnist and author Jacob Dlamini. In April 2010, writing in the *Business Day*, Dlamini offered a convincing piece under the header 'Why Malema is the South African Sarah Palin'. The idea for the column came from an American friend of Dlamini's, a person with a scholarly interest in US and South African politics, who emailed a list of parallels: the proud ignorance (Palin's enrolment at four colleges before she earned a communications degree, Malema's '100% Zuma, 20% woodwork'); the contempt for the media (Palin's phrase 'lamestream media', Malema's phrase 'bloody agent'); the shady financial dealings (the Palin Alaskan administration's friendship with the state's oil industry, Malema's 'National Tender Revolution').

There's also a strong similarity in how the two figures handle internal dissent. *Vanity Fair's* paragraph above on Palin's rule by fear is echoed in the following observation of Dlamini: 'It does not require a degree in political science to realise that the only people kept awake at night by thoughts of Malema are his comrades. They fear the little thug in ways they could never fear, say, the Democratic Alliance.'

Things get especially menacing, though, when held up against the final defining feature of Lukacs. Are Palin and Malema equally suspicious of other people within the same nation who do not seem to agree with some of their populist and nationalist ideologies? It goes without saying. Do they assign them the status of minorities, suggesting – and, at times, emphasising – that such minorities do not and cannot belong within the authentic body of the national people? Take your pick: 'hardworking, patriotic, liberty-loving Americans', 'the common people', 'bastard tendencies', 'counter-revolutionaries'.

Such rhetoric, for Lukacs, is not only the locus of hatred and fear to which populists must consistently return for succour and support, it is also the site of the potential breakdown of democratic values. In this, as he suggests himself, Lukacs echoes an observation of Alexis de Tocqueville: 'Majority rule is tempered by the legal assurance of the rights of the minorities, and of individual men and women. And when the temperance is weak, or unenforced, or unpopular, then democracy is nothing more (or else) than populism. More precisely: then it is nationalist populism'.

So, does America exemplify the defining qualities of a nationalist populist state? Does South Africa? The answer is clearly closer to yes for the latter. America under George W started to look remarkably like an idiocracy, but Barack Obama has done a lot to inject some rational perspective into the equation. Still, if there's one thing populists know how to do with aplomb, it's stage a comeback. Palin, who was essentially written off after the 2008 US elections, has returned to public life stronger than ever. In 2010 it looked likely that she'd make a formidable run for president come the next elections, and 7 000-word profiles in *Vanity Fair* – especially if they're self-proclaimed 'hatchet jobs' – are only going to help her cause. The common people have nothing but contempt for media outlets that employ words of more than four syllables.

Which brings us back to Malema. What to say, except that in 2010 he'd once again become the most prominent feature on the media horizon, like an endless worst-of-*Idols* loop. Populism only dies once it has swallowed itself whole, once it can no longer deliver on its promises and has run out of people to blame for its lack of delivery. Hugo Chavez remains in power thanks to Venezuela's vast oil resources; Palin's ascendant star has everything to do with the fact that Alaska's oil reserves are owned by the state. As Dlamini pointed out in 2010, Malema was not there yet, but he was heading – textbook-style and at impressive speed – in the right direction.

And Zuma's ANC, despite its best efforts to silence him, has no one but itself to blame. The country's slide from democracy into nationalist populism was confirmed at Polokwane. It's proving nigh impossible to put the beast back in the cage.

MALEMA'S MANUFACTURED MONEY

Only a month after Julius Malema appeared in court for money laundering, the Public Protector released her report into the company he co-owns, On-Point Engineering. The findings were damning and read like a guide on how to turn connections and lies into Range Rovers and Breitlings.
GREG NICOLSON, OCTOBER 2012

Aurecon South Africa must have been disappointed in October 2009 when its bid to the Limpopo Department of Roads and Transport was disqualified. The company, part of an international group of engineering and management specialists, had formed a consortium to win a tender for a new project management unit. Its bid was thrown out over of a technicality on the cover letter.

Sixteen bids were submitted to the Limpopo department. Six were immediately disqualified for being submitted in one envelope rather than two. Three more bids were disqualified for lacking qualifications, experience and skills. Cover letter technicalities claimed another three. In the end, 15 of 16 bids were disqualified. On-Point Engineering remained and was awarded the R52-million contract.

Public Protector Thuli Madonsela has released her investigation into allegations of misconduct and corruption in the awarding of contracts by the Limpopo Department of Roads and Transport to On-Point Engineering, Julius Malema's alleged cash cow. Madonsela said she would let the Hawks answer whether the awarding of the tender amounted to corruption, but in all other aspects, she was scathing.

The department's actions were 'unlawful, improper' and constituted 'maladministration', she said. Regarding On-Point's actions, she believes 'a crime has been committed'. She found that Malema and his business partner, Lesiba Gwangwa, had 'benefitted improperly from the unlawful, fraudulent and corrupt conduct of On-Point and maladministration of the department'.

While reputable companies were dismissed for the wording of their cover letter, On-Point failed to provide a tax clearance certificate, which was essential. Yet before the company was even recommended by the bid committee, the head of the department, Ntau Letebele, requested the certificate from On-Point. Letebele was appointed only ten days before the tender was advertised.

'The reality was that at the time of the submission of the bid document, On-Point had existed for approximately one month, had no employees, no assets or annual turnover and several of the purported key management personnel and staff members were not involved with it at all. It also had made no contribution to youth business development,' said the report, titled 'On the Point of Tenders'.

The bid was built on paper-deep lies that could have come

to light with a phone call – if anyone cared to call, that is. On-Point even said the company had been operating for nine years. When Madonsela asked Gwangwa why he lied, he explained that what he meant was that together the business partners had nine years in the business. Later, he said the problem was that English wasn't his first language.

That's just the start of it. The bid included a detailed list of staff and a company hierarchy. In reality, On-Point had no employees and Gwangwa had used the CVs of potential employees. He lured them with faint proposals and job opportunities. After an initial meeting, a handing over of a CV or a proposal, the hopefuls never heard from On-Point again, while Gwangwa and Malema's company used their details to pretend they had a real company. Miraculously, it worked.

Gwangwa said at the time of the bid the company structure wasn't a reality, but it would be if they got the tender. For Madonsela, then, 'the department would have run the risk of awarding the tender to an entity that has no track record of its experience and achievements working together as a team, which was the essential requirement'. That's exactly what it did. On-Point won the tender as the head of department failed to vet the company or negotiate the price properly.

'On-Point should never have been awarded the tender for the PMU as it did not qualify by a long stretch,' said Madonsela. 'The bid it presented to the Department on 29 September 2009 for the PMU tender consisted of a deliberate and fraudulent misrepresentation in respect of the profile, composition, experience, personnel, assets, annual turnover and contribution to youth business development, and therefore the functionality and track record of the company.'

After the tender was awarded, said Madonsela, On-Point engaged in illegal 'back-to-back' deals. Its contract included managing and overseeing road infrastructure programmes and supervising service providers to ensure quality control. But while overseeing projects, it was also charging the service providers for work it was doing for them on the same job. On-Point effectively charged both the province and service providers for the same work and attempted to hide it through confidentiality agreements and misrepresentation.

'This constituted a direct conflict between On-Point's obligations to objectively manage and supervise projects on behalf of the Department, its own financial interests and that of Mr Gwangwa, its sole Director. These agreements clearly constituted kickbacks, a form of gratification under section 12(1) of the Prevention and Combatting of Corrupt Activities Act,' found Madonsela.

She recommended that the contract be severed immediately. She wants the Hawks to investigate the link between Gwangwa, Malema and department officials, and for the National Treasury to find all instances in which On-Point had been double paid and the money recovered. She recommended that the High Court take 'urgent steps to initiate an investigation into the administration and disposal of the trust property of (Malema's) Ratanang Family Trust and the Gwangwa Family Trust'.

She also called on the National Treasury to restrict On-Point nationally from doing business and for the Limpopo

Department of Roads and Transport to begin disciplinary proceedings.

In response to the report, Malema accused the Public Protector of finding him 'guilty in absentia'. On-Point's bank accounts show Malema's Ratanang Family Trust was paid an average of R100 000 in 21 instances. They also feature payments to 'Sandton Property', 'Sundowns Farm' and 'Ratanang Farm'. The farm payment of R1 million was made shortly after Madonsela says On-Point received a kickback of a similar amount.

It seems the sole purpose of forming On-Point was to win the Limpopo tender; Gwangwa's reasoning for including Malema was because '[h]is personal friendly relationships with business leaders across the globe have made him into an invaluable asset for any business'.

It was those personal relationships that appear to have won On-Point the contract and bankrolled South Africa's most controversial political figure. Without Malema, of course, a company like Aurecon South Africa would have been likely to win.

* On 27 March 2013, Nathi Mncube, National Prosecuting Authority spokesperson, clarified that the charges against Julius Malema still stood, with a court date set for September 2014.

LESSONS FROM A
ZAMBIAN VICE PRESIDENT

In an otherwise hilarious interview with The Guardian, *Zambian Vice President Guy Scott flouted the rules of diplomacy to launch an assault on our foreign policy, our president and our general*

disposition. Should we be insulted? Absolutely – but only because, like all the best insults, Scott's are very close to the bone.
SIMON ALLISON, MAY 2013

Interviewing politicians is, as a rule, not particularly exciting for journalists. Interviews can be a nightmare to schedule and, when they finally happen, it's hard to get politicians singing from anything other than their tightly scripted song sheet. At times, the whole exercise feels like a glorified press release, and we have to work really hard to fill the gaps and find an interesting angle.

Every now and then, however, someone will come along who wanders so far off-script that the headlines practically write themselves. In May 2013, that someone was Vice President Guy Scott.

In an astonishingly frank and frequently hilarious interview with *The Guardian*'s David Smith, Scott dispensed with all diplomatic niceties to offer his opinion on Robert Mugabe, gay rights, his government's human rights record and – most interestingly for us – South Africa and South Africans.

He's not very impressed with us.

Try this for starters:

'The South Africans are very backward in terms of historical development,' he told Smith. 'I hate South Africans. That's not a fair thing to say because I like a lot of South Africans but they really think they're the bee's knees and actually they've been the cause of so much trouble in this part of the world … I have a suspicion the blacks model themselves on the whites now that they're in power. Don't you know who we are, man?'

He continued in this vein: 'I dislike South Africa for the same reason that Latin Americans dislike the United States, I think. It's just too big and too unsubtle.'

Ouch. Arrogant, unsubtle troublemakers who haven't quite got over apartheid – surely he's got us all wrong? Doesn't he know we're the rainbow nation?

But much as I want to be offended, my inclination to argue with Scott is tempered by the fact that I've said almost the same thing myself. 'The rest of Africa doesn't like us very much,' I wrote in an analysis last year. 'Being a South African in Africa is like being an American in the rest of the world. We're looked upon with a mix of envy and resentment, our wealth and power relative to the rest of the continent ensuring that most of the time we get our way.'

All right, Scott, we'll cede this point to you – we can be a little overbearing when it comes to our interactions with Africa. And yes, our current leaders may have learned a few tricks from their apartheid-era predecessors, specifically the one about running an entire country for the benefit of a privileged minority (for 'whites' insert 'Guptas').

But Scott's not yet finished with his South Africa-bashing, going on to question the holy grail of South African foreign policy: our BRICS membership. 'They think in BRICS that the 's' actually stands for South Africa whereas it stands for Africa. Nobody would want to go in for a partnership with Brazil, China, India and South Africa for Christ's sake.'

Again, we must reluctantly concede that Scott has a point. South Africa's addition to BRICS has always been contentious, precisely because we do not wield anything near the kind of economic or political power of the other nations in the group (including Russia, which Scott failed to mention). As *The Economist* explained in March 2013, our primary qualification was geographic.

'There was just one problem with the BRICs: no African countries were included. This was a little embarrassing. Overlooking Africa suggested that the continent was an economic irrelevance, good only for providing raw materials to the rest. It also cast doubt on the group's claim to speak for the emerging world. Two African countries might have been candidates, Nigeria and South Africa. But only one would keep the acronym intact. And so, in 2010, the club of BRICs became the BRICS.'

Scott's final attack was even more personal, and won't make him any friends in the Union Buildings. He compared President Jacob Zuma to another South African president – and no, it wasn't Mandela.

'He's very like De Klerk,' Scott said. 'He tells us, "You just leave Zimbabwe to me". Excuse me, who the hell liberated you anyway, was it not us? I mean, I quite like him, he seems a rather genial character but I pity him his advisers.'

Again, this taps into a gnawing resentment from other African countries about South Africa's at times bull-headed foreign policy. The mediation efforts in Zimbabwe may formally be under the SADC banner, but Pretoria is setting the agenda, and has been since Mbeki's time in office. This is clearly beginning to rankle our regional neighbours. And the barb about Zuma's advisers is disingenuous, and is the only nod to diplomatic courtesy in the entire interview. For Zuma, ultimately, is responsible for appointing his pitiable advisors; to criticise them is to criticise him.

But perhaps Scott's most telling point is his position on who liberated South Africa. A number of factors went into the dismantling of the apartheid state in 1994, and a major one was the support of other African states for the anti-apartheid movement. Zambia in particular played a hugely significant role, hosting the ANC's head-office-in-exile where, for a time, a certain Jacob Zuma found a home.

For this, South Africa owes Zambia a debt of gratitude, but it's a debt that Zambia's vice president clearly feels has not been paid. This might be the underlying cause of his resentment, with our sometimes brash behaviour only making things worse.

Either way, it's clear that the South African government has a few bridges it needs to build with its Zambian counterpart, and it will be interesting to see how our top politicians react to Scott's frank, if insulting, assessment – which, like all the best insults, is just a little too close to the bone for comfort.

MY COMING-OUT STORY

In a strange way, announcing something this personal in a public forum is easier than doing so to friends or family. It's probably because Daily Maverick has been a beacon of liberal thinking and debate, something that hasn't always been true when discussing a topic as sensitive as this with one's parents. This is my coming-out story.

STYLI CHARALAMBOUS, MAY 2012

Not living in the same country as your parents has its own pitfalls, as well as its perks. The upside includes freedom from the intrusive village grapevine run by the old-granny mafia, and not subjecting my home to the total of 80 cigarettes my folks plough through in any given day.

The downside is that each visit will conjure up the inevitable conversation that begins with the 'so, what's new in your life?' stage and rapidly degenerates into a cold war between traditional and new-age thinking.

And when I use the term 'traditional', I expect that Jewish, Indian and fellow Mediterranean descendants will join me in a collective sigh of recognisable frustration. They will be all too familiar with the tribulations of arguing with people who grew up in a very different time, a very different world.

By 'traditional', I really mean old-school conservatism that often belies logic and reason for the sake of centuries-old customs that have never before been questioned because they were made customary law by some grey-bearded fellow with a big hat. So it's with a relative amount of trepidation that I look forward to my next sitting with Papa and Mama, where this bombshell will very likely result in my umpteenth expulsion from the family home.

Even in my formative years, I knew something wasn't quite right. For most of the time I believed the problem lay with me. Or so it felt. On the outside I was just another typical boy attending a co-educational Model C school in the windswept suburbs of Port Elizabeth. There was no traumatic event or unduly influential set of circumstances that caused me to drift from what my parents and teachers were advocating as 'normal' behaviour. Nor was I exposed to an excessive amount of offensive material to make me this way. It was simply a natural outcome to something that stirred within me.

As I write this, I recognise the anger I feel towards a system, both educational and societal, that I can now claim to be morally corrupt. For years, these standards and teachings made me feel inadequate as a person, merely because I was someone with an outlook that differed from the norm and who was too afraid to express it to the world.

Looking back, I can see how unjust it was for parents, teachers and clergy to enforce what they thought was acceptable behaviour upon me and others who were no doubt just like me. For the sake of the next generation, I sincerely hope the curricula of schools have been updated to remove the archaic biases that we had to endure.

It was only when I had the opportunity to leave home after university, to the big smoke of Jozi, that I felt comfortable exploring these feelings.

Mind you, it wasn't easy to begin with. Years of indoctrination don't simply unravel overnight and I often found myself, almost robotically, spewing bigoted arguments during our late-night philosophical digs debates. But slowly, my rational mind was waging war with years of misguidance.

Quite fortunately for me, this was around the same time as this internet thing and Google were taking off. With terabytes of material being uploaded each day, not even the hurdles of dial-up connectivity or Telkom could stop me from expanding my mind beyond the clutches of what society had deemed normal on my behalf and at my expense.

While I feel aggrieved by my parents, who had conditioned me into a particular way of thinking, I understand that they were just by-products of centuries of misinformation. They merely extended the ill-advised lessons their parents had taught them, and their grandparents before them. But that would turn out to be the deceitfully clever part of the propaganda campaign.

It had woven itself so closely into the fabric of what it meant to be Greek (or Jewish or Indian) that breaking out from the constraints of this thinking would be akin to denouncing your own culture, and bring shame on the family name. It's no wonder that so many like me choose to rather live behind closet doors, away from the prejudices of old.

I try not to think of how many major life-changing decisions I've made on the back of these lies. Or things I've said and done, knowing only too well the hypocrisy of those actions but still succumbing to the societal pressure to conform. I still easily recall situations where my life could have been very different had it not been for the conformist teachings drummed into my psyche.

And the years of guilt I carried for actions I was told were immoral according to this cultural code, I will never get those back. Worse, I shudder to think how many people have been persecuted, victimised and even killed for not keeping their views sheltered from bigoted bullies.

But if any generation can stand up to the closed-minded thinking and irrational teachings of the past, it's ours. With the freedom of information that the internet brings to personal experiences, hopefully we can reduce the stigma attached to the stereotypical thinking that has dominated our past.

In writing this piece, I am hoping in some small way that it will not only help me to come out but possibly spur others on to join me and publicly declare their allegiance in the fight against the persecution of our kind and freedom of choice.

And still, even after baring something so private, on a forum for thousands to see, it doesn't make the task of sitting down with my mother any easier and uttering the words, 'Mom, I'm an atheist.'

8

LESSONS FROM A MURDER

WHEN THE MEDIA CIRCUS HAS MOVED ON

As South Africans, Oscar Pistorius' fans and the media struggle to digest the truth of what may have happened at his home on 14 February 2013, the reality of the death of Reeva Steenkamp – someone's child, someone's friend – was banished to the margins of the tragedy. This cannot be allowed to happen.
MANDY WIENER, FEBRUARY 2013

Reeva loved tea. She thought it was a universal panacea and any problem could be solved with it. She also loved scones.

She was a Leo and we were planning her 30th in Vegas. She would drop anything to come to you if you needed her or felt sad.

She was mad about Oscar, completely in love with him, as he was about her.

She wanted to be famous.

The messages beeped through on my phone, amid an overwhelming bombardment of calls from global news networks and incessant requests for interviews. They were from a mutual friend, one who was mourning a deep loss. It was one of those poignant, unique moments in which I had to pause and shift from the sometimes surreal frenzy of the news machine and allow reality to sink in. Until then it had been all Oscar, Oscar, Oscar – the Blade Runner, Paralympic golden boy, worldwide icon, PR machine. I hadn't realised until that point that Reeva Steenkamp and I shared several mutual friends and yet had never before met. They all spoke glowingly of her with genuine love and affection.

While I fielded calls from radio and TV stations in the UK, Australia, Canada, Spain, the Czech Republic and other more remote countries, facts were regurgitated and so were the questions. Mostly all about Oscar. At home, as South Africans, we struggled to digest the news, not wanting to comprehend the truth of what may have occurred at Pistorius' home on Thursday morning. We justified, contemplated hypotheses and drove speculation about why he would have shot and killed his girlfriend. Then, true to form, we began to joke.

The reality was simply too much too bear. Oscar had brought us such pride on the world's stage and the veneer had shattered, the gloss was horribly tarnished. It cut the country to its very core.

But with those text messages staring at me on the screen, it was undeniably real. So real for those who called Reeva Steenkamp a friend and truly appreciated her love of tea.

Somewhere amid the chaos of the day, a lawyer with decades of experience in criminal matters phoned. She was frustrated at the media hype around the incident. 'I'm looking for a compassionate, female perspective,' she said. 'Whether the charges are legitimate or not, someone died today. Don't miss that point. Someone's child died today and she was also important.' It was yet another dose of reality. When the media circus of hired helicopters and global requests moves on, Reeva Steenkamp will still be dead.

The 29-year-old model was on the cusp of celebrity stardom. Her relationship with Pistorius had elevated her profile and she was due to feature in a reality show scheduled to start on the weekend of 16 February. Samantha Moon, the executive producer and creator of *Tropika Island of Treasure*, says there were intense deliberations about whether they should continue premiering the season on Saturday 16 February as planned.

'The more we thought about it, the more I felt quite strongly that right now the country and the world knows Reeva as a model with amazing images of this beautiful girl. But what we have is proof of how wonderful she was. For me, the fact that South Africa will get to know this girl that we love and feel the loss of very deeply, I feel that if we were not to air it, we would be in some way contributing to erasing her. I just don't think we can do that.

'I would like everyone to know her as an intelligent, fierce, fearless woman. She was exceptionally caring and generous and truly loving. One of the things the contestants often joked about was that you couldn't be in Reeva's company for five minutes without being afflicted by "Reeva Fever"', says Moon.

Sarit Tomlinson, the managing director of Capacity Relations, which managed Steenkamp, gushed about the law graduate and actress' approach to life. 'Everyone that met Reeva will tell you the same thing, that she was the kindest, most down to earth girl with the most endearing personality. She was always about making other people happy and ensuring her friends and family were smiling. She really was a pure soul,' Tomlinson recalled.

As a journalist who is forever chasing the next deadline, I always try to pause and take cognisance of a story. Step away and breathe it all in and appreciate the ramifications of what we've put out there into the world. Sometimes, it's hard to grasp when you're detached and merely stating the facts. You have to challenge yourself to always ensure that your humanity has not been abandoned and that you retain compassion. As a crime reporter, it is also not often that a story in this country can shock you. This one most certainly did. Somewhere between a call to a mourning relative and a two-way with a breakfast talk show in New Zealand, I stepped outside the madness, and took a moment.

South Africa repeatedly produces material that a best-selling crime writer could never conceptualise. In fact, best-selling author Deon Meyer once told me that if he were to write a novel based on the Kebble killing, no one would believe him. Perhaps that is why it is so difficult for us to deal with reality. It just seems, well, too unreal.

For Oscar Pistorius, the incomprehensible reality of the nightmare he is in will just be beginning to dawn. For Reeva Steenkamp's family, the reality of her absence will be unmistakable. For her friends, who were once afflicted by 'Reeva Fever', there will be no denying the reality of her bloody, tragic end.

In South Africa, truth is so often stranger than fiction. The reality can hurt so badly that we don't want to believe it.

LESSONS FROM A MURDER

A CONVERSATION ABOUT VIOLENCE

I admit it. I am afraid of white men who are strangers. This is especially the case when white men are in groups, but on occasions when I have seen a lone white man on a dark street at night, I have quickened my steps and crossed the road. I do not – of course – think that white men are by their nature evil or violent. Yet listening to Oscar Pistorius' court case has reminded me of how little we speak about white male violence in this country.
SISONKE MSIMANG, MARCH 2014

In part, admitting my fears sounds silly: almost satirical. This is because our society's fixation on the idea of the black male assailant is so all-consuming that it distorts the feelings and experiences of the majority of South Africans. Most of the racialised fears of violence that are given expression in the mainstream media revolve around black people as the perpetrators of crimes. In our national psyche, whites (and, of late, middle-class people of all races) are almost always the victims of black male violence. Blacks, on the other hand, are rarely worthy of mention as victims at all. If they are, it is at the hands of other blacks.

In a thoughtful article in *The Guardian* on 4 March 2014, Margie Orford rightly points out that 'the figure of the threatening black stranger has driven many South Africans into fortress-like housing estates, surrounded by electric fences, armed guards and the relentless surveillance of security cameras'.

Yet where has the figure of the malevolent white stranger driven South Africans who are afraid of him? Is our silence on white male violence an indicator that there is no fear? Is there a white corollary to the threatening black stranger that Orford so ably invokes?

Given the history of this country, the very idea that black people aren't afraid of white violence is absurd. In the same way that the threat of the 'black intruder' is both real and imagined, the figure of the grinning rage-filled frat boy with murder in his heart (think Reitz Four at UFS, Waterkloof Four in Pretoria, and any number of racially motivated assaults on black people's dignity) is also both real and imagined.

Just as the figure of the black man who rapes the daughter of the house is both real and imagined, so, too, is the figure of the white farmer who is so outraged that a worker has stolen/broken/forgotten something that he kills him. Just as the violent black drug fiend is both real and imagined, so too is the white father who beats his wife to punish her for coming home late from work.

Stories about white men who behave this way circulate at braais and form core parts of the legends of many black families. Just as the dinner party in the affluent suburbs eventually touches on 'crime', the black get-together also invariably turns to white impunity. Often the stories are of violent acts perpetrated by white men against black people who were simply minding their own business.

Somehow these conversations – which happen in informal black spaces – haven't taken up as many column inches as the fears that preoccupy white middle-class social gatherings.

When white violence is referenced in the media it is usually contextualised in structural and historical terms. The narrative goes something like this: 'A long time ago there were bad white people who colonised the country, killed some Africans and instituted an evil capitalist system that exploited black labour. These acts were violent and this structural violence – best embodied by the migrant labour system for example – continues to this day.'

The problem with telling the story of white violence in this way is that it distances real, living white people from everyday acts of here-and-now violence. It allows violence by white people to be seen as a collective historical fact rather than as an active part of how whites and blacks in South Africa have learned to express themselves. It makes whites the present-day victims of crime, and makes blacks the present-day perpetrators of violent crime.

Unless we name the fears of black people with as much frequency and volume as we name the fears of whites, we will continue to be surprised and fascinated when white-on-white crime occurs. Unless we explore the ways in which white people act out violence, we will continue to tell the individual stories of white victims of crime in poignant detail even as we relegate black suffering to the back page.

A less stilted conversation about race, fear and violence might translate into more empathetic coverage of all victims. Because we see whites as victims and blacks as perpetrators, our collective sympathies are always with whites.

We are stuck in this 'white innocence/black guilt' binary and this means that the stories of the thousands of farm workers and domestic workers who are physically assaulted each year cannot be told. When we do tell them, it is as though they are purely about labour relations and not about white violence.

Ironically, given the complete absence of black people in the cast of characters involved in the Oscar Pistorius case, the trial has lead to a surge in conversation about our fear of black men. There hasn't been a commensurate articulation of concern about white male violence as a threat to the fabric of our society.

We are long overdue for a national conversation about the fear of white male violence.

WHAT GOT LOST IN
THE OSCAR PISTORIUS FRENZY

While the media (including Daily Maverick) fed the public appetite for Pistorius-related news in the last two weeks of February 2013, life continued as normal for many. And in South Africa, 'life as normal' involves daily violence against women. Here are some of the stories that got lost in the Pistorius frenzy.

REBECCA DAVIS, FEBRUARY 2013

Butterworth, Eastern Cape, 9 February. It's a Saturday night, and a 110-year-old woman is sleeping alone in the house she shares with her 22-year-old granddaughter. At some point after 8:30 p.m., a man enters her house, pulls the woman from her bed on to the floor, and rapes her. He briefly breaks off, and she thinks the ordeal may be over. Instead, he returns with a knife to ensure her silence while he continues. Only when the woman's granddaughter is heard outside the yard, does he get up and flee.

The *Daily Dispatch* reported that when a neighbour was summoned to the house by the shocked granddaughter, they found the old woman 'still trembling with fear and shock'. Police questioned a man matching the woman's description of her rapist the following Monday. For the 110-year-old, however, trauma remains. 'I have lost my appetite, my heart is heavy and I constantly feel like throwing up,' she told the newspaper.

Carletonville, Gauteng. On 25 February, 12 men are expected to appear in the Carletonville Magistrate's Court. They are part of a group of 15 men in total who are accused of having gang-raped a 23-year-old woman last Wednesday. The woman was walking home with her friend when they were allegedly set upon by a group of men, who hit her over the head before dragging her to bushes nearby. Her friend escaped. The 23-year-old was allegedly raped by at least 12 men in the bushes, before being dragged to a nearby shack where another three men proceeded to rape her.

Tzaneen, Limpopo, 16 February. A two-year-old child is allegedly abducted by a 29-year-old man, a friend of her father. He allegedly took her into the bushes, raped her and abandoned her there. A man was arrested on 20 February and will appear in the Tzaneen Magistrate's Court on 25 February.

Heilbron, Free State, 22 February. Nine youths, aged between 15 and 19, appear in the Heilbron Magistrate's Court. They are accused of having gang-raped a 24-year-old woman, who was walking home with her husband after a family gathering. Her husband was able to escape, and ran to contact police. The woman was reportedly found near an open field.

Kimberley, Northern Cape, 22 February. It is announced that the 16-year-old boy who is accused of having killed a Griekwastad family in April 2012 will face an additional rape charge. The youth allegedly shot dead farmer Deon Steenkamp, his wife Christelle and their 14-year-old daughter Marthella. The state now contends that he raped 14-year-old Marthella before killing her.

Herbertsdale, Western Cape, 15 February. A 49-year-old woman enters the Kwanonqaba police station to report an act of domestic violence. A 52-year-old police constable on duty listens to her complaint. Then he allegedly locks the station's front door, drags the woman to the trauma room, and rapes her. When the woman reported the matter to the same police station the next day, she was assured by a different policeman that police officers would be sent to her home to listen to her account. They never arrived. She reported it to a local councillor, and subsequently the Independent Police Investigative Directorate (IPID) was made aware of the incident. The constable was arrested on 20 February.

Atlantis, Western Cape, 18 February. Twenty-year-old Melandri Bukkies is home alone. A man – allegedly her ex-boyfriend, against whom she had an interdict – enters the house and stabs her to death. The *Cape Argus* quotes local councillor Barbara Rass as saying that Bukkies' murder was the second in the area within a week. 'We've lost two girls – both inside their own houses,' Rass said.

Phoqukhalo, KwaZulu-Natal, 15 February. A 41-year-old man is arrested for having repeatedly raped his 12-year-old stepdaughter. After the girl fell pregnant, community members approached the police with their suspicions in October 2012, but when police questioned the girl's family, vehement denials ensued. A paternity test subsequently confirmed that the father of the girl's child was her stepfather.

Ga-Rankuwa, Gauteng, 21 February. The dead body of an eight-year-old girl is found near a shopping complex. Angie Mabutho's underwear was absent from the scene. Mabutho had gone missing on her way home from school four days previously. Two men have been arrested.

Winterveldt, Gauteng, 14 February. The dead body of 75-year-old Kate Legodi is found at her home. She had been hacked to death. The suspected murderers are her two sons. The younger son – aged 40 – had been adopted by Legodi. When his older brother (aged 43) was arrested, he went on the run.

Grabouw, Western Cape, 20 February. Two men accused of having raped the 22-year-old daughter of a Grabouw councillor are released on R500 bail each. The *Cape Times* reported that the woman considered the alleged rapists to be good and trusted friends. 'I feel ashamed and dirty,' she reportedly said. Her father was extremely opposed to the two men having been granted bail.

The crimes listed above likely represent only a fraction of the full number of incidents of violence against women that have taken place in South Africa only over the few days described. Rape, in particular, is believed to be massively underreported – by some estimates, as few as just one in nine rapes are reported. Many of the violent murders and rapes listed here would have warranted only a few paragraphs tucked away in the inner pages of South African newspapers. In fact, it generally takes a rape or murder characterised by extreme levels of violence or particularly grotesque details – like that of Anene Booysen – to warrant a front page. That, or the involvement of a very high-profile protagonist.

Even if newspapers were to resolve to report all violent attacks on women and all rapes, it's likely they would simply run out of space. Lerato Moloi of the Institute of Race Relations said: 'If data for all violent assaults, rapes and other sexual assaults against women are taken into account, then approximately 200 000 adult women are reported as being attacked in South Africa every year.' She added: 'The real figure is in all probability considerably higher.'

The grim truth is that violence against women in South Africa is so prevalent that individual cases are often not even particularly newsworthy. They are just a part of daily life.

9

OUR SCOURGE

**ANENE BOOYSEN: THE AGONY OF
SOUTH AFRICA'S DAUGHTER**

In life, the two young women were worlds apart from each other, but in death they were uncannily the same. Aside from their brutal gang rapes and mutilation, both the 23-year-old woman known as 'India's daughter' and 17-year-old Anene Booysen wanted their rapists to face justice. In death, they both demanded that their communities confront the horror of sexual violence.
RANJENI MUNUSAMY, FEBRUARY 2013

'Will South Africans ever be shocked by rape?' a BBC feature asked in January 2013. It provided a shocking insight into South Africa's apparent numbness to sexual violence, describing the country's citizens as 'unable to muster much more than a collective shrug in the face of almost unbelievably grim statistics'. It pointed out that while Indians were re-examining their society in the light of a single, horrific incident of gang rape, in South Africa 'there is no sense of a nation being galvanised'. This is despite almost 60 000 rapes reported to the police each year, and the fact that the true figure might be at least ten times that – 600 000 attacks.

'It is not that the issue is ignored – far from it. This week South African newspapers are carrying gruesome stories of what is being described as a new trend – the rape of elderly grandmothers, mostly in rural communities; an 82-year-old and a 73-year-old attacked on 2 January,' the BBC reported. 'In recent days commentators and campaigners here have looked, almost enviously, towards India, wondering what it might take to provoke a similar sense of outrage – and angrily debating whether outrage itself is enough, and who, or what, to blame.'

This week, we got the answer. It took a disturbingly similar incident to that which caused the mass uprising in India to trigger shock and outrage in South Africa, even from the Office of the President. Though there is no mass uprising, there is a realisation that something has gone horribly wrong in South Africa for its women to be subjected to such horror and violence.

Seventeen-year-old Anene Booysen, of Bredasdorp in the Southern Cape, was gang-raped and badly mutilated. Her mother, Corlia Olivier, recounted to the SABC the sight of her daughter after the attack: 'My child almost looked purple. She was in such a bad state. All her fingers were broken, her legs were broken. Her stomach had been cut up, you could see her intestines. Her throat was also slit open.'

Die Burger reported that a doctor who had first-hand knowledge of the emergency operation performed on Booysen said someone had put their hands inside her body and pulled out her intestines.

'She lost a large part of her intestines. That is also why

she didn't survive,' said the doctor. Police apparently found Booysen's intestines lying around her, covered in sand.

Before she died in hospital, Booysen identified one of her alleged attackers – Jonathan Quinton Davids, 22, who was apparently her ex-boyfriend. He appeared in the Bredasdorp Magistrate's Court on 5 February on charges of rape and murder. Another three suspects have reportedly been questioned.

The victim in the New Delhi attack in December had to have 95% of her intestines removed in three operations. She suffered brain injuries, internal infections and had trouble breathing, yet she managed to make two statements to police officers to help arrest her torturers before she died. Like her, Booysen wanted justice to be done and her attackers to be held accountable.

In her final act of bravery, her voice was heard.

On Thursday, President Jacob Zuma said the attack on Booysen was 'shocking', 'cruel' and 'inhumane' and called for the harshest possible sentence for the assailants. 'Impose the harshest sentences on such crimes, as part of a concerted campaign to end this scourge in our society,' said Zuma in a statement. 'It has no place in our country. We must never allow ourselves to get used to these acts of base criminality to our women and children.'

The president's statement was one of a volley of reactions from the government, opposition parties, civil society groups, womens' rights organisations and organised labour, expressing outrage and demanding action to stem the tide of sexual violence in South African society.

Cabinet has now decided to prioritise crimes against

women and children and wants there to be no bail for suspects and stiffer sentences. The ANC Women's League wants an official enquiry into gender-based violence.

'We will be calling for a national commission of enquiry into rape and gender-based violence in order to develop a national strategy to eradicate rape from South African society,' the league said.

But could a public inquiry help to stop endemic levels of sexual violence in South African society?

Dr Saths Cooper, president of the International Union of Psychological Science, says rape is not a new phenomenon in South African society; literature, research and the facts and figures are all at hand showing the nature and extent of the crimes. He said there were several root causes of sexual violence against women, including power relations, socialisation and economic and social conditions.

'In most societies where there is economic stability and social security, incidence of rape is fairly low. But when social and economic conditions are unstable, and there is a high level of uncertainty and anxiety, there are concomitant levels of rape and other aberrations,' Cooper said. 'We don't know to what extent the frustration of young and old males, at their wits' end in a society that has discarded them, where they have no jobs and women tend to get things quicker, exacerbates the situation. That is not a cause, but could be an underlying issue behind incidence of sexual violence.'

Cooper says in South Africa there are 'lots of people who are the walking wounded, who feel frustrated and oppressed, and who don't have the ability to discriminate [between] right and wrong'. He said the education system does not socialise children on appropriate relations with other people. Therefore, racial and gender behaviour tends to be socially transmitted generationally.

Cooper said that South Africa has a 'prudish, Calvinist, Victorian notion about sexuality' which is why issues like women's dressing and behaviour are factored into justifications for rape. The migrant labour system had forged a situation in which sexual relationships became based on convenience. 'This gave rise to a set of conditions such as single, vicarious parenting and a significant number of households without male figures who could instil a sense of respect for women and girls.'

He said violent behaviour was learned and that people who experience violence against themselves or others may perpetuate it: 'How we [are] socialised to deal with each other interracially and gender wise, that transmits itself. It may not be noticeable in certain urban contexts but in schools, playgrounds, townships and neighbourhoods, it is easy to do what you see so much of happening around you. Brazenness increases. Others do it and get away with it, so the behaviour is replicated.'

Uneven power relations are also a major contributing factor to the rampant incidence of sexual violence. 'We are notorious as one of few societies where children who can hardly walk and grandmothers are raped,' Cooper said. Women who are intellectually challenged have also been victims of gang rapes and exploitation.

Rape is often misunderstood as stemming from sexual desire when it is primarily an act of violence and aggression.

'Ours is a violent society. The first resort is a violent reaction. We think afterwards about the consequences and that is a problem,' Cooper said.

Like the apartheid past, during which violence was a daily feature of life in South Africa, we seem – again – to be getting accustomed to, and being numbed by, death and brutality in our society.

The Marikana massacre, rampant service delivery protests, murder, rapes, road deaths, police brutality and other horrors shock us when they happen, but society recovers and moves on quickly. Self-preservation takes precedence.

South Africa seems to be reacting to rape in the same way as to other forms of exploitation such as abuse of power and corruption. We are pounded daily with the rape of the public purse and the political elite using their positions to feather their own nests. Scandal fatigue is a new South African syndrome as acceptance of corruption as a norm has set in.

In all these instances, the powerful abuse the weak and society learns to look on dispassionately. This is a far cry from the society that stood up against a powerful oppressive regime and conquered it, where community activism was the frontline defence against tyranny.

Our numbness to all forms of violence and the extent to which we appear overwhelmed by scandal fatigue is a sad indictment of the psyche of our nation. The agony and death of Anene Booysen is a signal of a sick society, our society. Hers is more than a story of the violent rape of an innocent. Anene Booysen is our country. The abuse and defilement must stop. We must stop it.

WATCH. PRAY. SOUTH AFRICA.

After a week of horrifying violence, I let the trauma sink in and am left with more questions than answers. What can we do when the causes of violence continue to feed off each other? Sorry, but I don't know right now.

GREG NICOLSON, OCTOBER 2013

If you follow the media, you see a lot of shocking things. You see more if you work in it. In October 2013, Yonalisa and Zandile Mali were found dead in a Diepsloot toilet cubicle. The cousins, aged two and three, had been sexually assaulted, killed and dumped. The where, what, who, why, when and how explains a senseless atrocity, but it's almost too surreal, a tragedy that's hard to comprehend, like the endless reports of fatalities in foreign countries.

It took Prince (the artist formerly known as) to remind me of the horror. A day after the discovery of their bodies, as I was sitting down to write and police were narrowing in on the key suspect, iTunes played 'The Most Beautiful Girl in the World'. When the first of my sisters got married, she walked into the reception with this song playing. Her smile beamed across the room as she moved towards a new phase in her life, with a family of her own, a house, bills, nappies and new dreams. We'd spent most of our childhood together in various stages of warfare and peacetime. On that day, she felt she was the most beautiful girl in the world and at that moment everyone in the room knew it.

The song is a corny love jam. Heart-fluttering, 17-year-old blind love, and 27-year-old jaded, broken-hearted-but-somehow-found-love love. Sing it to an infant. Parody it with your friends. Get some candles, play it for your partner and hope he or she doesn't laugh (at you). Innocence, hope, joy, freedom, love, laughter – all that was taken from Yonalisa and Zandile when they were molested and murdered.

The toddlers won't ever know the feeling of getting married. Nor will they experience their first day of school, or a playground kiss. They won't have the chance to decide whether they want to be a doctor or teacher, a pilot or chef. They won't graduate, not from primary school, not from a university, not an FET college. They won't fall in love and they will never raise children while struggling to pay school fees and worrying about the safety of their kids. These are all gone.

Yonalisa and Zandile's parents won't see their daughters alive again. Their most beautiful girls in the world are gone. I didn't see the Mali family's anguish, didn't go to the funeral. I haven't discussed it with friends. But once I breathed the misery into my lungs, I couldn't help but feel that the country's soul has been slashed open to release a reservoir of tears. Or maybe that morality has been stabbed so many times that the tears are dry so we can no longer cry.

How much can we stand? This piece is already soaked in emotion so let me not hide the hurt. In 2013 there have been public reports on the killings of Anene Booysen, Mido Macia, and a whole family in Etwatwa. The last time I was in Diepsloot, it was because two men were killed, supposedly for making too much noise. The senseless silencing of life also continues beyond the front pages and after headlines. The Marikana massacre has spiralled into a war of assassinations.

Rape – horrendous, unbelievable and gruesome rape – and the assault against women and children continue. Political murders rocked the lead-up to the 2012 ANC Mangaung conference. There have been multiple deaths in Cato Crest, where residents just want to keep living in their informal settlement. While we were processing the news of the deaths in Diepsloot, we heard that another two young girls had been found dead in Katlehong, allegedly poisoned.

The crime stats for the worst violence – the crimes the cops need help from society to prevent – aren't seeing enough change. For the first time in a decade, the 2012/2013 crime statistics saw a rise in murder. 'Serious and violent crime is increasing in South Africa,' Gareth Newham of the Institute of Security Studies told *Mail & Guardian*. Chandre Gould, from the same organisation, told Daily Maverick that she believed that 'violence [was] the most serious and pressing problem that South Africa face[d] [in 2013]'. UNICEF's South Africa home page hurts: 'Violence against women and children in South Africa is extreme.'

Sitting in the old Women's Gaol – a monument to a legacy of brutality, oppression overcome, and the rights of the modern Constitution – in 2012, I heard multiple explanations for South Africa's violence. The migrant labour system. Breakdown of family units. A failure to confront the trauma of colonialism and apartheid. Inequality. Poverty. Unemployment. The whole system that blends it all together, spits it out for people to consume, and mixes and blends the horror all over again.

I think of another form of violence in Diepsloot and across the country. A scared mother told us, 'Our children are now not able to play freely. As you know, Diepsloot doesn't have the luxury of privacy. Will we now keep our kids in our one-roomed shacks? We are forced to use the same communal toilets. Things happen in those toilets late night or early morning, but it is our reality.'

What's a mother to do? How can she protect her kids so they can live fulfilling lives, so they can live long enough to get married, feel what it's like to watch their siblings get married, or choose not to get married? How can she fight the violence of poverty and the violence of individuals so that her children will not get killed before they can learn to read and write?

What escape is there when unemployment is rising and in many places the education system is a crippling rather than enabling offering? Who do we run to when politicians make election promises but the state's busy building the president's house rather than a local police station? Protest? There's a quick sniff of tear gas and the sting of a rubber bullet. Mob justice? It's hardly going to teach anyone that violence is the wrong option.

What the fuck can we do but watch and pray?

THOUGHT I'D SAY 'HI'
TO A COUPLE OF RAPISTS

Somewhere in South Africa are two men I have grown to hate. I have never met either of them. They raped the woman who is now my wife. She was 14 at the time.
ANONYMOUS, JUNE 2013

They were in the army. White boys. German-speaking.

Even if she wanted to, it is probably too late for my wife

to lay charges against these bastards. But it is not too late to remind them of the harm they did to a child 26 years ago. If they read this, they will know that I know. Even if nobody else recognises who they are – and the aim of this is not to reveal their identities – they will remember what they did on that hot summer's day in 1987 next to the swimming pool at a house in the Johannesburg suburb of Robindale.

Sandy (not her real name) never pressed charges for the same reasons that so many rape victims don't. Guilt, shame and fear kept her mouth shut for way too long. It was only years later that she told her parents what had happened. She is still angry with them for not picking up the signs at the time.

So how old are you now, guys? Mid-forties, I guess. Your kids must be in high school. I'm sure you both live in nice homes in affluent suburbs. Life has been good. I'm sure it still is. Relax, *kerle*. Have a beer. Wipe that sweat from your upper lip and stop trembling. I'm not going to bust you. All I want to do is remind you that somewhere out there, maybe even in the same suburb as you, is a woman who is profoundly damaged by what you did to her all those years ago.

And then there is me. Your actions have affected not only Sandy's life, but mine, too. This story, then, is my way of saying, 'Fuck you.'

First, let me tell you a little about what it's like living with a woman who has been raped.

Ours was one of those whirlwind romances, meeting, dating, moving in together and marrying within a few months. Some of our friends said we were mad, that we should take it slowly. Others said life is short, go for it. Looking back, I realise how little we knew about one another.

One thing I noticed early on is the frequency with which she made sweeping generalisations about men. We would be having a light-hearted argument about the differences between the sexes when she would suddenly grow angry and say something like, 'Men are all the same. They all cheat. You'll cheat on me, one day.'

Once, she said: 'All men fantasise about gang-raping a woman.' First I had heard of it. And certainly not something that had ever crept into my fantasies. I told her to stop her irrational negativity towards all men. Every time this happened, I would suggest that she rephrased her sentence. 'Why don't you say "some men" or even "most men"? How can you accuse all men of something just because of the actions of a few?'

But it continued. All men go to strip clubs. All men visit prostitutes. All men are misogynists.

Sex with Sandy has never been an altogether comfortable affair. She has never used the phrase 'making love'. When I used to talk about us making love, she would laugh cynically and say, 'What's love got to do with it?' To her, it was 'fucking'. Still is. I no longer mention the words 'making love' in the context of sex. Knowing what happened all those years ago, I can almost understand how she may never want to equate sex with love. For Sandy, sex is not a tender, gentle thing. It is a rough, almost brutal, act.

Something I still struggle with is the post-coital crying. It doesn't happen all the time, but now and again Sandy breaks down and weeps after having sex. When she cried the first time, I thought it was something I had done. Or hadn't done. Many times, I have asked her what's wrong. I have begged her to tell me why she is crying. To let me in and share what's going on in her head. But she never does. At most, she will tell me not to worry. That it's nothing. It's painfully clear that whatever it is, she doesn't want to talk about it. Frustrated, confused and angry, all I can do is hold her until it passes.

Some time after we met, I made the stupid mistake of asking her how many men she had slept with in her life. She asked how many women I had slept with, and I told her. She said she had slept with roughly the same number. I was appalled. Not because I had slept with an inordinate number of women, but because I am one of the millions of men who had succumbed to the patriarchal propaganda that says a woman who has slept with a substantial number of men is a slut, a whore, the type of woman you simply don't marry. I felt as if I had been duped.

She also told me that she had slept with about ten boys/men by the time she had finished matric. I was coldly derisive, asking her what it had been like to be known as the school bicycle. She wept and shouted and threw things at me and it was a frosty few days that followed.

A few weeks later, the subject came up again. This time I listened to what she had to say. Sandy explained that after she was raped, she felt the only way she could hope to carry on living would be to have sex again. On her terms. She said it was a bit like falling off a horse and having to get back on to conquer your fear.

Having casual sex was her way of devaluing sex, of minimising its significance. Engaging in a string of meaningless physical relationships meant that to her, sex became of no more consequence than a workout at the gym. In doing this, she convinced herself that the rape itself had simply been a physical assault. I don't know how effective this was, because 26 years down the line, Sandy is still obviously damaged.

I am quite a tactile person, but Sandy struggles to show affection. She isn't one who hugs or touches easily and this has been the source of many arguments. 'How do I know you love me if you never show it?' I ask, frustrated by her emotional distance. Our sex life is so erratic that I am no longer sure she even enjoys sex. And who could blame her if she doesn't?

Sandy drinks too much and takes sleeping pills at night. She also suffers from depression and shows symptoms of borderline personality disorder. And she tried to kill herself a few years before I met her. She still talks a lot about suicide. I don't know what to do.

It's been months since we spoke about the rape. Perhaps she still needs to talk about it. But I don't know what more there is to say. It would be easy for me to say, 'It's been 26 years. Get over it.' Somehow, I don't think that's what she needs to hear.

All I can really do is keep trying to understand what it is like to be her. This isn't always easy, especially when I'm being singled out to take the rap for the sins of other men. Sometimes, when things are bad, I think it would be best if we got divorced. My life would certainly be a lot easier if I could share it with someone less damaged than Sandy.

So, Mr X and Mr Y, what did you think of my little story? Took you back, didn't it? I bet you thought nobody would ever mention the bit of fun you had at my wife's expense so many years ago. Least of all on the internet. Oh, and in case either of you is wondering, the scar on Sandy's thigh has never healed. Do you still have the bayonet?

IN DEFENCE OF A LION KILLER

The outrage about an American hunter, Melissa Bachman, who bragged on Twitter about bagging a splendid male lion, was terrifying to watch. Terrifying, but also deeply troubling on many levels. Emotive outrage and smug judgement are no substitute for rational thought and pragmatic policy.
IVO VEGTER, NOVEMBER 2013

Every year, game hunters travel to South Africa, pockets stuffed with dollars. Most of them are men, who quietly come and go, leaving R6.2 billion in industry revenue behind, according to Environmental Affairs Minister Edna Molewa.

But when one hunter, an American television host named Melissa Bachman, dared to boast about her wonderful African hunting safari, posing with a dead lion, she got more than she bargained for. Her Facebook page and Twitter feed were overrun with vicious hate mail. She was described as the most hated woman in South Africa. Ricky Gervais was scathing, though cleverly so: 'Spot the typo,' he wrote, about her boast: 'What a hunt!'

I don't know Ms Bachman, so I can't speak for her character. I've seen no suggestion that she failed to obtain a legitimate hunting permit, complete with the required CITES documentation. The Maroi Conservancy, which hosted her, seems legitimate too, although its website has also been barged offline by angry internetters.

I can't say I'm a big fan of hunting either. I've been invited on hunting trips, but declined for two reasons: one, I prefer to avoid media junkets, lest I be accused of being a shill for Big Hunt; and two, I prefer to avoid killing animals personally, even though I happily eat meat.

It is quite reasonable to dislike sport hunting. It is an emotional subject. But is it not curious that a perfectly legal hunt justifies crudely insulting a woman in sexist terms?

Writer and artist Sarah Britten wondered if it would have had as much impact if it were a male hunter with a lioness. She says she doesn't like hunting, but likes the reaction to Bachman's lion photo even less.

The answer seems quite obvious. Loads of men shoot loads of lions all the time. None of them makes it to that interminable aggregator of dodgy viral clickbait, Buzzfeed.com: 'TV Presenter Melissa Bachman Angers Entire Internet After Shooting A Lion'. None of them gets called sexist names by Ricky Gervais.

But let's stipulate, for the sake of argument, that we don't like hunting, and we don't like Ms Bachman. Does this justify the ugly, hypocritical anger? If her hunt was legal, what did she do wrong? Should it be made illegal?

In 1960, there were only three game farms in South Africa. There were only half a million head of game. Changes in the law to permit private ownership of game and commercialise big game hunting coincided with the sea change that we see in 2013: 10 000 game farms, supporting 20 million head of game on as many hectares. By contrast, the government formally protects only 7.5 million hectares as national parks.

The game farm industry employs 100 000 people, which is reportedly three times more than employment in ordinary livestock farms. Income from game breeding stock sold at auction rose almost 15-fold in just six years, from R60 million in 2006 to R864 million in 2012.

Is that mere correlation, or is there some causation at work here?

The knee-jerk reaction of the chattering classes is that you don't protect animals by killing them. That seems self-evident, but, as Mark Twain said, 'It ain't what you don't know that gets you into trouble. It's what you know for sure that just ain't so.'

The notion that hunting harms the survival of species – or the environment, more generally – happens to be false, and demonstrably so.

Commenting on Botswana's recent decision to ban professional hunting in the hope that it would stop poaching, Professor Melville Saayman of the North-West University observed: '… the problem is that it is going to have a reversed effect.'

Says Saayman: 'Kenya followed the same path. They also banned hunting and currently have a huge game poaching problem, so much so that some of their species face total extinction. The strategy proposed by Botswana is short-sighted and is not going to work. Game numbers will decline and this will have a serious impact on the hunting and game farm industry in the country.'

In Kenya, hunting was banned in the late 1970s, but the country has since lost 85% of its wildlife. Go figure.

'Case studies from South Africa,' says Saayman, 'have shown that as soon as the hunting of a species is allowed, it leads to the breeding as well as conservation of the particular species. Botswana's policy is definitely going to lead to job losses.'

In the early 1990s, I was on a guided tour of the Pilanesberg Game Reserve. I looked around at the devastated landscape, with nary a tree taller than a man. The ranger told me that the park had 60 elephants too many, but that nobody wanted them, because they all had their own elephant problems, and transport was too expensive.

'So what are you doing about it?' I asked.

'We hunt them, from the north of the park, out of sight of the regular tourists, who tend to get terribly upset about it,' he replied. 'The revenue helps, but we can only host one hunt a month, which isn't enough.'

The upshot of the misinformed anti-hunting and anti-culling sentiment of the dinner party set was that an entire park ecosystem was put at risk, just to 'save' a few elephants, of which there were plenty.

It is true that some lion populations in Africa are under pressure. However, an academic study undertaken by Peter Lindsey and others in 2012 found that even in countries where the threat is severe, prohibiting hunting – instead of just issuing fewer permits – would prove counterproductive, reducing habitat protection, reducing tolerance for lions among local populations, and reducing funds available to combat poaching.

In September 2012, I wrote about a story from Texas, where hunting ranches host large herds of endangered antelope like Addax and Dama Gazelle, which are extinct in the wild in their native Africa. The reason they're there? They earn their keep by supplying the hunting industry. What will happen if hunting these animals is banned? They will cease to exist. Entirely.

As it happens, that story also involved vile vitriol directed at a professional hunter, Corey Cogdell. That hunter was also female. Coincidence? I think not. It looks like Britten and Davis are right. Bachman's big mistake was not the hunt itself, nor even bragging about it – it was being female.

Let's consider the story of the Maroi Conservancy, where the hunt in question occurred. It consists of several private properties along the Zimbabwean border in Limpopo Province that have agreed to pull down the fences between them.

A profile of the conservancy is quite clear about the change that hunting has made: 'In the past, parts of the conservancy were intensively farmed for citrus and other crops, and some landowners tried running cattle. None of them managed for game. Poaching was common, with people cutting the fences to trespass. Now, all the meat from animals that are hunted goes to the local community to encourage them not to poach.'

In other words, where there used to be a few crop farms with poaching problems, Maroi is now a fully functional breeding game conservancy, supported by revenue from hunting.

Presumably, Maroi charged Bachman in the region of $30 000, which is the going rate for a full-maned lion. By comparison, most animals cost under $10 000. An elephant typically goes for $100 000, and a rhino – yes, hunting them for trophies is legal – fetches even more. And here's one for the trivia buffs: What is the cheapest animal on a typical trophy price list? Even cheaper than an impala female, a jackal fetches just $100. Poor put-upon vermin!

In terms of their vulnerability, lions aren't under nearly as much pressure as rhinos. What has hunting done for the rhino population? Extending full private property rights to the animals and legalising trophy hunting arguably saved both the Black and White Rhino from becoming extinct decades ago, according to a detailed study conducted by environmental economist Michael 't Sas-Rolfes.

As we all know, rhino are not out of the woods, and the recent spike in poaching is a grave concern. However, the solution is not to continue the ban on trading in rhino products, which is failing, but to lift it, and to let rhino farmers like John Hume breed the animals for their horn. It is gratifying to see that Minister Molewa thinks along the same lines, and will apply – against all odds – to CITES to lift the ban on the trade in rhino products.

As a child, on game viewing holidays, I remember learning how rare the Roan Antelope, Bontebok, Sable Antelope and Black Wildebeest were. Today, they are relatively common, and the Professional Hunters' Association of South Africa (PHASA) names them among the species that were once on the brink of being wiped out, but are today thriving on private game farms supported by hunting revenue.

'I am of the firm belief that the hunting industry and the game farming industry are important partners, who play a key role in terms of conservation, tourism and economic development,' Molewa told a hunting indaba in 2010.

In November 2013, she reiterated the government's policy to promote South Africa as 'a destination of choice for hunting'.

David Mabunda, CEO of SanParks, agrees: 'As a developing country, it would be suicidal to want to make trade-offs between hunting and photographic ecotourism. We don't have the luxury of choice. We need both.'

In light of all this, does the massive outcry about Melissa Bachman make sense? No, unless you're a misogynist or simply dislike American braggarts. Her public boasts about her kills may be tacky and decidedly ill-advised but, frankly, she appears to be someone who is passionate about the hunt, and isn't ashamed of her prowess.

This is not about her feelings. Anyone who dresses up like Lara Croft in *Tomb Raider* is probably tough enough to handle the hate directed at her by Internet trolls. If she's at all typical of professional hunters, she can comfort herself with the knowledge that she is more in tune with nature and its conservation than most of the haters.

Her detractors might brag about 'shooting' animals with cameras, but if my safari-company contacts are any guide, most of them are shallow tourists who demand to be driven about in air-conditioned luxury, to see all of the Big Five in one day, as if that is a more informed reflection of nature than a professional hunt.

South Africa officially considers Bachman a welcome and valued visitor, and rightly so. Even if you disagree, and you arrogantly think you have the moral authority to judge her arrogance, the real story is this. Your smug superiority risks depriving South Africa of tourism revenue and employment. It risks depriving the country of much-needed funding for conservation. It risks reducing the value of our wildlife, which reduces the incentive for private farm owners to breed and protect game. Hypocritical anger is a greater threat to conservation than Bachman's rifle will ever be.

Think about that, the next time you pen a bullying comment, safely hidden behind your screen. Moral superiority cuts both ways.

10

THE R-WORD

**BLACK ANGER AND
WHITE OBLIVIOUSNESS**

Artistry – or lack thereof – aside, Brett Murray's painting The Spear *will go down as a symbol of a moment in South Africa's reconciliation process. So much overlaps in this one painting that I probably won't capture it all here. The net effect, though, is chilling.*

OSIAME MOLEFE, MAY 2012

I can't remember how old I was when it happened. I was young enough that I couldn't see out the car window without taking off my seatbelt. So I didn't see what set it off. But when my dad, forced to the shoulder of the road by a bakkie, opened his driver's side door, the word rang out like cannon fire. 'Kaffir!'

Of all the insults in the expletive-laden rant that the bakkie driver – a white Afrikaans-speaking policeman – hurled at my dad, that word stung the most.

Powerless, and fearful of what might happen next, my mom, siblings and I watched the large man take my dad by the scruff of his neck. Thankfully that was where it ended, with an apology from my dad. We drove home in silent shame, teeming with anger that we had no choice but to swallow. This was not an incident of road rage or an officer doing his job. It was racism. But this was Pretoria in the early 1990s, so it was to be expected.

That man who traumatised my family, for no reason other than a palpable hate for the colour of our skins, has disappeared. He's blended into a fallacious rainbow nation amid accepted apologies that were never offered in the first place. Was it he who asked the other day, after the second attempt to pronounce my name, 'Don't you have a nickname?'

I found myself growing angry listening to a 2012 panel discussion on SAfm about online racism and the infamous racist model tweets. One of the panellists, AfriForum's Kallie Kriel, repeatedly pronounced Tshidi, the name of one of the models, as 'Tee-dee'. He had no problem saying 'Jessica', the name of the other model.

At the same time as Kriel was denouncing racism, regardless of the colour of the racist, he was displaying a more insidious bigotry that black South Africans have been forced to endure. In this country, you're likely to find more Tshidis than Jessicas. What reason exists for Kriel's inability to say Tshidi, other than the casual dismissal that says you can get along just fine in this country without learning to say African names or speak African languages? If he wanted to say it properly, he would have learned how to do so.

In that moment, I was angry not just about Kriel's mispronunciation. I was angry about all the occasions on which my own name had been mangled and – without my permission – shortened to 'Os'. I was angry about the adjustments I had had to make to survive in a Eurocentric work and university culture – a culture that made little adjustment for me. I was angry about how others who could not make the adjustments fell by the wayside. I was angry about these and the many other slights and humiliations, overt and subtle, that I, my dad and other black South Africans have had to endure without remedy.

For as much as white South Africa says it is opposed to racism or committed to building a united, non-racial South Africa, that commitment has largely been non-performative. Those familiar with this will realise I've referenced Andile Mngxitama.

Mngxitama's views are radical, but that does not detract from this being a valid point.

Colonialism and apartheid cloistered opportunity and privilege behind walls of whiteness. Even today, to access that opportunity, blacks need a *dompas* that says: You're acceptable. You've left your tribal, savage ways behind.

When apartheid's walls were removed, only one side shifted towards the other. Where being black means constantly changing, evolving and moving to find a place in a world not designed for you, being white means remaining unmoved. Worse, it also means being oblivious to that lack of motion or to the adjustments that the other has had to make. And when you do become aware of it, seldom does it mean wanting to give up the privilege.

This is why many black South Africans are angry, and this is the nerve that Murray's painting struck.

Regardless of the artist's intentions, *The Spear* became a proxy for the anger about the many unremedied injuries, large and small, that blacks have suffered at the hands of whites and for the lack of cognisance of these offences. By taking on traditionalist African practices and black sexuality (one of many possible interpretations of the painting), doing so in a way that challenged African conservatism, and because of the still-unresolved anger, Murray's painting became open to interpretation as 'yet another white, phallocratic avenue for bragging about European civilisation'.

That same anger insulated an equally 'offensive' painting by Ayanda Mabulu from the same kind of backlash, once his ignored work re-entered the public consciousness.

Some might view this anger as something black South Africans need to 'move on' from or get over. After all, whites voted 'Yes' in the referendum. Whites happily participated in the first free-and-fair elections in 1994 and the Truth and Reconciliation Commission thereafter. Whites volunteer their time in townships and support affirmative action, mostly. But beyond that, the commitment has been largely non-performing in that it does nothing to dismantle white privilege, creating a space in which even valid white commentary about black figures is received with anger.

For many, white privilege is a difficult concept to understand, mostly because it averts the eyes of those who enjoy it from seeing it. But *The Spear* came to our aid again in providing us with a clear example of the phenomenon in which two men who committed an act of vandalism were treated in glaringly disparate ways. It was no coincidence that the one head-butted and body-slammed was black and the one treated genially, and almost allowed to go free, was white.

It does not matter that the security guard was black. He was a representative of a system that associates black males with criminality.

In addition to the lack of action, FW de Klerk's interview with CNN's Christiane Amanpour demonstrated that it is fair to question whether white commitment to building a united South Africa has ever been genuine, or as honest as it should have been. De Klerk claims to have made a 'profound apology' for apartheid, yet during the interview perversely clung to the belief that the system was created in the interests of justice for black and white South Africans. I can accept that as a young man he genuinely believed this. Socialisation is powerful and can blind one to the glaringly obvious. But for him to look back and still claim the same, in the face of irrefutable evidence that justice for blacks was the last thing apartheid had in mind, renders his apology hollow.

I know he is not alone in thinking an apology and dismantling apartheid as a formal system absolves all sins. He's also not alone in believing that apartheid was not that bad. To back this claim, proponents tally up deaths under apartheid and compare it to Jewish deaths in Nazi Germany. They compare methods by which the deaths were inflicted and relative rights and wrongs under each regime. They do this to avoid the fact that the commonality was a deep racial and ethnic hatred that relativism can't wash away.

With the publication of Samantha Vice's paper on whiteness (called 'How do I live in this strange place?'), I thought we had reached an important point in the reconciliation process. Whereas Mngxitama argues Vice's paper to be yet another example of white, non-performing anti-racism, I thought it an avenue to performance, if taken further.

But many whites were too angry about Vice's answer to respond, let alone respond honestly, to her question: What role do whites have in post-apartheid South Africa, given the grievances committed in their name?

Vice's answer, from her individual perspective, was that whites should feel shame and withdraw from society. But fear, self-interest and – paradoxically – shame drove the closing of ranks; Vice was shouted down to avoid dealing honestly with the question.

The consequences of this lack of white engagement are too gruesome to imagine.

I am chilled by how many black South Africans allowed political forces to whip up and abuse their legitimate anger about white immutability to protect a man who has acted in a manner that dishonours African traditions and the office behind which he hides. One after the other, the ANC and its alliance partners tapped into this black anger, to the point at which some were calling for Murray's head.

I am chilled because this kind of anger and its cousin – fear – has, in the past, been used in the gruesome offences that humanity has visited upon itself. Over and above massive levels of inequality, youth unemployment, the failing education system and corruption, which are all serious too, this points to disaster ahead.

RACISM KILLED THE RAINBOW NATION

It is a Friday night with one of my aunts. We are overeating, as Jews do on Friday nights. I am settling in to being bored for at least the next hour. The conversation drifts around the table for a few minutes until one of my uncles brings his particular brand of wit and insight to the proceedings.

PAUL BERKOWITZ, MAY 2012

'I've just bought a new gun. Think I'll use it to shoot some kaffirs.' And then he giggles nervously.

This happens in 2005 or 2006. I don't remember exactly what happens next in this story. Obviously there's a change in the room's atmosphere and an awkward silence. I remember that there is no strong rebuke of this uncle. By all accounts, he is the black sheep of the family and his siblings don't act like this. Maybe he gets it from his friends. He is not told off, set straight, labelled, rebuked, chided or shamed. Certainly not by me. I sit there, silently judging him and saying nothing.

There are other times in my life when I am in the company of other white people and I hear 'kaffir', things like it, or 'darkie' racial slurs. Many times people won't even use these words, but they'll manage (blacks are stuffing up this country) politely (mentality of a black) to dehumanise. I do not remember saying or doing anything.

I am attending King David Victory Park High School. Every year there is a day to commemorate the Holocaust. We are shown movies of the death camps. Sometimes a survivor (very old) tells us personal experiences. We are told how the Nazis switched from using carbon monoxide to Zyklon

B in the gas chambers as it was more effective. We are shown actuarial records of how many Jews lived in each European country before the war.

Friends from school sometimes refer to black people in Yiddish terms that are derived from the Hebrew *shoch* or a slightly warped form of the German *shvartzer* for 'black'. Just like the Spanish *niger* equivalent, with the patina of time and context *shoch* and *shvartzer* take on a new meaning ('nigger').

The story of the Holocaust is drummed into me. I increasingly feel the message is sensational and manipulative. We Jews have been honorary whites for at least 30 years in South Africa. I become uneasy with what I see as a victim mentality that justifies a hardening of the heart. I am embarrassed by what I see as provincial-mindedness and double standards. As a teenager I have impeccable moral absolutes. By matric I have more or less lost my religion.

My nose is clean personally. I respect black people. In my romantic life I like to tell people I only discriminate against ugly girls, in a smug and self-congratulatory sort of way. My friends are diverse in their middle-classness. Things are good for me, good for the country; the racism is an aberration.

When technology connects me with mouth-breathers and trolls via internet forums and news sites, I marvel that there can still be so many morons around. For a few years I spend hundreds of hours combating their stupidity online. Maybe I express myself better when I write. Maybe I'm brave enough when there's distance and anonymity. I don't think I convince anyone.

When Jessica Leandra dos Santos uses 'kaffir' in a tweet in

early May 2012, I'm not surprised. I don't feel sorry for her when she loses her career. I make a few jokes about the incident on Twitter and I manage to piss off a few people with a detached intellectual take on the flurry of appeals to the HRC. These days I am cynical, but optimistic. Optimistic, but cynical. I accentuate the cynicism at bad times like these to elide the pain.

That week brings more hate and denigration from all sides. Two days after the racist tweet, there are now four young people (all under 40 by my calculations) hated by the general public. There are two women (one black, one white) and two men (one black, one white). I joke to a friend that we are demographically diverse in our hatred.

On 10 May, FW de Klerk is on CNN telling the world that the Nats tried their damnedest to make the homelands work. I remember how strenuously he fought for his name to be blacked out of the TRC books. I have long held that FW is an opportunist who was just the brightest politician in power at the time. With PW Botha and the HNP/CP around as competition, it was not difficult.

I have never liked him or held him in high regard. He was smart enough to know the writing was on the wall and smart enough to cover his tracks. I am reminded of Tom Lehrer's immortal words that 'political satire became obsolete when Henry Kissinger was awarded the Nobel Prize'. I guess the Nobel Prize for the Politically Pragmatic would be wordier and less of an honour, although it would be vastly more accurate in FW's case.

And then I reach my breaking point. My detached

cynicism hasn't stopped this awful, shitty week from reaching me. Like a cheese-grater abrading away, it's finally reached my endodermis. I tell friends that there should be a national campaign to strip this fool of his Nobel Prize and there is no irony or dark humour behind these words, just anger and exhaustion.

The racism is not isolated and it's not going away. It is a blood cancer, requiring constant transfusions; it is a tubercular hip that leaves the patient deformed; it is oral herpes periodically flaring and causing shame. It is scoliosis, it is brain damage, it is cataracts. It is HIV/Aids.

My dear mother tells me that this is the pain from the loss of what psychologists call 'the good thing', the object or concept that is mythologised as the repository of hope. South Africa, the rainbow nation, was the good thing, lost in the bog of apartheid denialism, shrouded in the fog of racism.

We have built on poor foundations. The TRC was a political solution that whitewashed the guilty on all sides and protected most of the generals. Some token payments were made to the families of victims. We compounded this fudging of financial restitution with the BEE framework. Whatever the merits of economic empowerment objectives (and there are many), there is no way to unscramble the omelette of proper restitution.

Let me acknowledge that the government since 1994 has made many mistakes and that in the last few years it has been mostly rubbish. This is not because it is a black government or an African government. It is because governments the world over are middling to crap. I also defy anyone to show another example of a post-independence government anywhere in the world with the inherited challenges of South Africa. Even if our government had not put a foot wrong, I believe unemployment would still be in the double digits and there would still be service delivery backlogs.

The ANC has also provided a convenient justification for anti-black racism with racially polarising rhetoric. They haven't contributed to keeping the good thing safe.

Neither has the DA, sprinkling us with fairy dust, telling us to clap our hands and believe we're all born equal. Look at the numbers, Tinker Bell: white unemployment hasn't gone above 7% through a global recession. African unemployment hasn't fallen below 25%.

Please, let us not outsource our social ills to politicians. No more model shoots at Mmusi's house, no more hotline to Zuma or Jesus.

The country took a gamble on reconciliation over justice and it failed. Maybe it's time to go the Jewish route. A week ago I would not have advocated it, but I see the logic. There is still anti-Semitism, but it's muted in most countries. The Jews got Israel. They managed to win huge reparations from Germany. And the concept of the Holocaust became so repugnant that a generation of Germans wore the hair shirt. They purged themselves, as a country, of that evil. They damn near puked out their guts but the chemotherapy worked.

South Africa is not Germany. Blacks and whites have to live side by side. The issue of financial restitution is also dead in the water. Most of the apartheid-era gains are overseas anyway. But black South Africa can still force white South Africa to respect it and treat it as human. I used to argue against this route because I thought cultivating a full-blown victim mentality was the worst thing to do. Can't be worse than the status quo, though, can it?

The book of Kohelet (Ecclesiastes to you *goyim*) says there is a time to build up and there is a time to break down. It is time to break down this rickety foundation of forgiveness. Black people have been doing the forgiving and white people have been doing the forgetting.

It is time to insist that the last few generals alive (on all sides) be brought to trial, that we have a proper court with powers of subpoena to reopen the TRC files and that the school history curriculum devotes at least a year to apartheid studies. For good measure, FW de Klerk should be stripped of his Nobel, apartheid denialism should be made an offence and all white people should be required to visit an apartheid museum.

Middle-class black people accept white people living next to them, and they are not even trying to agitate for a wealth tax on white people, but they draw the line at being treated like shit. If we have to take a sledgehammer to this sham, sooner is better than later.

SHOULD SOUTH AFRICA'S BLACK PEOPLE GET OVER APARTHEID? HELL, NO!

I've just about had it with being told to get over apartheid. It is a deeply dishonest assertion to make. And honesty is a vital step in this scary and confusing journey we've taken together as South Africans.

SIPHO HLONGWANE, JULY 2011

I was invited by YFM to attend a dinner to be held on 30 June 2011. It was part of a 'Generation Y' series of discussions that aimed to reawaken the spirit of the youth in confronting their own problems. The keynote speaker at this particular discussion was Nkosinathi Biko, son of struggle stalwart Steve Biko.

As I sat there in the ballroom at the swish Hyatt Hotel in Rosebank, surrounded by accomplished, well-read and well-spoken young South Africans, it hit me that most young South Africans weren't represented in the room. Take a South African between the ages of 18 and 24: chances are he or she is unemployed, unemployable, with little or no chance of getting ahead in life.

Yet there we were, tweeting on our Blackberrys, mocking each other's Model C accents, brushing our car keys away to make room for the Cabernet Sauvignon that was being passed around. We were talking about the problems facing young South Africans and we weren't hearing from those who are hardest hit by poverty, poor education, unemployment and crime. What right did we have to speak for them?

Why are more than 50% of young people in South Africa unemployed? Whose fault is that?

Here's an outrageous idea – it is apartheid's fault. That is the reason why apartheid was such a horrible thing. It not only disenfranchised the majority of South Africans based on their skin colour, it did its damnedest to make sure they would forever be poor and uneducated. Its effects will remain with us for decades, perhaps even centuries.

Apartheid's victims should remain angry for as long as apartheid's effects are with us.

A mistake that is always made (and will no doubt be repeated in the comments below this column) is that whenever it is said that black anger at apartheid should not subside, we mean that blacks should be angry with apartheid beneficiaries. No. Blacks should be angry at apartheid because trying to come to terms with it in any other way would blunt the eagerness of our response to it. Our solutions in 2011 will not be as vigorous or thorough as they should be. (Here's another outrageous idea – could this partly explain why our government fannies about with its responses to the poverty problem: they're not angry enough?)

If we stop being outraged by apartheid, we take the foot off the accelerator. We will begin to excuse it and finally tolerate it.

I get mad at those who benefited from apartheid when they try to prescribe to its victims how they should deal with its legacy emotionally. There have been a series of enlightening articles sparked off by a paper written by Samantha Vice, entitled 'How do I live in this strange place?' Vice attempts to grapple with the issue of being white – and therefore a beneficiary of apartheid – in the new South Africa. She concludes that regret, shame and a withdrawal from the public space is the correct response. Political commentator Eusebius McKaiser countered that assertion, saying that whites needed to engage with their apparently problematic whiteness publicly. The response to Vice and McKaiser by Pierre de Vos – 'On being white and feeling ashamed' – is also a must-read.

What astonished me most about this conversation was the attitude of some commentators. They blatantly refused to accept that being white under the previous regime meant you were a beneficiary of apartheid. While I understand why many white people would have difficulty adopting Vice's position about their skin colour, I can't fathom how any white person could deny the dynamics of apartheid.

I start to understand a little how so many white people can shamelessly say that blacks should get over apartheid. After all, if whites didn't benefit from it, what's the big deal? That's the problem, though. Don't look at me, or the sort of young, black South Africans who tweet from dinner at the Hyatt. Think of the destitute young South African in Diepsloot. Should she get over apartheid when it put her there in the first place?

And when we sit in a room to grapple with these issues, the people it really affects aren't there. White South Africans look at Sipho Hlongwane and think apartheid died in 1994. They forget that I'm an outlier.

Dear white person, whenever you're tempted to tell blacks how they should feel about apartheid, think of that poor youth in the township or rural area. See if your words sit as comfortably then as they do now.

Until the political freedom and the right to be fully recognised as human beings in their own country begins to have material, economic results, black people must remain angry. Anything else would mean selling out our children's futures. It is as simple as that.

THE MYTH OF THE COMPETENT APARTHEID GOVERNMENT

Competence in the apartheid government? Yeah, right. This is a myth that has to die, if only because it will inevitably – fairly or

> *otherwise – be read as racist. Although the differences between today's government and that of pre-democratic South Africa are profound, especially from a moral point of view, there are many policy similarities.*
>
> IVO VEGTER, AUGUST 2012

The comments on Daily Maverick are seldom as shrill and offensive as the anonymous screeds on some other South African news sites. However, a few classics of racist myth-making do slip through.

One I noticed recently was made in response to an article about the corruption and inefficiency of the ANC-led government of South Africa. It said that the apartheid government, for all its faults, was much more competent.

While the ANC doesn't get nearly enough credit for its successes, and its great merit is racial justice and democratic fairness, it is hard to dispute that on balance, it fails at many basic duties of an effective government. Criticising it for these failures does not amount to racism. However, to go further and claim that the apartheid government ran the country more competently does go beyond the pale.

It is a scurrilous lie, a myth that begs to be busted, because it strengthens the race card that so often poisons our public debate. Merely dismissing those who perpetuate this myth as racist isn't good enough, even if that is true for some – or even most – of them. The danger is that a few may be honestly convinced that the myth is true. There is an underlying misconception at work that deserves to be separated from the *ad hominem* charge of racism.

The truth is that the apartheid government was just as crony-capitalist and corrupt as the ANC government. The economic policies of the ANC and the apartheid state's National Party government are almost identical, and have a lot in common with national socialism.

National socialism, wrote Emile Lederer in 1937 in *The Annals of the American Academy of Political and Social Science*, 'is an economic system based on a totalitarian concept of the state to which everything – economics included – must conform, under coercion if necessary.'

The approach to economic recovery and development favoured by the fascists was likewise one of state corporatism.

In his great treatise *Human Action*, which appeared in German in 1940 but in English only in 1949, the economist Ludwig von Mises warned: 'All varieties of interference with the market phenomena not only fail to achieve the ends aimed at by their authors and supporters, but bring about a state of affairs which – from the point of view of their authors' and advocates' valuations – is less desirable than the previous state of affairs which they were designed to alter. If one wants to correct their manifest unsuitableness and preposterousness by supplementing the first acts of intervention with more and more of such acts, one must go farther and farther until the market economy has been entirely destroyed and socialism has been substituted for it.'

If these policies sound familiar, it is because the dynamic epitomises the economic policies of both the NP and the ANC.

Here's the difference: the apartheid government only had to keep a constituency of a few million happy. For a while, it was possible to support five million whites in state-corporatist luxury on the backs of 50 million people. Half of the white population had protected jobs in the public sector, complete with dinky little government-subsidised houses. Many of the rest would get rich working for the Broederbond-controlled big business cartel. In the face of the glaring racial injustice, what was less frequently noted was that the prosperity-generating private sector was, in fact, tiny.

By comparison, the ANC also supports a crony-capitalist elite, and also promotes public-sector employment and labour-intensive public works to keep the masses supplied with bread and circuses. The ANC's problem with exactly the same economic policy is that it has to keep all 50 million South Africans happy, with exactly the same resources at their disposal and similar constraints on the vigour of the private sector, both formal and informal.

The NP's economic policy was corrupt, inefficient and rapidly failing, even with the advantage it had in the unjust years of what they euphemistically called 'separate development'. Why would the very same policies suddenly produce a cornucopia large enough to support all South Africans?

The ANC of today is no more corrupt than the old NP. It is no less competent, no matter how different it might appear to whites who only noticed their own preferential treatment under apartheid, but who now live as equals with their fellow South Africans. It is no less efficient, either. The only difference is that the ANC's problem is ten times larger: it promised to provide a better life for all, not just some.

The claim that the apartheid economy failed is not some

sort of historical revisionism. The question was addressed in 1991 by Terence Moll of the African Studies Centre of the University of Cambridge, in a paper published in the *Journal of Southern African Studies*. 'It is often claimed,' he wrote, 'by analysts right across the political spectrum that the apartheid economy grew "exceptionally rapidly" until the early 1970s. Rarely, however, is evidence provided to back up this claim ... [The] apartheid economy did not surge forward after 1948, as did other developing economies, its comparative output and productivity growth record is poor according to a range of measures, and its share of world and developing country manufactured exports fell steadily from 1955 to 1985, suggesting that the apartheid economy grew curiously slowly and can be said to have "failed" – partly because the apartheid superstructure impeded economic development, and partly because of the constraining effects of a range of short-sighted and ill-directed state economic policies.'

In a third-year history lecture, Wallace Mills, a professor at St Mary's University in Canada, stated: 'Although the National Party government claimed to be committed to capitalism, apartheid involved massive interference in the market; there was little "free market" under apartheid.'

Mills went on to detail the failure of job reservation for whites, in that it caused high wage inflation and skills shortages that weren't being filled fast enough by the oppressed non-white population. He explained that marketing boards and other protectionist measures that favoured the white farming sector contributed noticeably to rising prices and inflation. By the early 1970s, South Africa was mired in a combination of stagnation and inflation, predating the oil shocks that caused the problem in the rest of the world, and enduring long after the rest of the world got inflation under control and rediscovered economic growth.

In *The Concise Encyclopedia of Economics,* Thomas Hazlett, professor of law and economics at George Mason University's School of Law, viewed apartheid as socialism even more clearly: 'The now-defunct apartheid system of South Africa presented a fascinating instance of interest-group competition for political advantage. In light of the extreme human rights abuses stemming from apartheid, it is remarkable that so little attention has been paid to the economic foundations of that torturous social structure. The conventional view is that apartheid was devised by affluent whites to suppress poor blacks. In fact, the system sprang from class warfare and was largely the creation of white workers struggling against both the black majority and white capitalists. Apartheid was born in the political victory of radical white trade unions over both of their rivals. In short, this cruelly oppressive economic system was socialism with a racist face.'

When evaluating the economic policy performance of the ANC government today, it is worth comparing it with the apartheid government, but not because the latter was any better. It is worth comparing because the same fallacies of state-led growth and crony protectionism hobbled the apartheid economy, too.

To address South Africa's official corruption, lack of service delivery, stubbornly high structural unemployment and persistent poverty, we ought to focus on the proper role of a government in the economy. Instead of promoting favoured interests at the expense of others and pursuing vanity projects that aggrandise socialist leaders, our government should limit itself to its most basic duty: establishing and protecting the right of every South African to life, liberty and property.

Instead of relying on the government for 'service delivery', we ought to realise that nobody other than the citizens of South Africa can, through their own labour and innovation, create the means to provide the services they need.

Nostalgia for the 'good old days', days that weren't even very good for those who were supposed to benefit to the exclusion of everyone else, recalls a false history. Perpetuating such a myth will do nothing to improve the government's economic policy performance today.

On the contrary, it is a distraction from the real danger – namely, the popular demand for service delivery – which calls upon a well-meaning government to intervene in the market in the vain hope of providing a better life for all. Like all national socialist governments before it, including the apartheid state, it will inevitably 'fail to achieve the ends aimed at by [its] authors and supporters'.

Besides, perpetuating the myth of a competent apartheid government is racist.

11

MADIBA

MADIBA, I LET YOU GO

Madiba is hanging on to life by a thread at a time when South Africa seems to have dived into the bowels of hell. Our heroes are falling one by one, our police don't protect us and our politicians are weak and vicious. And we're hanging on to Mandela as though our lives depend on it, not his – when what we should be doing is using the great gift of introspection that he gave us to pull ourselves from the wreckage.

MARELISE VAN DER MERWE, APRIL 2013

South Africa is, once again, on tenterhooks, wondering if Madiba is going to make it. Newspapers are ensuring they are on standby in case *the* news breaks – so much so, in fact, that a DStv channel aired an obituary in error earlier in the week, much to the righteous rage of the ANC. The country doesn't want to look away, in a mixture of mercenary alertness (God forbid we are the newspaper that misses it) and heart-wrenching sadness (he is our everything).

After the DStv obituary aired, ANC spokesperson Jackson Mthembu flew off the handle, and I can't say I blame him. To me, the incident symbolised everything that is wrong with this compulsive Madiba-watching. 'This was uncalled for and totally insensitive,' Mthembu fumed. 'President Mandela is alive and receiving treatment for a recurring lung infection, as reported by the Presidency.

'We join millions of South Africans and people all over the world in wishing Madiba a speedy recovery and discharge from the hospital. We also join all those who are offering their prayers for the old statesman to get better.'

DStv apologised, although it's unclear whether it will be able to bounce back from such a boo-boo.

I must say, though, that Mthembu is wrong on one count. My prayers are not for Madiba's speedy recovery. My prayers and good wishes are that he will not have a long, drawn-out death; that he will be peaceful; that he will be surrounded by loved ones and look back with satisfaction on the life he lived. He is an old, old man – one who crammed more into his active years outside of jail than most people would do in two lifetimes. He used his jail time, too, to good effect, educating himself and others, spreading messages of peace and, most importantly, working on his inner world – coming to terms with the abuse he had suffered, so that when he came out of jail, he was able to lead us all to genuine reconciliation.

What I don't want for him is speculation, the endless watching for whether he made it through the night, the long process of going into hospital, coming back out, labouring for air. There is a reason pneumonia is known as the old man's friend: it is quick and usually not painful. We should let him take that gift.

If there is anything Madiba taught us, it was gentleness and humanity – not to mention the stupendous power of forgiveness. In my own life, this struggle for forgiveness has been massive, for reasons unrelated to the political climate. But every time the anger comes, I look towards Madiba and remember what the human soul can overcome. He has had a profound influence on my life, and I am sure I am not the only one. Part of what makes him such a remarkable human being is that one would be hard-pressed to find a person who has not been influenced by him in some way. He is the person who looked through the vicious shells of apartheid leaders, prison warders, the insensitive crusts of self-righteous whites who did not want to change. He looked through them all, saw the human beings inside and reached out to them. He gave us all the mercy we so desperately wanted, and he led others to it, too.

It is time for us to show him some of that same mercy. To stop staring and instead to honour him quietly in our lives going forward, to grant him his peace. Madiba has earned his rest. He has earned the right to sit quietly with the people he loves most in this world, and drift gently into the next one. He gave us his life in service – but we don't even want to grant him his death.

Why do we keep on wanting him to get better, just so that he can go back into hospital? Selfishly, we don't want to let go of all he symbolises, so we are forcing him to cling to a life that he has, in all honesty, lived out.

Madiba withdrew himself many years ago, as we all know. He no longer wanted public life; what he wanted was a life, a good life, with his family. He was done fighting and wanted happiness. And that, ironically, seems to be the one thing that – for all the love we claim to have for him – we don't want to grant him.

If you have ever read fairy tales or epics, you will know that a typical plot manoeuvre is for the main character, at the critical stage, to lose his mentor. South Africa is at that critical stage: we are staring into the abyss, the crisis times have come, and we are about to lose our father figure. But what happens in these stories? The fighter gets up and carries on; he moves forward with the tools the mentor has given him already. And if it is a good story, he emerges victorious.

Madiba gave us many tools. He is done giving now, and we should be ready to accept that. What we can do if we want to honour and respect him is use those tools and remember those lessons. The way I see it, if we really want to show love for Madiba, we should not be praying for the antibiotics to work. It's not him who needs fixing. We should be praying for ourselves.

We should pray that we can learn to forgive like Madiba.

We should pray that we learn to sacrifice, without complaint, for the common good.

We should pray to learn that even time we believe is wasted can be used to achieve so much good – in learning, in thought leadership, in becoming greater within ourselves – while we wait for circumstances beyond our control to change.

We should pray that we learn his great gift of introspection, so that we never let the bitterness grow inside us, even when it seems nothing is changing.

We should pray that we have the courage to speak up and be honest, even if there are grim punishments in store for us when we do.

We should pray to be gentle, but not meek – to fight for what we believe in.

We should pray that even when we are good, good people, we remember that nobody likes a goody-goody: that it's still nice to dance, crack jokes and wear a loud shirt.

And most of all, we should pray to remember that all great changes begin with the person in the mirror: our own transformation leads it all.

If all South Africans strive for this, maybe, just maybe, we will be able to give Madiba the same gift that he tried to give to us: a country that works.

He has paid his debt to South Africa, and more. He has led each one of us to be a better person, to be part of a stronger South Africa. Surely it is time for us lovingly to let him go, and to move forward with the lessons he sacrificed so much to teach us.

OPEN LETTER TO
SOUTH AFRICA FROM FOREIGN MEDIA

Daily Maverick is happy to publish this letter, addressed to the citizens of an increasingly maudlin South Africa. The contents provide a fine primer on what to expect in the days of Nelson Mandela's hospitalisation, and how we should behave while those days unfold. Oh, and don't forget to floss – you're on TV!

RICHARD POPLAK, JUNE 2013

Dear South Africa,

Please get the fuck out of the way.

Wait, that probably came out wrong. Let us explain.

As you may have noticed, we're back! It's been a long while since the Oscar Pistorius bail hearing thing, and just as we were forgetting how crappy the internet connections are in Johannestoria, the Mandela story breaks.

We feel it is vital that locals understand just how big a deal this is for us. In the real world – far away from your sleepy backwater – news works on a 24-hour cycle. That single shot of a hospital with people occasionally going into and out of the front door, while a reporter describes *exactly* what is happening – at length and in detail? That's our bread and butter. It's what we do.

And you need to get out of the way while we do it.

It's nothing personal. In fact, we couldn't do this successfully without you. In many cases, our footage is made more compelling by your presence. Specifically, we are fond of small black children praying and/or singing in unison. Equally telegenic are the Aryan Übermensch blond kids also praying/singing, who help underscore the theme that Mandela united people of all races under a rainbow umbrella.

Also very important, thematically speaking, are Mandela's successors. We very much like the idea that your ex-president was one of a kind, and that despite his best efforts, the current batch of idiots prove that he was an exceptional presence, *sui generis*, and we don't have to worry about someone else like him coming along in Africa ever again. We enjoy your leaders' bumbling ways, their daft non sequiturs, the glint of their Beijing-bought Breitlings. That 'Vote ANC' truck parked outside the hospital? If that doesn't speak to moral degeneration of the first order, what does? In other words, this story would lack a tragic arc without Jacob Zuma. May he keep on keeping on.

Then there's the Mandela family. Really, where would we derive our soap-operatic undertones if it weren't for the infighting and the blinged-up brashness of that clan? We love subtly implying that a saint sired a generation of professional shoppers and no-goodniks. In our biz, we call that irony. Makes for great copy.

In fact, we love everything about the country that *doesn't* live up to Mandela's legacy. We will take every opportunity to mention how everything you do flies in the face of everything Mandela would've wanted from his people – how you're basically a nation of underachieving screw-ups. All of this is fantastic – we thank you profusely for your individual and collective contributions to this essential storyline, and urge you to keep squandering your potential.

But, as we said, we're busy.

We need to be fed, constantly and without respite, big juicy mouthfuls of new information regarding every aspect of the story. Each piece of data, no matter how seemingly trivial or inane, is to us the rich, fatty gravy that we will slather over this one essential fact: the father of your nation is gravely ill, and we're banking – literally, *banking* – on his not making it. The geraniums in the hospital planter, beating the chill of winter? Metaphor. Again – no detail too small.

Indeed, you need to brace yourselves. We're about to engage in the single greatest orgy of industrial-grade mourning porn the world has ever known. Your little country will forever be honoured as the site that made the Princess Diana thing look like a restrained wake for a loathed spinster who perished alone on a desert island. Oh man, this is going to be big.

But that's then. For the meantime, we need you to behave yourselves. We're going to be pushy, and we make no apologies for it. This is the news – and news, after all, is the concrete foundation of democracy, a principle Mandela was willing to die for long before he was dying.

Note the solemn tone of our television reports. Ken the funereal passages published in our great papers. At times, the scramble for information may seem like a pursuit entirely free of dignity. But remember that watching a sausage being made can be a grisly process.

We would like to respect the fact that you're going through a period of great sadness and protracted grieving. But we all need to be grown-ups about this.

So, we ask again, and this time with feeling:

Please. Get the fuck out of the way.

A STADIUM FULL OF TRUTHS

The booing of President Jacob Zuma at Nelson Mandela's memorial service was, like the rain, unscheduled and, for some, unwelcome. But it tells us a few important things about the Zuma presidency and Madiba's legacy.

STEPHEN GROOTES, DECEMBER 2013

There are moments in politics when something happens that really knocks you sideways. Something that no one saw coming. The set-piece event of saying goodbye to Madiba, the one occasion on which we were all supposed to come together as a nation, was such a moment. Our everyday frustrations, our usual arguments with ourselves and one another, were supposed to be put on hold. At least until the mourning period was over.

Instead, as Zuma's arrival was announced at the stadium, sections of the crowd began to boo. Then they raised their hands over their head, rolling them over each other, which started as the change or substitution sign in football, and has come to mean political change here. Then the chanting. One word. 'Mbeki'. (He, too, was in the stadium.)

Eventually the chanting died down and the service continued. Until the big screens showed Zuma again and, again, the booing started. It became a game: wait for the screen, listen to the boo. Unkindly, when the screen picked up Barack Obama, the stadium erupted in a huge cheer, and then went back to Zuma. The auditory responses from the crowd could not have been more different.

Eventually, the big screen was turned off for a while. Then, while Obama was speaking, the chant came back, but this time it said 'screen, screen'. It was just too obvious, and so it was turned back on. After Obama, Master of Ceremonies (and the ANC's Number Two to the country's Number One) Cyril Ramaphosa called for discipline. In Zulu, he said what was translated to me as, 'Don't embarrass us, we have overseas visitors here. We can deal with present-day stuff once the visitors have gone.'

Imagine if he had said that in English.

At the end of the long list of well-wishers, Zuma's speech was announced. There was some booing, but it was drowned out by cheers. Then came the praise singer and the choir, which really fired up the crowd. By the time Zuma spoke, the booers had been thoroughly defeated. Or had just left, joining the crowds who departed after Obama's speech finished.

Some people will claim that this is a turning point, that what happened at the FNB Stadium on 10 December 2013 marked a major change in our politics. As *City Press* editor Ferial Haffajee tweeted, it seemed that people had come to say goodbye to two presidents, not one.

Certainly, it did mark some sort of turning point in our public discourse, in the language that we use in our politics. To be blunt, if people are prepared to show their frustration with Zuma, during the funeral of Nelson Mandela, imagine if it had been a mere sporting event.

So, the gloves are off. Respect for the Presidency will no longer protect Zuma from this kind of treatment. For someone who used to be met with rapturous ululation wherever he went, this is a huge change. Expect him to spend more time speaking in KZN than anywhere else in the future.

His political handlers are also going to have to plan for this kind of eventuality in the future, and particularly during the election campaign. That Zuma has enemies is no secret. That they have the daring to disrupt Madiba's funeral is something new. And if they feel that strongly, then they may well decide to do the same thing on the campaign trail, even if it does hurt the ANC in some way. Their hatred of Zuma could well outweigh their love for the ANC.

It's important at this point to look at who was doing the booing. This was a long way from the rural poor. And it certainly wasn't the urban white minority. Rather, it was the middle-class black urban resident. The person who has the time, money and resources to take a day off and get to the stadium. If you think I'm describing someone who looks an awful lot like the type of person who could have voted for COPE in 2009, you're absolutely right. The point is, if this had been in KZN or the Eastern Cape, this probably wouldn't have happened.

That said, another important dynamic is playing out here.

One of the many defences that Zuma uses, apart from the usual conspiracy crap, is an appeal to racial solidarity. It's never explicit, but the subtext is often there. A message that if you are not for us ('us' being the ANC and Zuma, as one identity), then you are against us, and against yourself, because you are black.

What happened at the memorial service was a complete rejection of that appeal to racial solidarity. There was no way that sort of argument would have worked on the people booing Zuma. They rejected him – what he stands for and how he behaves – and no spin in the world would have changed their minds.

One of the other questions that arose from this was an inevitable one in ANC politics. Was this planned? Was it a co-ordinated attack on the dignity of the president during the most high-profile (and highly exposed) moment of his career, just when the international stakes are at their highest? And, if so, by whom?

The fact that the service was held in Gauteng could immediately point a finger of suspicion at the Gauteng ANC. They are no fans of Zuma. They backed Kgalema Motlanthe at Mangaung, and have been strong enough to make sure that none of their people has been purged by Zuma since that conference. They may have lost the fight, but the war continues. Of course, there's no proof that it was co-ordinated, or that it was the Gauteng ANC.

But, if I were Zuma, it might be worthwhile to find a way to make the claim publicly. It would put the pressure back on them, to explain why they used this funeral to make this particular political point. And even if it wasn't them, it would still put an enemy under pressure.

In the end, this sort of behaviour diminished the memorial service of Nelson Mandela. I will always be sad about that. No doubt it will be argued that as a democrat, he may not have minded too much. It still diminished the occasion. And that diminishes all of us as South Africans.

Just like Jacob Zuma sometimes does, as our president.

FOG DONKEY: THE ONLY
HONEST MAN IN A STADIUM OF FOOLS

The Memorial Signer – the man standing alongside speakers at Nelson Mandela's memorial service at Johannesburg's FNB Stadium – was called out as a fake, but was, apparently, suffering

> *from a 'schizophrenia attack' brought on by happiness. Which begs the question: who, or what, at FNB Stadium on that fated day was real?*
> RICHARD POPLAK, DECEMBER 2013

'Dollhouse. Petrol. Road sign. Interested nail. Icon. Much cardboard. Weather. Tile. Tiles. Sheet. Poptart.

'POPTART!'

I knew that it would not be long before the industrial mourning machine delivered its ruling metaphor, its Neo, its Christ-figure. It took no time at all before we tumbled down the Cartesian rabbit hole, before we found ourselves in a netherworld governed by topsy-turvy nonsense verse, in which the man flapping his hands meaninglessly was the only man making any sense at all.

His name is Thamsanqa Jantjie. But, for one glorious day, he was beyond the banality of names.

Let's back up a moment. As thousands of mourners filed into the FNB Stadium, they had a very simple role to play – that of background colour. As they arrived, the media asked them the usual groaners – 'Why are you here? What did Madiba mean to you? How far did you travel to get to the stadium?' – and they gave their stock answers – 'Because I loved Madiba. He was bigger than Jesus. I walked 12 000 km from Paris over the past three days.' These paradoxically smiling, tear-stained faces were meant to provide the backdrop to the proceedings, singing happy songs, singing sad songs, and offering doses of curative African 'spirit' for television viewers in Milwaukee and Swansea and Perth.

They had their shot, these good people, and they blew it.

'Many files.'

'Wiper blade. Banana cheese.'

Arriving next were our local leaders, who roared over in their motorcades with blue lights flashing and sirens bleating: the signs and signifiers of power in this newly gilded age. The media asked them the usual groaners – 'Why are you here? What did Madiba mean to you? How far did you travel to get to the stadium?' – and they gave their stock answers – 'Because I loved Madiba. He was bigger than Jesus. I flew in a gold-plated jet from Nkandla to Waterkloof.'

To say that this cohort didn't quite rise to the occasion would be, in fairness, an untruth, because I'm not sure what occasion they imagined they were rising to. Was this a memorial, a campaign stop, a meet-'n-greet? Their words were the carefully measured pabulum served to a sick baby, so tasteless and easily digestible that they steamed through the intellect's digestive tract to emerge as puffs of noisome air, drifting away with the rain.

They had their shot, these good people, and they blew it.

'Ducting volume. Me.'

[redacted]

Then we had the guests from afar, the super-celebs, the high-wattage smilers. They were here to speak above and beyond the assembled crowd, to measure out small political gestures, to take photographs with the features on their smartphones, to emit enormous words into a cavernous stadium and buff their brands before Clio, History's muse, who was almost certainly in the stands taking notes. Their words were boxes and boxes of Cocoa Puffs, served up on the silver of a Versailles dinner set, sugared cereal masquerading as haute cuisine.

The Obamatory was pitched high – so high, in fact, that it laid everything around it to waste, like a Hollywood tent-pole opening a Rwandan film school year-end screening. But what did it all mean? What did it amount to?

They had their shot, these good people, and they blew it.

'Mango tank. Sad chair talks.'

'Jam angel. Fisheries.'

'Shiny duck. Shiny ducks.'

And so it was left to one man to make sense of it all. His job, as I understand it, was to interpret the words on stage for those who hear darkness. It is an ingenious process – by an agreed-upon code, spoken sounds are transformed into gestures which, in turn, become language. The language is a gesture itself: by providing the deaf with a signer, we are saying that everyone must be allowed to participate – that everyone, regardless of disability, is part of the polity.

The problem was simple: the signer did not know the agreed-upon codes. Or rather, the problem is complicated: the signer could not deliver the agreed-upon codes. The signer strode onto stage, stood alongside the most important people in the world, and made gestures that had no meaning to the hard of hearing – that had no meaning to *anyone*, it turns out, except perhaps the signer himself.

He had his chance, this beautiful man, and he absolutely fucking nailed it.

'Biltong!'

The deaf are offended, but they should count themselves among the very lucky few – they were the only people being spoken to like adults, like citizens, like *humans*. The nonsense that travelled through Thamsanqa Jantjie's hands, conjuring images of Fog Donkeys and Mango Tanks and Moontrumpets and Maximum Coffee Extinguishers, was the best possible language available to describe what has happened to us, what is happening to us, what will happen to us. The deaf saw, through his hands, the only possible truth – an upside-down gobbledygook of streaming rubbish, a meaningless void of nothingness, a sales pitch selling nothing but the pitch itself.

We will leave aside, for the moment, the wisdom in placing a schizophrenic alongside the great men and women who spoke for us – a schizophrenic who, if he is to believed, was having a full-blown attack when their empty words travelled into his bustling mind. I believe that the Memorial Signer – not Jantjie himself, but the avatar he represented in that moment – will emerge as the only figure in the stadium that Clio shall reward with historical standing. He is the man of our age, a truthsayer, a sage, a Fog Donkey. The *only* way to understand all this is through the mind of a schizophrenic. Alternatively, can anyone of us describe the current malaise better than the Twitter handle attributed to him, which noted 'Sausage blubber pencil/Prison/Magic lion everywhere'?

The Memorial Signer holds the only flashlight in the midnight dark of the rabbit hole. Follow him, my friends, and no other. For he leads us to the only truth worth hearing: there are no truths at all worth hearing.

MY OLD
SOUTH AFRICAN FLAG

> *I have a secret. Since 1994, I have kept, hidden in the back of my closet, a tattered old orange, white and blue South African flag. This is the story of that flag. It is also the story of my life. And a tribute to Nelson Mandela.*
>
> IVO VEGTER, DECEMBER 2013

By the time you read this, more than 100 hours would have passed since the death of Nelson Mandela. He was the icon of the liberation struggle in South Africa, a road that was long and bloody, but righteous and victorious.

Better journalists than I am have written obituaries and analyses; more of them than anyone could possibly read. They've had years to prepare the perfect front page, the perfect cover tribute, the perfect editorial, the perfect eulogy. I do not propose to try to best them, or even add to them.

I do not wish to add to the platitudes and superlatives, all of which the real Mandela exceeds. I will not contribute to the beatification of a man who was fallible and human beneath the mask of miracle-worker.

Instead, I will tell a personal story. It is a short story, but to understand it, you need to know me, and what Nelson Mandela meant to me. That is a long story. Call this a long-form anecdote.

I want to tell you the curious history of the skeleton in my closet. I own a genuine flag of the old South Africa, made of 100% polyester, with faded orange, white and blue bars, and a torn bottom-right corner.

'Skeleton' is a good word for it, not only because it is a long-held secret, but also because it represents death.

It represents the death I felt in my marrow when I had a rare opportunity, while Mandela was president, to visit Liliesleaf Farm and Vlakplaas. They were grim time capsules, as yet untouched by renovations, and closed to the public except by special arrangement. They were the sites where security police arrested, tortured and murdered people on suspicion of fighting for freedom. They were haunted by the shades of evildoers still living, like Eugene de Kock, and by the ghosts of their victims, like Griffiths Mxenge.

It represents the death I witnessed through the lenses of Ken Oosterbroek, Kevin Carter, João Silva and Greg Marinovich.

It represents the death that resounded in the written words of reporters I greatly admired, like Allister Sparks, Max du Preez, Joe Tloloe, David Beresford, Christelle Terreblanche, Ivor Powell, Thami Mazwai and Anton Harber.

I have always hated that flag.

As a child, I went to an Afrikaans school. I was ordered to treat this flag with reverence. I learned the meaning of its colours, and of the small flags it contains. I was taught to stand at attention before it, with my thumbs pointing down the seams of my grey school trousers.

I was instructed how to raise it, how to salute it, how to strike it, how to fold it and how to carry it. I was warned that if I ever let it touch the ground, it would be desecrated, and the wrath of the headmaster, as the duly authorised representative of Prime Minister John Vorster and God, would descend upon me, and there would be great weeping and gnashing of teeth.

I hated that flag.

My parents were immigrants who knew little about South Africa's history when they brought me here in 1976. Aged only four, I was too young to argue.

They never had much interest in politics. With hindsight, they would have chosen differently, but at the time, their life savings had been invested in the move. They tried to make the best of what they found in South Africa, without either actively making themselves guilty of complicity, or drawing unwanted attention by causing trouble in a country that was not their own.

They didn't make waves, but they were good Christians who taught me liberal virtues that clashed with what I was being taught at school.

I was to treat all people with kindness, decency and respect. If it was Afrikaans custom to address my seniors as *'oom'* and *'tannie'*, however odd that sounded to us, I would do the same for the help. We called her '*Tannie* Victoria'.

That it was also Afrikaans custom to call her '*kaffermeid*' seemed inconsistent to me, but if we discussed it, I can't recall. Perhaps how other people behaved towards her was just not a matter for my conscience. I did not reconcile these questions for myself until many years later.

Once, in primary school, we were asked which party our parents would vote for. The class was mostly divided between the ruling National Party and the right-wing opposition Conservative Party. I did not really know what the difference was. When my turn came, I said that my parents weren't allowed to vote, but if they could, they would vote for the

Progressive Federal Party. I did not know who Helen Suzman was, or that the PFP was the only party in South Africa's parliament that openly opposed apartheid. I was denounced by the teacher, to the jeers of my classmates, as a '*kafferboetie*' (little kaffir brother).

I hated that flag.

For outstanding performance in Afrikaans and history, I won a prize. I was proud of it, because Afrikaans was not my home language. The prize was sponsored by the Junior Rapportryerskorps (the Junior Despatch Rider Corps), which was the youth wing of the secretive, quasi-masonic and powerful Afrikaner Broederbond. It was a book about the Israeli offensive against Syria in the Golan Heights during the Six-Day War. To me, it was just an adventure story. I was ten years old.

I wore glasses. I sucked at sport. I read biographies of the classical composers, for heaven's sake. To teachers, I was a precocious pain in the neck. To my peers, I was just a nerd, and a weakling at that.

I was also an immigrant. Even my friends called me '*kaaskop*' (cheese-head). It was as unremarkable to me as calling the English '*rooinek*' (redneck) or '*soutpiel*' (a rather more crude term), or calling black people '*houtkop*' (blockhead) or 'kaffir' (which surely needs no explanation).

Who was I, a foreigner, to question a culture I did not like? My objective as a child was just to fit in. To be accepted. I joined in their jingoistic jeering, and never mentioned the PFP again.

But I never did fit in. I hated that flag.

Our history curriculum always started with the arrival of

Jan van Riebeeck in 1652. I was Dutch, so that we were important to South Africa once was a source of pride. The rest of the lessons were limited to wars featuring brave Afrikaners defending themselves against cruel and inhuman Englishmen, or wars featuring pious Afrikaners trying to civilise an array of godless and inhuman black tribes, and failing that, to drive them off or shoot them. Always in self-defence, of course.

At face value, those lessons explained why Afrikaners had to stand together against the threat of outsiders. How was an immigrant kid to know this narrative was both selective and biased? I was in love with a singer, Sonja Herholdt, and if this story was good enough for her, it was good enough for me.

My father's youngest sister was a student in Holland, and wrote a sociology thesis on multiracial churches in South Africa. She visited in 1983, on a research trip. By then, I was 12, and multiracial churches struck me as a sufficiently curious phenomenon to be studying.

My parents were Protestants, and our Afrikaans church wasn't for black people, so we took her to Catholic and Anglican churches. The home-made ginger beer after the service at Regina Mundi in Soweto burnt my throat. I did not know it was an important church. The stones of St Mary's Cathedral in Johannesburg were old and cold. I did not know that Desmond Tutu was its dean. I did not know who Desmond Tutu was.

When I went to high school in 1984, some of us were assigned to sweep the classrooms for bombs before school started. We had to be on our guard. *Paraat*, they called it. Always ready. It was drummed into us.

The Church Street bombing only a year earlier proved that blacks were terrorists who were out to kill women and children. That the two bombers accidentally blew themselves up proved how stupid kaffirs were. Weren't we proud to be white, God-fearing Afrikaners? Wasn't that worth defending? I checked under desks with nervous trepidation about what I might find, and mortal fear of missing something.

On Fridays, we were made to come to school in army browns and, after school, we would learn to drill. Our instructors were teachers, but they had real army ranks. The highest-ranked was a lieutenant. Even the other teachers saluted him.

Sometimes, we got to shoot .22 rifles. My father said it reminded him of the Hitlerjügend. I didn't understand. Those history lessons, which I dropped as soon as I could, never did cover World War Two. I'm not even sure I connected 'Hitlerjügend' to Nazis. If I did, they were just outlandish baddies in films, like the mafia, or Red Indians, or Martians.

The aunt who had visited us a few years earlier mailed us some ANC brochures and information about the Dutch anti-apartheid movement. I worked out later that it must have been 1987, on the occasion the 75th anniversary of the founding of the ANC. At the time, my father placed an expensive telephone call overseas to explain just what would happen if we were found to be in possession of subversive literature.

We were not revolutionaries. We were not part of the struggle. South Africa was a dangerous, confusing country that we only half-understood. We wanted no trouble. We rarely raised our heads above the parapets, and never boldly or for long.

At the age of 15 years and six months, I received South African citizenship. I didn't ask for it, but they couldn't call me up to the army at 16 otherwise. Officially, I had to fit in. Going to the army was my duty. It would make a man of me. If I didn't like it, I should go back to where I came from. Corporal punishment was still frequently applied with sadistic pleasure, so I didn't dare say that this was exactly what I wanted to do. I hated that flag.

The indoctrination was effective in that while I knew enough to realise I did not want to live in South Africa, I did not know enough to explain why. I felt I was just kicking against a culture that rejected me, and in which I never felt at home. Between God, PW Botha, the *dominee* (pastor), the cadet drill sergeant and the headmaster, there was a great deal of authority to fuel youthful rebellion.

At school, I was into mathematics, computers and science. I neither liked nor understood what passed for history at school. Politics and sociology was something other people studied once they grew up. The only copy of the anti-apartheid newspaper, the *Rand Daily Mail*, I had ever seen was its last edition in 1985.

It never occurred to me to call what I hated 'nationalism', or 'authoritarianism', or 'racism'. I didn't think to describe South Africa as a 'police state', in which a 'black majority' existed whose members were 'oppressed' as 'second-class citizens'.

I didn't even know the words I'd need to use to explain why was I unhappy in this country. All I knew was that as soon as I grew up, I wanted to leave. I hated that flag.

None of this is an excuse, or an abdication of responsibility.

Although it was less common among Afrikaners than among English liberals, some of my school friends tell me they did rebel against apartheid. If they could understand it, why didn't I?

Perhaps it was my need to fit in. Perhaps it was a sense of caution instilled in me by immigrant parents who had learned to keep their liberal values to themselves. Perhaps the craven knowledge that I could escape back to the Netherlands played a role. It shames me now that I wasn't as smart as I thought when I was young.

I passed matric at the top of my school, although admittedly in a weak year, and after my main rival had left to complete his matric at a classy private school. I was admitted to university, where I signed up for computer science and applied mathematics.

And there they were: everyone PW Botha had warned us against. *Die swart gevaar* (the black threat). *Die rooi komplot* (the communist plot). *Die goddelose sondaars* (the godless sinners). They were all real. It was glorious. And they all hated that flag!

The year was 1989. It was not a good time to sound like a Boer. In a matter of months, I got rid of my heavy Afrikaans accent, and constructed myself a new one. To this day, people don't know where in England I'm from.

As early as orientation week, I met the riot squad, whom we called 'the pigs'. We got tear-gassed for singing *Nkosi Sikelel' iAfrika* at them. I didn't yet know all the words, but in defence of the baton-wielding thugs, we did sing it with vicious intent.

I found that I could muster deep reserves of anger. Not anger at being oppressed, of course, but anger at being betrayed. My country, my government, my church and my school had all lied to me. They had pretended that South Africa was civilised. That we were the good guys, with God on our side. They tried to turn me into a white supremacist who wouldn't baulk at murder, and they had almost succeeded.

I learned an astonishing amount of politics and philosophy in a very short time. Like a pinball I bounced about, talking to anyone and learning from everyone. Except the communists. I discovered to my dismay that you can't argue with hardline communists, because they're even more dogmatic than Afrikaner nationalists. If I can't argue with you, we can't hang out.

I never knew the United Democratic Front existed, but discovered they'd been there all along, risking their lives for freedom and human rights while PW Botha was wagging his finger at us. I discovered that white anti-apartheid activists existed, in the Black Sash and the National Union of South African Students. That same year, the Mass Democratic Movement was formed, uniting the union federation Cosatu, the UDF and other organisations into a single-minded defiance campaign to break the back of apartheid.

I could not have hoped for a better time and place to imbibe politics, and discover what it was that I had hated so much.

I had a great deal to learn, and I didn't learn quickly enough to consider refusing to vote in the whites-only election of September 1989 seriously. Having turned 18 six months earlier, I reasoned that having a vote was a rare privilege, and that the responsible way to use it if I wanted an end to apartheid was not to abstain, but to vote for the Democratic Party.

That choice was vindicated, or at least made moot, on 2 February 1990. I was walking across Eastwood Street in Turffontein, when a friend called me back to listen to the car radio. The African National Congress, the South African Communist Party, Cosatu and a host of other organisations had been unbanned. I was elated. I re-crossed that street as if walking on clouds. Momentous change was in the air and I, as a raw 18-year-old, felt part of history in the making.

Nine days later, after 27 heroic years in prison, the mythical struggle hero whom I knew only from stickers and t-shirts and protest songs walked onto our television screens. Nelson Mandela was free.

He immediately made a great impression. He laid the remainder of his life at our feet. He said that a majority, both black and white, recognised that apartheid has no future. He said that the defiance campaign and the armed struggle would continue, until the conditions for a negotiated settlement had been created. He called upon whites to join the freedom movement, and evoked a vision of a free, democratic and peaceful South Africa on the horizon.

I admired the conciliatory messages he so pointedly added to his appeals to the struggle base.

He repeated his memorable words at the Rivonia Trial in 1964: 'I have fought against white domination and I have fought against black domination. I have cherished the ideal of a democratic and free society in which all persons live together in harmony and with equal opportunities. It is an ideal which

I hope to live for and to achieve. But if needs be, it is an ideal for which I am prepared to die.'

His was a vision I accepted, not only with my head but with my heart. I marched often, and learned to toyi-toyi, as badly as only white people can. But when the defiant harmonies of struggle songs echoed *a capella* from a full-throated crowd, all self-consciousness was sublimated in a sense of justice and unity.

To be fair, I also partied; I was a student, after all. The Woodstock era, with its strong anti-establishment and anti-war message, was appealing for the many parallels to the South African struggle I was witnessing. I was a political searcher rather than a fanatical activist. I was an enthusiastic amateur, not a hardened political operative. The lines between rebellion against the establishment and protest against apartheid were fuzzy. But things were moving in the right direction and, for the first time, I felt like I fit in.

I met icons of the struggle, like Joe Slovo and Thabo Mbeki, while working at the campus radio station. They were kind, intelligent and charismatic.

We began to broadcast without a licence, having decided that we no longer accepted the authority of the government to grant us official permission to speak. We were shut down a month later, but we had made our point.

We played African jazz, revolutionary reggae, hardcore punk, hippie-era rock and a fresh wave of home-grown protest songs in all languages, Afrikaans included. The ideal of non-racialism and reconciliation was very much alive on campus, and in the bars and clubs of Hillbrow, Newtown and

Yeoville. As whiteys, appropriating that sentiment for our own was grandiose and sanctimonious, but it was visceral. We didn't want to spoil it by over-analysing it.

I joined the End Conscription Campaign, because although military service had been reduced to one year in 1989, those call-ups were still coming. By now I knew that I would be expected to defend an unjust regime and shoot people I considered compatriots. I also knew that objectors like David Bruce and Saul Batzofin were still in prison for refusing to serve.

In 1992, I failed to apply for academic deferment, and I ignored my call-up. I got a letter warning me that next time, they'd arrest me. I figured that if the military police weren't already knocking on my parents' door, they'd never do it. I got another call-up later that year, and wrote a letter to Magnus Malan, the hated Minister of Defence: 'Dear Magnus, Thank you for your kind invitation to an all-expenses paid trip to Upington. Unfortunately, I have prior arrangements. Yours, Ivo Vegter.'

I never heard from them again. It wasn't a grand gesture. I wasn't risking my life. My liberty was probably not at great risk, because I sure wasn't the only one no longer reporting for military service. But it felt good to register this formal act of defiance, two years before conscription was finally abolished in 1994.

It was as if I was getting to know my country for the first time during those tumultuous years of South Africa's transition. Everything I'd been taught I assumed to be false, and I adopted the *Vrye Weekblad* and *Weekly Mail* as my textbooks.

These were the publications that exposed the scandals, the plots, the assassinations, and the murders. They were guiding readers through the complexities of electoral systems, human rights and constitutional principles.

I finally learned why it made perfect political sense for the Broederbond to give a young child a book about the Six-Day War if he were to grow up in a country that had few true friends, and saw itself as a white David fighting for its survival against a black Goliath, supported by the red Soviets.

I realised that the anti-British propaganda that was drummed into us at school not only explained Afrikaner nationalism, but rather more than they probably wished to admit. As the acts of an abuser can often be traced back to his or her own abuse as a child, the history taught by the apartheid state told an all-too-candid tale of a nation humiliated by the British. Once they threw off the shackles, they picked up the tools of their former masters and became even more cruel oppressors themselves.

I read political essays and political philosophy, and began to realise that the end of apartheid did not merely signal a victorious campaign of armed resistance, or an effective campaign of economic sanctions, or a change of heart by the white oppressors. I started thinking of the fall of the Berlin Wall in 1989 as the trigger. Before the end of the Cold War, South Africa was a proxy in the global standoff between the West and the East. That explained the link that was always drawn between *die swart gevaar* and *die rooi komplot*. The apartheid government's black threat propaganda, used to maintain the delusion of white supremacy at home, was anathema abroad.

Not so a communist plot, which was a legitimate danger that kept Western powers, however grudgingly and reluctantly, on South Africa's side. When the Cold War ended, so did the strategic reason to prop up the whites-only regime for the sake of stability. On its own, it could no longer sustain itself in the face of armed struggle, sanctions, ungovernability campaigns and open defiance.

I followed the negotiations obsessively. Several times, as the talks deadlocked, I feared a civil war. Every time, political divisions were bridged, and catastrophe was averted. My faith in humanity grew.

Many times, violence with complex causes erupted, causing heart-wrenching pain and blood-boiling anger, no matter who stoked it. Every time, the flames of hatred were doused, and war was averted. My faith in humanity grew.

The March 1992 referendum was a nervous time. It was the last time whites would go to the ballot box alone, with the power to call an end to the reform process that had begun on that summer's day in February 1990. I was terrified that Mandela's hope that whites would join the freedom movement would be dashed. It wasn't. The turnout was huge, and more than two-thirds of whites voted to end apartheid. My faith in humanity grew.

I was especially afraid after Chris Hani was assassinated. Even if you were a right-winger opposed to a negotiated settlement, it seemed, to me, stupid to try to provoke the angry, disaffected youth into a genocidal bloodbath by killing one of the leaders they respected most.

I was on my way to his memorial service in 1993, only to

meet Archbishop Tutu walking in the other direction. In a nearby square, anger had erupted into violence. I followed. Things were about to get ugly and, being white, I was allowed to cross the police line.

Minutes later, they opened fire on the crowd. I helped a man wounded by birdshot, and he spat in my face. I had hoped my long hair would distinguish me from the pigs who had shot him, and from the lunatic who had shot Hani, but I couldn't blame him.

Later that day, Tutu mustered reserves of moral authority that gave the lie to his diminutive stature and squeaky voice, to calm the angry crowd. And my faith in humanity grew.

On New Year's Eve of that year, a group of friends and I celebrated the death of apartheid. We had decorated a friend's parents' house with editorial cartoons photocopied from the newspapers, documenting all the heroes and villains of the transition years. They'd been splendid years for cartoonists, and we had a nostalgic time constructing our collage.

At midnight, we sang *Nkosi Sikelel' iAfrica*, which must have surprised the neighbours in these posh northern suburbs. But we knew the new year would bring the long-awaited New South Africa. We couldn't wait.

With a swelling heart I, and millions of South Africans, watched an unprecedented three-day election begin on 27 April 1994. We saw voters of all races smile in long, snaking queues that needed no barriers. We watched old people vote for the first time. White and black shared camp chairs and picnic lunches. We witnessed the infinite patience and good humour of a rainbow nation that had struggled for freedom, sacrificed for peace and thirsted for this moment. When I drew my cross next to the face of Nelson Mandela, it felt like the consummation of a sacrament.

Two weeks later, I stood on the lawns of the Union Buildings, watching Nelson Mandela take the oath of office. I felt at one with the multitude as we sang *Nkosi Sikelel' iAfrika*. There was no venom left in the singing. We did not get tear-gassed for it. I watched the Air Force fly over, painting the sky in the colours of the new South African flag and, for the first time, that Air Force protected us all. We were one. Free at last!

I had learned many things during South Africa's transition years, but that was the day on which I realised I didn't hate South Africa. I loved it, deeply. I knew, on that day, that I could never leave. Mandela had made South Africa my home.

When I heard that Nelson Mandela had passed away, I cried, remembering my tears of joy on that day. I grieved, knowing that Madiba, more than any other influence, defined my adult life. He may have meant even more to millions of other South Africans, but his was a heart big enough to share with the country, and the world.

I paid no heed to those who tried to deny people the right to eulogise him because of their anti-ANC positions of the past. I paid no heed to those who said Mandela supped with communists, or endorsed an armed struggle in which innocent people were killed.

If Mandela taught us anything, it is that we must acknowledge faults and remedy failures, but we cannot let guilt or grievance, however justified, waylay us on our quest to forge a peaceful, prosperous country from the shattered fragments of our divergent pasts.

I have kept many mementoes of that period. Among the most treasured are a 1994 election ballot paper, and near-complete sets of back-issues of my student texts: the *Weekly Mail* and *Vrye Weekblad*.

But this is about the skeleton in that closet of mementoes: the old South African flag I own.

A few months after Mandela's inauguration, I was rummaging for second-hand furniture at a pawnshop in Ontdekkers Road. I bought a rickety coffee table that I still have, and a few other bits and pieces. I needed to get them home, but I had no trailer or roof rack. The pawnbroker went inside and returned with a tatty old South African flag to protect my car's roof when we tied the furniture to it.

It was startlingly absurd. That flag, which I had once been taught to revere above all else, was being given away by a pawnbroker. That flag, which must never touch the ground, was reduced to packing material.

That this flag no longer held any value could not have been demonstrated more eloquently. Even to burn it would have given it back some of its significance, because you cannot desecrate something that means nothing.

I realise that the flag holds different memories for different people, which is why I have never taken it out since that day. But for me, it signifies the cathartic private realisation that apartheid had truly been consigned to the dustbin of history. I look on that flag as I imagine Germans might look upon pieces of the Berlin Wall: not as an offensive celebration of the past, or a defiant statement about the present, but as reminders of an evil empire that holds no terrors any more.

All of my subsequent political thought has its roots in those transition years, when both communism and apartheid – each for its own reasons, but one ironically dependent on the other – collapsed.

It would take many more years of reading history and economics for it all to crystallise into a coherent world view that I was prepared to debate openly in opinion columns. However, it was Mandela's ability to negotiate with his enemies that taught me to always focus on the substance of an argument, rather than a caricature of the speaker.

Mandela drank tea with Betsie Verwoerd, the widow of the architect of apartheid, HF Verwoerd, in the remote Afrikaner enclave of Orania. Who are we to dismiss our fellow South Africans simply for who they are, or to denounce all they say simply because we don't share their ideology?

If we do that, then everyone who has ever disagreed with Mandela – about communism, foreign policy, the armed struggle, voting age, or HIV/Aids – would also have to reject the manifest greatness of his ability to lead a divided country to peace, reconciliation, justice and freedom.

Rejecting both communist totalitarianism and racist discrimination remained fundamental principles for me. Mandela taught us that a just society is based on certain fundamental principles, and that those principles are non-negotiable. But he also showed that human dignity demanded the inclusion and consideration of all, from the powerful rich to the outcast poor.

In those formative years, Nelson Mandela taught me that what I hated wasn't the country, but its government. Never again have I confused the two.

He restored my faith in humanity. He reduced what I hated to nothing, and taught me to love freedom. He demonstrated that free people, together, can achieve miracles.

I no longer hate that flag, because it is no longer worth hating. Its meaning is that it no longer has meaning.

That is why I thank Nelson Mandela. Rest now, Madiba. The walk has been long, and you carried so many people. I was just one of them.

LIST OF CONTRIBUTORS

BRANKO BRKIC

Branko is the founder and editor of Daily Maverick. In his 30 years in publishing, he has been the editor of business, politics, technology and wildlife magazines. He has also published fiction and non-fiction books, most of them in Serbian. Although he has never pretended to be a reporter, his wide knowledge of politics (especially in America), combined with his experiences in a disintegrating Yugoslavia, gives him an unusual outlook on events in South Africa.

GREG MARINOVICH

Greg is a Pulitzer Prize-winning photographer and co-author of *The Bang-Bang Club*. He has spent 25 years as a conflict, documentary and news photographer around the globe. In 2009 he was the recipient of the Nat Nakasa Award for courageous journalism, and is a current Nieman Fellow. His photographs and articles have appeared in top international publications such as *Time*, *Newsweek*, *The New York Times*, *The Washington Post*, *The Wall Street Journal* and *The Guardian*, among others.

GREG NICOLSON

Greg left his hometown of Melbourne to move to Johannesburg, beset by fears that Australia was going to the dogs. With a camera and a Mac in his bag, he ventures out to cover power and politics, the lives of those included and those excluded. He can sometimes be found at the tavern, searching for a good story or drowning a bad one.

IVO VEGTER

Ivo is a columnist and the author of *Extreme Environment*, a book on environmental exaggeration and how it harms emerging economies. He grew up in the deep south of Johannesburg, and learned his politics reading the *Weekly Mail* and *Vrye Weekblad* at Wits University during the early years of the country's transition to democracy. Ivo approaches issues from the perspective of individual liberty and free markets. He recently left the city for the peacefulness of living in Knysna, where he continues to write about everything under the sun. He is always right.

J BROOKS SPECTOR

Brooks settled in Johannesburg after a career as a US diplomat in Africa and East Asia. He has taught at the University of the Witwatersrand, been a consultant for an international NGO, run a theatre and been a commentator for South African and international print, broadcast and online media, in addition to writing for Daily Maverick from day one. He learned everything he needed to know about politics from *Casablanca*. He might be cynical about some things, but a late Beethoven string quartet, John Coltrane's music and a dish of Pad Thai will bring him close to tears.

JAY NAIDOO

Jay is the founding general secretary of Cosatu and a former minister in the Mandela government. He is currently chair of GAIN, a global foundation fighting malnutrition. Not shy of an opinion or outspoken word, Jay sits the on the board of numerous other global civil society foundations and is busy establishing a leadership school and community centre in the rural Free State.

KALIM RAJAB

Kalim Rajab is a director of the New National Assurance Company, South Africa's oldest black insurance company. He has worked in the diamond industry and was educated at UCT and Oxford. He writes in his personal capacity about South Africa, current events, film appreciation and culture.

KEVIN BLOOM

Kevin has written for a wide array of South African and international publications, including *Granta*, *The Times* and *The Guardian*. His first book, *Ways of Staying*, won the 2010 South African Literary Award for literary journalism, and was shortlisted for the Alan Paton Award. Kevin is currently an Honorary Writing Fellow at the University of Iowa and is working with Richard Poplak on a book about the changing Africa.

MANDY DE WAAL

Mandy de Waal reports on technology, corruption, science, the media and whatever else she finds interesting. She loves small stories and human narratives, and dislikes persistent evangelists, bad poetry and the insane logic that currently passes for political rhetoric. Back in journalism after spending time in the corridors of corporate greed, De Waal has written for *Mail & Guardian*, *Noseweek*, *City Press*, *Rapport*, *Moneyweb*, *Brandchannel* (New York) and a number of other good titles.

MANDY WIENER

Mandy is a senior reporter at Eyewitness News and the author of the blockbuster *Killing Kebble – An Underworld Exposed* as well as *My Second Initiation*, co-written with Vusi Pikoli. She was also the series editor of *The Youngsters*.

MARELISE VAN DER MERWE

Marelise van der Merwe writes a lot about gender, which has led people to ask whether she is perhaps a lesbian or, worse, a feminist (at the very least, an oddball with a unibrow). By day she is production editor at Daily Maverick, and by night she is also production editor at Daily Maverick. If you spot a spelling error on the site, it is her fault. When she's not obsessing over comma placement, she wires her heart to Facebook, falls asleep at parties, or makes a mean butternut soup.

MARIANNE THAMM

Marianne Thamm is an award-winning and best-selling author, columnist, editor, journalist, satirist and occasional stand-up comic whose work has appeared in a variety of international and local publications during her 30-year career. She is the author of nine books and assistant editor at Daily Maverick.

OSIAME MOLEFE

Osiame Molefe is a freelance writer with a keen interest in the space in which personal and societal ambitions intersect with technology, politics and economics, having written most recently for *The New York Times*. When he is not writing news, analysis and opinion, he reads speculative fiction and writes some, too. In a former life, he

LIST OF CONTRIBUTORS

worked as a chartered accountant in New York, Bermuda and Johannesburg, but has since fled that industry in pursuit of a life less grey. He holds a bachelor's degree in accountancy from Rhodes University, but don't let that fool you into believing he has a head for numbers. He does not.

PAUL BERKOWITZ

Paul has worked at Econometrix, FNB and the University of Witwatersrand. Despite having a head for numbers, Paul is equally at home formulating incisive essays ranging from social commentary to political economics.

RANJENI MUNUSAMY

Ranjeni Munusamy is a survivor of the Salem witch trials and has the scars to show it. She has a substantial collection of tattered T-shirts from having 'been there and done that' – from the government and the Zuma trials to spin-doctoring and upsetting the applecart in South African newsrooms. Following a rather unexciting exorcism ceremony, she traded her femme fatale gear for a MacBook and a packet of Liquorice Allsorts. Her graduation *cum laude* from the School of Hard Knocks means she knows a thing or two about telling the South African story.

REBECCA DAVIS

Rebecca Davis studied at Rhodes University and Oxford before working in lexicography on the Oxford English Dictionary. After deciding she'd rather make up words than define them, she returned to South Africa in 2011 to write for Daily Maverick, which has been a magnificilious decision. She is now fully conversant in legalese, following countless hours spent covering the Oscar Pistorius trial.

RICHARD POPLAK

Richard is an award-winning journalist, author, graphic novelist and doggerelist. He is currently a senior writer at Daily Maverick. His first book was the highly acclaimed *Ja, No, Man: Growing Up White in Apartheid-era South Africa* (2007), which was long-listed for the Alan Paton Non-Fiction Award and short-listed for the University of Johannesburg Literary Award. He has spent the past four years travelling Africa, researching a book that interrogates the notion of a rising Africa, entitled *Continental Shift*. He is the author of Daily Maverick's first book *Until Julius Comes: Adventures in the Political Jungle*, published by Tafelberg.

SIMON ALLISON

Simon Allison covers Africa for Daily Maverick, having cut his teeth reporting from Palestine, Somalia and revolutionary Egypt. He loves news and politics: the more convoluted, the better. Despite his natural cynicism and occasionally despairing tone, he is an Afro-optimist, and can't wait to witness and chronicle the continent's swift development over the next few decades.

SIPHO HLONGWANE

Sipho was a writer and columnist for Daily Maverick before migrating to the dark side of big media. His other work interests also include motoring, music and technology, for which he has won some awards. In a previous life, he drove forklift trucks, hosted radio shows, waited tables and was once bitten by a large monitor lizard on his ankle. It hurt a lot. Arsenal Football Club is his only permanent obsession.

SISONKE MSIMANG

Every night after eight, once the wine and the tranquilisers have kicked in, Sisonke writes. Daily Maverick, *The Times* and the

Mail & Guardian pretend to take her seriously. A few international publications have been duped too. Sisonke Msimang writes about race, gender and politics in Africa and beyond. In addition to writing, Sisonke does work for several civil society organisations, including Sonke Gender Justice.

STEPHEN GROOTES

Grootes is the host of The Midday Report on Talk Radio 702 and 567 CapeTalk, and the senior political correspondent for Eyewitness News. He has been part of the political hack pack since before the Polokwane Tsunami, and covers politics in a slightly obsessive manner. He is the author of *SA Politics Unspun*, a look at demystifying the state of South African politics. Those who love him have recommended help for his politics addiction. He quotes Amy Winehouse.

STYLI CHARALAMBOUS

After being expelled from the halls of finance houses for possessing an inkling of wit, this entrepreneur enjoys birdwatching and writing not-so-subtle yet moving social commentary pieces for South Africa's bastion of journalism excellence (that's Daily Maverick, in case you were wondering). Having escaped the Port Elizabeth mis-education system, Charalambous now resides in Jo'burg and can sometimes be spotted quality-control testing the water of the city's watering holes. In his spare time he is also the chief expense-claim officer (CEO) and publisher of Daily Maverick.

VUKANI MDE

Vukani is the opinions editor for Independent News Media. He was previously political editor for *The Weekender*, *Business Day*'s Saturday sister publication, and SADC editor for *Southern Africa Report*. Vukani has also worked as communications advisor and media liaison for the Minister of Trade and Industry and as national head of communication for Cosatu. He writes in his personal capacity.